USING FILM TO
TEACH NEW TESTAMENT,

WITHDRAWI

Mark G. Boyer

University Press of America,® Inc.
Lanham · New York · Oxford

Copyright © 2002 by
University Press of America,® Inc.
4720 Boston Way
Lanham, Maryland 20706
UPA Acquisitions Department (301) 459-3366

12 Hid's Copse Rd.
Cumnor Hill, Oxford OX2 9JJ

Library of Congress Cataloging-in-Publication Data

Boyer, Mark G.
Using film to teach New Testament / Mark G. Boyer.
p.   cm
1. Bible. N.T.—Study and teaching. 2. Motion pictures in
Christian education. I. Title.

BS2530 .B65 2002
225'.078—dc21   2002020141 CIP

ISBN 0-7618-2242-9 (pbk. : alk. paper)

⊖™ The paper used in this publication meets the minimum
requirements of American National Standard for Information
Sciences—Permanence of Paper for Printed Library Materials,
ANSI Z39.48—1984

Dedicated to

Bernard Brandon Scott,
who taught me
how not to become a living dinosaur!

and

Gerrit J. tenZythoff,
1922-2001,
who gently encouraged
the completion of this work

Contents

Introduction

Several years ago, I attended an adult continuing education course taught by Bernard Brandon Scott from Phillips Graduate Seminary, Tulsa, Oklahoma. One day he reflected on the challenge he faced teaching the New Testament to traditional students. He said that he was a literate person, but his students were graphic people. Because of his literacy, he called himself "a living dinosaur" in a video society.

What he meant was that his primary source for information is reading, while his students' primary source for information is pictures-- television, movies, computers, photographs. He learns by reading the printed word on a page; they learn by watching a videotape or moving icons on a screen. From their point of view, he was a dinosaur. From his point of view, the New Testament wasn't on videotape or DVD.

In that course, Scott demonstrated how he bridged the hermeneutical gap between his method of learning and that of his students. He used feature-length films which employed themes similar to those in the New Testament. By showing the film and having the students discuss the themes they encountered, he was able to construct a bridge from the film to the New Testament text. The scenes forming the plot of the film served as a coat room peg bar upon which he could hang the scenes forming the plot of a New Testament book.

At that point in time, I had been teaching New Testament for several years, and Scott's insight opened up a whole new world for me to explore with my students. I began a search for movies that I could use to bridge the gap between me and my students, as I had experienced exactly what Scott had spoken about. My search for films continues, as I examine each new movie I view with the hope that I will find something in it that I can use to communicate more clearly a scene or a theme from a New Testament book.

In the first part of this book, I introduce the literate reader and teacher to the graphic world of the student. After reviewing the parts of a story and demonstrating how to use the historical-critical methodology of biblical scholars, I illustrate both with "Dreamer of Oz: L. Frank Baum" and "The Wizard of Oz." The study of these films can help students grasp not only the parts in a story, but how we have a tendency to read back into a story that which wasn't there in the beginning.

In order to communicate the concept of tragedy to students, who desire that every story ends with the main character "living happily every after," I present "The Good Mother," a film that was a box office flop. It helps communicate the tragedy of abandonment found in Mark's Gospel. Also useful in exploring Mark is "Phenomenon," "Sommersby," and "The Shawshank Redemption," although the latter works better with John's Gospel.

The irony found in Matthew's Gospel is also found in Peter Seller's last movie, "Being There." Just as those who listen to Chance Gardener conclude that he is speaking about the economy, when in fact he is talking about gardening, so does the Matthean Jesus speak about the kingdom of heaven, which is not understood by his listeners as the reign of God on earth but as a movement to overthrow Roman rule. Also helpful in grasping Matthew's view of Jesus as a type of Moses is "Willow," a film set in a world where little people are stronger than their giant enemies and a girl-child is the long-awaited redeemer.

The Gospel of Luke's theme of giving witness, which culminates in martyrdom, is displayed in "Witness," staring Harrison Ford. Luke's second volume, the Acts of the Apostles, can be grasped by students after viewing "The Mission," a film based on the history of the Catholic missions in South America in the middle of the eighteenth century.

"Jeremiah Johnson," a film with little dialogue, affords the student the opportunity to learn how to read signs, such as those found in John's Gospel. For an understanding of the cosmological movement of the pre-existent Son who comes down from heaven to save the world and, then, returns to where he came from, "Powder," with its young man who survives a lightning strike which kills his mother and who, before he disappears in a flash of light, spreads goodness even as he is persecuted for his albino appearance, communicates that theme extremely well. The born-again theme comes clearly into focus after having students watch "The Shawshank Redemption," in which the main character is initiated or born again into prison life with water from a fire hose and escapes from prison through a birth-canal pipe that leads him to a river and, finally, to the ocean.

Because Paul's letters are more philosophical theology and less story than the gospels, "Regarding Henry" and "The Doctor" can spur students to investigate Paul's themes of death and resurrection and conversion and change in lifestyle. In "Regarding Henry," Harrison Ford portrays a man who is shot and, during recuperation, becomes the loving human being he had not been previously. His conversion sparks the conversion of his wife and daughter to a new way of life. In "The Doctor," William Hurt, as a doctor teaching future doctors, explores what it is like to be a patient, an experience which sparks a change in his methodology.

The Book of Revelation presents a special challenge because of its apocalyptic genre of literature. However, "Pale Rider," whose name comes from one of the four horsemen in the Book of Revelation, can help students grasp how evil is defeated by good in the apocalyptic genre. "The Milagro Beanfield War," with the appearance of an "angel" who sparks new life into an old town, serves the same purpose. To see what the earth would be like after a great flood, "Waterworld," staring Kevin Kostner, captures the Book of Revelation's theme of the search for a new world, paradise.

Because the metaphor of "vineyard" permeates both the Old Testament and the New Testament, viewing "A Walk in the Clouds" provides students with not only a good love story, but the experience of how the vineyard serves as the metaphor for a family who has worked the land for over 400 years.

And, finally, I present a film that offers a way to teach students how to engage in hermeneutics. By watching the latest version of "Romeo and Juliet," they experience how one can take Shakespeare's text from the past and give it new life and meaning in the present. Hermeneutics, the art of translating or bridge-building, helps students take the biblical text and answer this question: What does the text say today?

The teacher who uses film should keep in mind that all analogies between movies and the New Testament will limp. What I mean is that things are both like and unlike. As much as possible, I have chosen to illustrate the likenesses between some of the books of the New Testament and movies. The differences will become apparent as the films are viewed.

In my method of teaching, I instruct students to watch a film and then to read the biblical book which I think it illustrates. As they interact with the graphic screen and the literate text, they begin to make connections. They do not always connect in the way that I presume, but that is the learning that I do from them. By not controlling their insights, I gain new understandings from their paralleling of characters or themes from films and New Testament books. Respecting each other's perspective, of course, plays an important role in the exchange of learning in my classroom. What is important is not that students come to the same insights as I do, but that they learn the scenes and can explain how they interact to form a plot for a biblical book.

Following each chapter in this book the reader will find exercises and questions for discussion. After students have viewed a film and read a biblical book, they should process what they have learned through exercises and the discussion of questions which will both confirm and challenge what they have discovered in their study. Some of the exercises and questions can be prepared by students before class and some can be saved for in-class discussions. Teachers should make use of the materials as they see fit and add their own to what I have provided as a starter.

I hope that this book will help teachers to communicate the variety of themes and character portrayal found in the New Testament. By bridging the gap between literate and graphic societies, teachers are also spanning the world of the first century and connecting it to the world of the twenty-first century--so they won't end up being living dinosaurs!

Teaching Literature

The New Testament is Literature

The body of written texts of a culture is called literature. It consists of legal documents, scientific reports, works of fiction, true stories, wisdom material, parables, healings, and much more. Each piece of the body of literature has its own unique literary form or manner of transmission. Some of the texts began in an oral style and were told and retold before finally being written on something.

When approaching the Bible, a person is attempting to read a collection of literature spanning several cultures and thousands of years. Like any other literature, to unlock the meaning of the texts, one must understand the world out of which they emerged as well as the world out of which the reader emerges. If the reader is not aware of his or her own biases and presuppositions and prejudices, he or she may read these into the text of a culture that never had them.

In teaching the gospels of the Christian Bible (New Testament), it is important to keep in mind who the intended reader was. Mark's Gospel, the oldest of the canonical four and written around 70 C.E., was written primarily to a peasant Gentile-Christian audience, while Matthew's Gospel, written around 80 C.E., was penned primarily for Jewish-Christian readers. Likewise, the author of Luke's Gospel, written between 80 and 90 C.E., intended it to be read by upper class, elite Gentile-Christians. John's Gospel, written near the end of the first century or the beginning of the second, was intended for Jewish-Christian readers who were moving away from Judaism and seeking their own identity.

A gospel, no matter, which one chosen, is a complete story. There is no reason to go outside of the story to fill in what the reader may perceive to be missing pieces. Likewise, attempting to harmonize all the various events in all four gospels into a single story erases the uniqueness of each story and removes the traces of the author's perspective from his narrative. In fact, the best way to read a gospel is in one sitting while pretending that one has never read it before.

A gospel's uniqueness will begin to come through as the reader determines whether it is a comedy or a tragedy. In the classical distinction, a story is determined to be a comedy if the hero or heroine wins the battle or fight and is still alive at the end of the story. A story is declared to be a tragedy if the hero or heroine loses the war and is killed by the time the story ends.

Mark's Gospel is a tragedy. There are no post-resurrection appearances by Jesus. They women go to the tomb, find it empty, hear the proclamation from the young man sitting in it that Jesus has been raised from the dead, and they leave saying nothing to anyone. The hero of Mark's Gospel, Jesus, once he is dead and buried, is never seen again by the reader in the story.

Matthew's Gospel, Luke's Gospel, and John's Gospel are comedies. Jesus makes two post-resurrection appearances in both Matthew's Gospel and Luke's Gospel, and four in John's Gospel. By appearing, the reader "sees" that the hero is alive.

The reader should also pay attention to the rest of the elements that go into making a good story, such as the author, the person who writes the story. Every author has a biased point of view, a definite perspective or lens through which reality is viewed, the culture is understood, and the world is made meaningful. The anonymous authors of the gospels--the current names were not assigned until the second century-- are subject to time, place, language, and the customs in which each lived.

The author who writes the story may or may not be the same as the narrator, the person who tells the story. In the gospels, the authors function as the narrators, leading the reader, the person who reads the story, from one event to the next. This linear progression of the story is called the plot. It is composed of every small scene in the total story and carries the theme of the author and the action of the characters from one point on a linear continuum to another. Closely tied to the plot is the setting or settings of the story--the places, such as houses, fields, lakes-- where the scenes of the story take place. The setting or backdrop for a story often contains clues for understanding the meaning of the story or the author's intent in recording it.

In addition to the hero, Jesus in the gospels, the narratives also contain major and minor characters. The major characters are those who join the hero, the savior, the redeemer, the liberator, the protagonist. The leader of a cause or champion gets others either to join or oppose him. In the gospels, the major characters are John the Baptist and Peter, the crowds, Pilate, etc. Minor characters, those persons who support the hero or those who oppose him, keep the action of the story moving. They have minor roles and may appear only in a single scene. In the gospels, minor characters consist of people like Bartimaeus, James and John, Martha and Mary, etc.

The writer crafts the characters to fit the plot of the gospel. Their descriptions may be based on historical persons and even what historical persons may have said, but they are, nevertheless, the re-creation or product of the writer, who puts dialogue, words and sentences, on their lips in order to have them interact with each other.

Early in the story, after the reader is introduced to the hero and those who need to be rescued, a bonding scene is usually presented. The union of the hero with those who need to be liberated can consist of a meal, a dance, a long discussion, or, in our culture, sexual intercourse. If the bonding is not effectively done by the writer, then the hero stands out as a loner with no support from the rest of the characters in the story. While the gospels are weak in bonding scenes, the call of the disciples serves the purpose as does the many meal-eating scenes. The reader is bonded to Jesus as he or she listens to the sermons he gives, watches the healings he does, and tries to figure out the parables he tells.

When the writer thinks that the reader needs more information in order to understand a scene in a story, he may employ a flashback. A flashback, usually portrayed as a fade-out in film, is an event outside of story-time that happened in the past but the reader needs to know it for the present. A flashback is sometimes portrayed as a dream during the night or a day dream. The infancy narrative at the beginning of Matthew's Gospel contains several dreams in which the reader learns about Joseph's dreams and the instructions he received in them. That information is crucial to understanding Joseph's consequent actions.

Sometimes, the possibility of an event outside of story-time is information which the writer thinks the reader ought to know about. Called a flashforward, information is given to the reader about the future. A flashforward is like a prediction. It serves to keep the reader reading the story in order to find out if it comes true. The authors of Mark, Matthew, and Luke portray the hero, Jesus, as three time predicting his death and resurrection in Jerusalem before it actually happens in the story.

As the story progresses the hero is tested. A trial or a problem is presented and the hero overcomes the trial or solves the problem, proving that he is strong, reliable, and worthy of trust by both the characters to which he bonds and the reader. The one who provides the test or problem is the adversary, the opponent, the antagonist, the force which usually personifies that which is undesirable or evil. In the gospels, the adversary consists of Satan, the devil, unclean spirits, demons, etc. Jesus is tested in the desert during a 40-day trial. He overcomes the trial and immediately emerges from the wilderness to begin his public ministry of continuing to defeat evil in all its forms.

The story reaches a crescendo when the conflict seems to be as great or greater than the hero. Conflict, the competitive or opposing action of incompatibles, can be either internal or external. Internally, it may be a doubt that the hero has. Externally, it may be the fickleness of some of the major characters. In the gospels, conflict reaches a crescendo when Jesus is arrested by the authorities and the disciples flee the scene.

Conflict leads to the crisis in the story. The crisis is the turning point where the hero must overcome evil (comedy) or evil overcomes the hero (tragedy). In the gospels, the crisis occurs when Jesus stands before Pilate, is sentenced to death, and made to carry his cross to the place of execution. Even though the reader wants to believe that this is not the end, in Mark's Gospel it is. The hero is crucified, dies, is buried, and never seen again in the story. The only resolution or solution to the problem is the young man's announcement to the women that God raised Jesus from the dead.

In the other three gospels, the resolution occurs through the post-resurrection appearances. Those who needed to be saved, rescued, redeemed, etc. are saved, rescued, redeemed. Death did not end the life of Jesus. His followers, who have managed to find each other, discover him alive in their midst. The hero tells them that he is with them until the end of the world as he sends them on a mission of proclaiming what he taught them. Ideally, all live happily ever after--either in this life or the next.

One element of story that is not often discussed but which is very important in understanding a gospel is mapping. A map is a geographical drawing of the parameters of the location(s) or place(s) where the story unfolds. It may include houses, gardens, cities, states, countries, our world, other worlds, and shows how these are inter-related. In Mark's Gospel, it becomes clear to the reader that the author knew little or no Palestinian geography as he portrays Jesus zipping across the land from one place to the next. By attempting to draw a map of Mark's Gospel, the reader begins to see that except in story time it is impossible to get from one place to the other in the short time the author gives.

As the elements of a story are understood, in relation to gospels, the reader begins to understand why gospels are not biographies of Jesus of Nazareth. Jesus of Nazareth lived for about thirty years at the beginning of the first century. However, the first gospel, Mark's, wasn't written until about forty years after his death. The synoptic gospels (Mark, Matthew, Luke) portray no more than a year in the life of Jesus. John's Gospel portrays three years. Either a year or three years of a hero's life hardly makes a gospel a biography. No gospel writer was interested in a biography, even though each writer may have included some biographical details. The author's interest was in telling a story that disclosed to the reader who the author believed Jesus of Nazareth to be and what he wanted the reader to believe about him.

Exercises and Questions for Discussion

1. What are the two types of stories? Prepare a definition of each.

2. Distinguish between an author, a narrator, a reader, and a hearer.

3. Define "plot." How doe the individual scenes of a movie, TV program, or book form a plot for a story? What role does "setting" play in the plot?

4. Distinguish between "flashback" and "flashforward."

5. Explain how "dialogue" functions in a work. Who creates dialogue? Can there be dialogue without words? Explain.

6. What is the difference between "major characters" and "minor characters"?

7. Define "bonding." In our culture how is "bonding" usually accomplished in books, movies, and TV programs?

8. Why is it important that the hero or heroine be tested? Who does the testing? What is the result of the testing called?

9. What are the "crisis" and the "resolution" in a book, movie, or TV program? Define each.

10. A "map" is a geographical drawing of the parameters in the location(s) where a story unfolds. Draw a map of a book you have read, a movie you have seen, or a TV program you have watched recently.

11. Choose a book which you have recently read or watch a movie or TV program and identify the following in it: author, narrator, reader (viewer, hearer), setting(s), plot, flashbacks, flashforwards, dialogue(s), major character(s), minor character(s), bonding, testing, adversary, conflict, crisis, and resolution.

Teaching Literature

Literary Redaction Criticism:
Dreamer of Oz: L. Frank Baum and *The Wizard of Oz*

In 1991, ABC released a made-for-TV movie titled "Dreamer of Oz: L. Frank Baum." The film is the biography of the author of "The Wizard of Oz"--Limon Frank Baum. As such, it provides us the opportunity to teach redaction criticism, to understand what the original author wrote in his book, as well as what influenced his writing before the book was turned into a movie.

"Dreamer of Oz" also gives the opportunity to see how perspective influences the way a book or film is produced. Because "The Wizard of Oz" preceded the "Dreamer of Oz," the latter is biased insofar as it focuses on the origin of "The Wizard of Oz" through the people and events in Baum's life. Events not related to the production of "The Wizard of Oz" in Baum's life are considered to be of no importance.

The year is 1939; it's the opening night of the film, "The Wizard of Oz." A reporter is interviewing Mrs. L. Frank Baum (Maude Gage), the narrator of the "Dreamer of Oz," in an attempt to get the story behind the story. Like "The Wizard of Oz," "Dreamer of Oz" is filmed in black and white which fades into color as Mrs. Baum's words turn into a flashback and characters take over acting out the story.

We see that Baum is an actor in a Shakespeare Company and has nose bleeds. His sister introduces him to Maude Gage, whom Frank courts and teaches "to see in her mind" the stories he tells. In a dream within the flashback (a second level of redaction), there are scenes of Emerald City and the countryside. Baum proposes marriage to Maude. Her mother opposes it, but it takes place nevertheless.

The narrator returns to tell the viewer about their first years of marriage. Baum gets a decent roll to play as an actor only to watch the theater burn and to be told by Maude that she is pregnant. On December 4, 1883, F. Jackelyn Baum is born, and Baum gives up acting and moves to Syracuse to work for an oil company. In a scene with Jackelyn at a window, Baum tells a story about getting to a magic land by way of a cyclone.

On February 12, 1886, a second child, named Robert Stanton Baum, is born to the Baums, . During a visit from Maude's mother and while Baum is writing, he tells a story about a witch in a magic land. As he sees the story in his mind, he pictures Mrs. Gage as the Wicked Witch and Maude as the Good Witch.

During a discussion about Maude's sister, Helen, and her husband, Charlie, living in the Dakota Territory, the Baums decide to move to Aberdeen, where Baum meets a little girl named Dorothy. For livelihood, the Baums open Baum's Bazaar Store. Frank tells Maude that the store will be a success. Thereafter, Baum meets Ned Brown, a midget. During the grand opening of the store, no one buys anything.

Baum tells a story about a little farmer (midget) who didn't give his scarecrow a brain. First, the farmer made the nose on the scarecrow. Then, he painted ears on him so he could hear, eyes so he could see, and a mouth, but he couldn't talk. The farmer put the scarecrow in a cornfield, and the crows talked to him.

Meanwhile, Harry Neil Baum is born December 17, 1889.

Baum visits and speaks to Dorothy, whom he discovers is in bed, coughing, and very sick. He tells her a story about a little girl in a magic land who was born in the Dakota Territory and named Dorothy and lived with her Uncle Henry and Aunt Emily. She flew to the magic land in a house and met little people and a scarecrow. Dorothy also met a man made out of tin who lived in a cabin in a forest. He needed oil and had no heart. He didn't like to chop down trees. One day while he was chopping at a tree, it began to rain and he rusted in place and couldn't move. Dorothy dies.

In his quest for a livelihood for his family, Baum buys a newspaper. However, a misprint causes an angry man to force him to a duel with guns. In the gunfight scene, the bearded man runs away. The Baums leave the Dakota Territory and, in 1891, move to Chicago.

Baum tells a story about a cowardly lion and pictures the bearded man. He says that he didn't know why the cowardly lion needed courage because his roar caused everything to be frightened of him.

In Chicago, Baum works as a buyer for the crockery department of a company. On his birthday, Maude gives him a diary called "The Magic Land" into which she tells Frank to write his stories.

Baum next gets a job as a traveling salesman for Pitney Books. In a rail passenger car he speaks with a man who wears a mustache and smokes a cigar. His name is Sullivan, and he identifies himself as a salesman extraordinaire. He is a total humbug.

While in Lawrence, Kansas, in a hotel room, Baum gets another nosebleed, and he begins to write his story. When he returns home to Chicago after weeks on the road, he discovers that his mother-in-law is there. She offers him a manager's position. Baum is more interested in writing, but realizes that his story needs a plot.

In a flashback to the passenger car, he begins to envision a plot for his story. Dorothy's house is in a cyclone with Toto, her dog. They come out of the house and see a beautiful land and meet four Munchkins. Dorothy's house landed on the Wicked Witch's sister, another Wicked Witch, and Dorothy is in danger. Dorothy must go to see the Wizard, a powerful magician, like Merlin in the King Arthur tales. Dorothy seeks the Wizard by following the yellow brick road. The name for the magic land comes from the label on the drawer of a file cabinet, O-Z or Oz.

During lunch, Baum meets a friend who is a writer and tells him about his Oz story. Chauncy Williams wants Baum to write a book about Mother Goose. Baum writes *Mother Goose in Prose* in October 1897. The book is not a financial success, so Baum goes back on the road as a salesman, gets sick, and faints. He discovers that he has a heart condition and his doctor recommends a sedentary lifestyle.

William Denslow, an artist, illustrates Baums September 1899 *Father Goose* book, which sells 75,000 copies. Mrs. Gage doesn't like it. Baum proposes the Oz story, named *Emerald City*, to Denslow. Denslow likes the idea and they work on the new book together. The story takes shape as Dorothy kisses the lion, oils the tin man, and hugs the scarecrow and cries.

However, *Emerald City* is rejected by five publishers. Baum enters into a state of depression and claims that he is a failure. Maude reassures him that he's not, but he can't sleep, breaks pencils, plays with the lamp, wads up paper, and experiences what is called writer's block. Maude stops him and tells him that he'll find a way out if he stops pitying himself.

Baum decides to publish his book himself. By signing away his royalties to *Father Goose*, he is able to afford the printing of 2,000 copies. Maude, who has been supportive up to this point, doesn't think this will work and becomes angry. Baum tells her that he needs her to believe in him and to help him.

Mrs. Gage suddenly begins to support Baum. She says that all

his books are good, and she tells Maude to support him. She says that she
sees the need for fantasy literature. Mrs. Gage suggests that Baum change
the title of his book because using the name of a jewel (emerald) is bad
luck. She suggests the title be *The Wonderful Wizard of Oz.*

Baum sees his publisher for a royalty check on the Oz book,
which is a success. The check amounts to $3,344. With part of the
money, Baum gives Maude an emerald for never losing faith in him.

The Baums move to California. Within two months, first 25,000
copies of the book are printed, then another 30,000. By January 1901,
90,000 copies have been printed. And by 1939, 4,000,000 copies are in
print.

The narrator tells the viewer that Baum wrote thirteen more
books about Oz. In 1902, a musical was developed, and in 1910, a silent
film was made. Baum died in May 1919, only after he and Maude had
exchanged much love and traveled to far away places. The film ends with
the words, "There is only one dreamer of Oz: L. Frank Baum."

Summary: Elements of a Story and *Dreamer of Oz*

Author: Screenplay by Richard Matheson
Narrator: Maude Baum and reporter
Reader/Viewer: me, you, us
Settings: Syracuse, Aberdeen, Chicago, Lawrence, California
Plot: get *The Wizard of Oz* published
Flashback: whole film except for scenes with reporter
Flashforward: none
Dialogue: all major and minor characters have speaking parts
Major characters: L. Frank Baum, Maude (Gage) Baum, Mrs. Gage
Minor characters: children, Dorothy, Ned Brown, publishers, artist
Bonding: dancing and marriage
Testing: meeting defeat before getting a book published
Adversary: book publishers, Mrs. Gage (at first)
Conflict: L. Frank and Maude Baum between themselves, Mrs. Gage with
    Baums, book publishers and L. Frank Baum, public
Crisis: L. Frank Baum decides to publish *The Wizard of Oz* himself, ill-
    ness
Resolution: F. Frank Baum publishes is his own book and becomes suc-
    cessful as a writer
Map: A map of "Dreamer of Oz" would consist of lines drawn from one
    town to another indicating where the Baums lived, along with railroad
    tracks to the towns to which L. Frank Baum traveled as a salesman.

Further Exploration of
The Wizard of Oz and *Dreamer of Oz*

Historically, L. Frank Baum was an actor, playwright, newspaper editor, store owner, and salesman. He was forty years old in 1896 when he began writing *The Wonderful Wizard of Oz*, which became the best-selling children's book of 1920. The book was adapted for the musical stage in 1902 and toured for almost a decade.

Baum's story of Oz was not fashioned as a dream or a state of unconsciousness; Dorothy's adventures really happened to her in the book. The author, in response to children requesting to know more about Dorothy and her exploits, wrote fourteen other books about the girl from Kansas, the Scarecrow, the Tin Woodman, the Cowardly Lion, and other characters before his death in 1919. Other writers continued Baum's series until 1963 when the number of titles had reached forty.

Silent films based on several of the Oz series of books were made in 1908, 1910, and 1914. In 1925, a silent version of *The Wizard of Oz* was released by Chadwick Pictures, but it hardly followed the original story. Thereafter, Samuel Goldwyn purchased the rights to *The Wizard of Oz* which he sold to MGM in 1937. Judy Garland was cast as Dorothy, Buddy Ebsen as the Scarecrow, Ray Bolger as the Tin Woodman, Bert Lahr as the Cowardly Lion, and Frank Morgan as Oz. Later, Ebsen and Bolger switched roles.

The entire movie was filmed in the studio. No exterior work was even planned. By 1938, filming was ready to begin. The original person cast to play the Wicked Witch, Gale Sondergaard, was replaced with Margaret Hamilton. After a little over a week, things began to fall apart. Ebsen got sick from the tin powder used in his makeup. Richard Thorpe, the original director, was replaced by Victor Fleming. Jack Haley replaced Ebsen as the Tin Woodman. Filming resumed in early November 1938 and continued through February 1939.

Other problems continued to plague the filming. Toto got stepped on and had to be replaced by another dog for a few days. Two actors playing the flying monkeys crashed to the stage floor when their support wires broke. Hamilton suffered burns from her witch's broom and was off the stage for a month. When Fleming was asked to take over the floundering "Gone With The Wind," King Vidor was brought in to finish the picture, especially the Kansas sequences.

One good omen did present itself, however. Frank Morgan, Oz, needed a long-tailed coat. Someone from the wardrobe department went to a second-hand clothing store and found just the right item. One day Morgan turned out one of its pockets to find the name L. Frank Baum sewn into the lining. After tracing down the tailor, it was discovered that he had once make the coat for Baum.

After some sneak previews, some of the Wicked Witch's scenes were trimmed, other brief scenes and random lines of dialogue were cut, and three musical numbers were deleted. First deleted was the huge procession through Emerald City as Dorothy and her friends returned from the Wicked Witch's castle with her broomstick (to a reprise of "Ding! Dong! The Witch is Dead!"). Second to be cut entirely was "The Jitterbug." And the last piece to get the ax was Bolger's specialty dance in "If I Only Had A Brain."

Portions of "If I Were King of the Forest," a reprise of "Over The Rainbow," and a scene in which the Tin Woodman was turned into a beehive by the Wicked Witch were also cut. By July 1939, all the work was done; it had cost MGM three million dollars. The film premiered in August 1939.

On the 50th anniversary tape can be seen the promotional trailer (preview of coming attractions) used for the 1955 re-release of the film--all alternate takes of different versions of familiar scenes in the film, Cavalcade of the Academy Awards--a short featurette of the history of the Oscars with excerpts from the ceremonies during which the film won five in 1940, the Texas Promotional Trailer--a quick look at three of the stars of Oz, "If I Only Had A Heart"--Buddy Ebsen as the original Tin Woodman before illness forced him out of the role, "The Jitterbug"--a deleted song and scene set in the Haunted Forest, and "If I Only Had a Brain"--a dance by the Scarecrow which was deleted from the film.

By the time "Dreamer of Oz" was made in 1991, all of the later influenced it. Baum's life is interpreted from the point of view of writing his book and the making of it into a movie. Thus, scenes from what had already become the movie were read back into the film about Baum's life to serve as a prophecy-fulfillment literary form. In other words, Baum's dreams are not predictions of the future (the making of "The Wizard of Oz") because the future had already occurred when the film about Baum's life ("Dreamer of Oz") was made.

The prophecy-fulfillment device was used by the biblical authors in the same manner. For example, writing forty years after Jesus of Nazareth was crucified by the Romans outside of the city of Jerusalem, the anonymous author of Mark's Gospel portrays his Jesus-character as predicting (prophecy) his own death on three different occasions in story-time. That prophecy is fulfilled when it happens in story-time. Writing after the fact, the author of Mark's Gospel keeps the reader interested in the story by telling him or her what will happen next. The reader continues to read to see if what was predicted will, indeed, take place. No writer would predict something to happen outside of story-time--an event that has not already taken place in historical time. Otherwise, he or she would risk his or her credibility by predicting something to happen that didn't.

That is why "Dreamer of Oz" presents a truly biased biography of L. Frank Baum. The film-maker interprets his whole life through the lens of "The Wizard of Oz." Certainly, he experienced other events in his life which had no influence on his writing or the turning of his writing into the movie.

Exercises and Questions for Discussion

1.   For each of the major characters indicate whether he or she is considered to be good or evil. Explain why for each. Do any of the major characters change from good to evil or evil to good? Who? Explain how the transformation takes place.

2. Outline the plot of "Dreamer of Oz" by scene. For each scene indicate its importance to the whole story and what purpose it serves. Also, indicate how each scene points toward a scene in "The Wizard of Oz."

3.   What do you think is the major truth which the movie attempts to communicate? Is this truth one that endures? Explain.

4. Explain how "Dreamer of Oz" uses the literary device called prophecy-fulfillment. In what ways does "The Wizard of Oz" serve as a bias for L. Frank Baum's biography?

5.   Why is it important that there be so many dream scenes (flash-forwards) in "Dreamer of Oz"?

6. According to "Dreamer of Oz," from where did each of the characters come in "The Wizard of Oz"? Be specific for each.

7.   According to "Dreamer of Oz," from where did the title for "The Wizard of Oz" come?

8. According to "Dreamer of Oz," from where did the plot for "The Wizard of Oz" come?

9. How does the "Dreamer of Oz" illustrate redaction criticism when it is compared to "The Wizard of Oz"?

Teaching Literature

The Elements of a Story:
The Wizard of Oz

Most students emerge from a graphic culture today. They are more familiar with TV and movie screens, computer monitors, and the Internet than they are with books. Add to this the fact that few of them are exposed to some of the great pieces of literature, and it comes as no surprise that few students understand how a story works. That, of course, is a crucial element in studying a gospel.

An analysis of the two-hour film "The Wizard of Oz" (Loew's Incorporated, 1939; 50th anniversary edition by Turner Entertainment Co., 1989), a film based on the book *The Wonderful Wizard of Oz* by L. Frank Baum and an American classic, can attune students to the various elements of a story as well as provide an exercise in understanding how the pieces of a story are inter-related.

Victor Fleming directed Judy Garland (Dorothy), Frank Morgan (Wizard), Jack Haley (Tin Woodman), Ray Bolger (Scarecrow), Bert Lahr (Cowardly Lion), Billie Burke (Glenda), and Gale Sondergaard (Wicked Witch) in a simple story of good versus evil. The viewer is introduced to all of the characters at the beginning of the movie, filmed in a sepia tone (a brown tint which first appears to be black and white), as a tornado is beginning to brew on the plains of Kansas. In the screenplay by Noel Langley, Florence Ryerson, and Edgar Allan Woolf, there is no narrator. The viewer must rely upon the writers to tell the story through the characters.

Once the tornado hits and Dorothy, the name means "gift of God," is hit on the head, a "dream scene," filmed in Technicolor, comprises the rest of the film. The scene is set in Munchkinland, and, as Dorothy so aptly puts it, speaking to her dog Toto, "I have a feeling we're not in Kansas anymore."

The characters the viewer met before the tornado now return as the major characters in Dorothy's state of unconscious dreaming. The heroine is Dorothy. She is supported by the Munchkins, the Scarecrow, the Tin Woodman, the Lion, and finally, the Wizard. Her adversary is the Wicked Witch of the West, only one half of the evil, since Dorothy's house landed on the other half--the Wicked Witch of the East--and secured freedom for the Munchkins. In other words, the heroine has already saved a group of people before she even begins her journey down the yellow brick road. Furthermore, she has received the ruby slippers worn by the Wicked Witch of the East. The slippers are the coveted prize of her sister, the Wicked Witch of the West.

The minor characters supporting Dorothy include the Good Witch of the North, Glenda, and Toto, Dorothy's dog. The minor characters on the side of the Wicked Witch of the West include a group of flying monkeys and an army of guards.

The plot of "The Wizard of Oz" is for Dorothy to find her way home to Kansas, or to put it in biblical terminology, Dorothy needs to be saved. That can be accomplished, she discovers from Glenda, by consulting the Wizard in Emerald City. And the way to Emerald City is clearly outlined with the yellow brick road. Then, as Glenda disappears in a bubble, Dorothy says, "My, people come and go so quickly."

No journey is complete without companions. The first person she meets is Scarecrow, who doesn't scare crows or people and wants a brain because he thinks he is a failure. Having a brain is a sign of being able to think. The Scarecrow's major fear is a match, because he is nothing other than straw stuffed into a man's clothes. In biblical terminology, he is a shell of man needing a soul. Once Dorothy invites him to join her on her journey, they embrace and begin to dance and sing, "We're off to see the Wizard, the wonderful Wizard of Oz." The dance is the bonding between Dorothy and the Scarecrow.

The next person to join the troupe is the Tin Woodman, who has rusted in place in an apple orchard. Once Dorothy oils him loose, he tells her that he wants a heart, a sign of emotion. Up to this point Dorothy has not yet been tested. Suddenly the Wicked Witch appears on the top of the roof of the cottage in the orchard and throws fire toward the Scarecrow, who ignites but is smothered out by the Tin Woodman. The Witch threatens to use the Scarecrow to stuff a mattress and to make a beehive out of the Tin Woodman. But because under Dorothy's leadership they have conquered her this time, she disappears, promising to return, and the three lock arms together, begin to dance, and sing, "We're off to see the

Wizard, the wonderful Wizard of Oz." Now, three are bonded, the heroine has been tested, and met head-on the conflict which emanates from the Wicked Witch.

Dorothy, Scarecrow, and Tin Woodman dance their way to the edge of the forest, where they meet the Cowardly Lion, who needs courage. He fears lions, tigers, bears, and his own tail. After a momentary roar and a minor attack on Toto, Dorothy slaps Lion for attacking her dog and tells him that maybe the Wizard can give him some courage. All three join hands with Dorothy, begin to dance, and to sing, "We're off to see the Wizard, the wonderful Wizard of Oz." In biblical language, Dorothy, the heroine, now has three disciples.

Gazing into her crystal ball, the Wicked Witch of the West casts a spell on the poppy field through which the four travelers must pass on their way to Emerald City. As they run through the poppies, they begin to get drowsy, but their protectress, Glenda, deactivates the spell with snow. Thus, good overcomes evil again. Lion says, "Unusual weather we're havin', ain't it?"

The four arrive at the huge doors which either permit people to enter or serve to keep people out of Emerald City. The bell boy, who is the Great Oz in disguise, answers the door and tells the travelers that no one has ever seen the Great Oz. But after showing her ruby slippers, Dorothy and company are permitted to enter.

Emerald City in biblical terms is the Book of Revelation's new Jerusalem which has come down out of the heavens. It is a place of laughter and joy. The four travelers get cleaned up, re-stuffed, polished, and groomed in preparation to see the Wizard of Oz. Meanwhile, the Wicked Witch does a little sky writing: "Surrender Dorothy."

When the four ask to see the Great Oz, the porter tells them that no one can see Oz. The biblical critic will recall that no one could see God and live in the Hebrew Bible (Old Testament). The testing of the heroine continues, and Dorothy explains that she is the Dorothy mentioned by the Wicked Witch in the sky writing. She and her friends have their hopes elevated. However, they are quickly dashed when the porter says that Oz will not see them. However, he eavesdrops on their conversation and feels compassion as he sees Dorothy crying.

Soon, the doors of the hall swing open and the four companions begin to walk down a long hall to where the Great Oz awaits them. Biblically, the hall is a temple, and the travelers are headed to the Holy of Holies. Needless to say, they are wrapped in fear.

In the inner sanctuary there is a type of Ark, a face projected on the wall, and lots of fire emanating from torches. The fire increases when

Oz speaks. The Great Oz knows all. He knows why the travelers have come and what they want. The viewer knows that Oz knows because the porter was Oz in disguise. But Dorothy and her three friends don't know this piece of information.

Dorothy, like Moses in the Hebrew Bible (Old Testament) Book of Exodus, dares to talk back to Oz, who promises to grant her request, but she must prove that she is worthy. It will mark the crisis point of the movie. She must bring the broomstick of the Wicked Witch of the West to Oz. In order to do that she will have to kill her; Dorothy will have to finish defeating evil. Once this is done, the Great Oz will grant her request to return to Kansas. When she begins to speak, he says, "Go."

Into the Haunted Forest the four companions go. The Wicked Witch watches their activity in her crystal ball and sends an army of flying monkeys (minor devils) to attack them, capture Dorothy and Toto, and bring them back to her. Leaving behind the dismembered Scarecrow, the Tin Woodman, and a shaking Cowardly Lion, the monkeys accomplish their mission.

In her castle, the Wicked Witch threatens Dorothy by taking away Toto. She wants the ruby slippers which belonged to her sister, the Wicked Witch of the East. When she attempts to remove them from Dorothy's feet, she is hurt by a ray of fire. She realizes that Dorothy must be killed before she can have the slippers. Toto escapes, avoiding the spears of the Wicked Witch's troops. But Dorothy is given only a one hour glass of sand before she will be put to death.

At this point, the heroine faces imminent death. It looks like one-half of evil (Wicked Witch of the West) is going to defeat the totality of good (Dorothy). But gazing into the Witch's crystal ball, Dorothy sees her Auntie Em from Kansas and is reminded of her mission--to get back home to Kansas. This gives her hope that she will triumph.

Meanwhile, Toto goes to Dorothy's three companions and leads them to her. They plan a rescue, climbing up rocks to the castle, watching the guards, killing three guards, putting on their clothes, and joining the rest of them marching into the castle. Once inside, they take off the guards' uniforms and begin looking for Dorothy.

The battle between good and evil begins. The guards discover the intruders and chase them around the castle. Some guards are knocked down by a falling chandelier. Chasing them around the ramparts of the castle, which are illuminated with torches, the Wicked Witch sets Scarecrow on fire as the guards trap the four companions. Dorothy, picking up a bucket of water, throws it toward Scarecrow in order to save his life. In so doing, she douses the Wicked Witch, who immediately begins to melt.

In other words, the Wicked Witch is exorcised with the water; evil is destroyed with baptism. The other half of evil is defeated. The guards rejoice at her death. Dorothy asks for her broom. And the four are off to see the Wizard one last time.

When they arrive to see the Great Oz and present the broom to him, he wants time to think about what he is going to do. Toto yanks back a curtain to reveal that the Great Oz is only a man standing near a microphone, pulling the levers which create the blazing fires. Dorothy declares him to be bad for having tricked them. He says that he is really good, just a bad Wizard.

The Wizard gives the Scarecrow a diploma to certify that he has a brain. The Lion gets a medal to recognize his courage, and the Tin Woodman gets a ticking watch as a testimonial that he has a heart. The gifts they sought were the gifts they had all along--a brain, courage, a heart--and used in their quest not only to get to Emerald City, but to kill the Wicked Witch.

Now, the viewer is told how the Wizard got to Oz. During the Omaha State Fair, his balloon floated away to Oz, where the people acclaimed him their Wizard. Using the balloon, he promises to take Dorothy back to Kansas.

After making his farewell speech, he appoints the Scarecrow as the new ruler of Oz to be assisted by the Tin Woodman and the Lion. Just as the balloon is beginning to lift, Toto escapes from Dorothy's basket. She runs after him, and the balloon goes off with the Wizard and without Dorothy.

After having survived so many tests, Dorothy is tested again. Good comes to her rescue in the person of Glenda. She tells Dorothy that she has had the power to return to Kansas all along--the ruby slippers. She has had all the power she needs; she just had to learn how to use it. While repeating the sacred mantra, "There's no place like home," and tapping together the ruby slippers three times, Dorothy returns to Kansas and the film color returns to sepia again. Good has triumphed over evil, and all live happily ever after.

Dorothy is found in bed. The resolution of the mission is now complete. Dorothy is back in Kansas. All the characters who have been in her dream pass by the window in her room or through the room to see how she is. She was knocked unconscious, they tell her. Her final line, "There's no place like home," brings the film to an end.

Summary: Elements of a Story and *The Wizard of Oz*

Author: L. Frank Baum (Screenplay by Noel Langley, Florence Ryerson, Edgar Allan Woolf)

Narrator: none

Reader/Viewer: me, you, us

Settings: Kansas, Munchkinland, Cornfield, Orchard, Forest, Poppyfield, Emerald City, Castle of Wicked Witch

Plot: return to Kansas

Flashback: none

Flashforward: Dorothy's state of unconsciousness indicated by change from sepia to color and back to sepia

Dialogue: all major and minor characters have speaking parts

Major characters: Dorothy (heroine), Scarecrow, Tin Woodman, Lion, Wizard, Wicked Witch of West, Good Witch of North (Glenda)

Minor characters: Toto, Uncle Henry, Auntie Em, Munchkins, army of winged monkeys, Wicked Witch's guards

Bonding: dancing down the yellow brick road

Testing: Dorothy is tested by having to get the broom of the Wicked Witch; Scarecrow is tested with fire several times; Tin Woodman is tested with emotion; Lion is tested with courage

Adversary: Wicked Witch of East, Wicked Witch of West and her army of winged monkeys and troop of guards

Conflict: Dorothy and Wicked Witch of West, who wants ruby slippers

Crisis: Dorothy and trio of companions are trapped on the ramparts of the Wicked Witch's castle by her guards

Resolution: Dorothy throws water on Wicked Witch and melts her, brings her broom to the Wizard, and returns home to Kansas by tapping together heels of ruby slippers

Map: Here's what a map of "The Wizard of Oz" might look like:

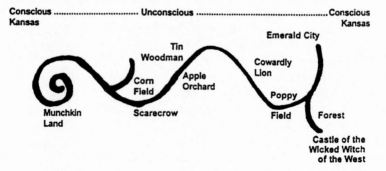

Exercises and Questions for Discussion

1. For each of the major characters indicate whether he or she is considered to be good or evil. Explain why for each.

2. Outline the plot of the film by scene. For each scene indicate its importance to the whole story and what purpose it serves.

3. What do you think is the major truth which the movie attempts to communicate? Is this truth one that endures? Explain.

4. What is the biblical significance of the following: a tornado; the name Dorothy, meaning "gift of God"; Dorothy's three companions on the journey; two Wicked Witches and one Good Witch (Glenda); journey through a cornfield, an orchard, a forest, and a poppy field to Emerald City; ruby slippers; Wizard of Oz's sanctuary or temple; water used to kill the Wicked Witch; the refrain, "There's no place like home."

5. Why is it important that the majority of the movie be cast as a dream, the state of unconsciousness of the heroine, Dorothy?

Teaching Mark's Gospel

The Good Mother

Mark's Gospel presents the reader with a tragic hero in the person of Jesus of Nazareth. Likewise, "The Good Mother" (Touchstone Pictures, 1988) based upon the novel of the same name by Sue Miller, presents the viewer with a tragic heroine, Anna Dunlap (Diane Keaton), who is a recent divorcee and the mother of a young daughter named Molly (Asia Vitira).

The film begins with an adult Anna narrating her life's story. She says, "When I was a child, I spent summer with my grandparents at their vacation home in Maine." Then, as flashbacks of a teenage Anna rowing a boat appear, the adult Anna continues,

> In those days there was no road to the house. So one of my favorite chores was to row visitors across the lake. My mother had three sisters and a brother, my Uncle Oric. In August the men would join their wives and the children, and for two weeks the family was fully assembled.

Flashbacks of the summer home and the gathering of members of Anna's family accompany the next part of the story. Anna continues, "My grandmother seemed overwhelmed in their company, but she was the one I loved the most. We were all dominated by my grandfather. He demanded ambition and achievement, and we all tried to please him."

Then, the viewer is introduced to one of Anna's mother's sisters. Anna, the narrator, says, "The only one who ever stood up to him (grandfather) was Babe. She was my mother's youngest sister--twenty years younger than my mother." Because of their closeness in age, Anna states,

Through those long summers, Babe became my friend. I was, well, I was the oldest grandchild and I was shy already. I was a conformist. Compared to the others, you see, Babe just seemed so glamorous and unconventional, and I adored her.

Babe becomes Anna's idol of nonconformity. Anna continues to narrate Babe's story, saying, "I remember there was a time when Babe was gone a lot with young men in their power boats from the other side of the lake." Babe got pregnant. She is not reticent in showing her enlarged breasts and extending stomach to Anna and, thus, paving the way for Anna's unconventional lifestyle. Then, Anna states, "A week later, Babe left for Europe with one of my aunts. I learned later that she'd had her baby in Switzerland and gave it up two days afterward."

Filling in the years between Babe's pregnancy and Anna's growing up, she says, "... As I grew up and began to drift away, I saw Babe less and less, though she'd appear at family gatherings often having had a lot to drink." In the next scene Babe appears at a summer family gathering, drinks too much, and drowns herself in the lake. But before doing so, she had taught Anna to take risks and to be passionate.

Anna explains, saying,

In the years after Babe's death, I often thought of what she offered me during those summers. In her presence it just seemed as if anything was possible. And I wanted to be like her. I wanted to take risks, and I wanted to feel. I wanted to be a passionate person. And even now, in spite of everything that has happened, I feel, I really, really had to try.

To some students, Babe is a type of John the Baptist. In Mark's Gospel, John is usually found near the Jordan River after emerging from the wilderness and calling for repentance. Both John the Baptist and Babe are unconventional. Just as Babe teaches Anna about her way of life, so John not only teaches others about his way of life, but he baptizes Jesus, another unconventional character, who leads a lifestyle of healing, exorcising, and parable-telling.

After a six- or seven-year time lapse, the narrator in "The Good Mother" disappears and the viewer is presented with the adult Anna and her daughter, Molly, in a breakfast scene immediately followed by scenes revealing that Anna works in a lab with a man named Alex, that she gives piano lessons to students, that she and Molly share a special relationship, and that she is uninhibited in teaching Molly about sex.

Anna is a type of Jesus in these scenes. She travels from one place to another, like Jesus makes his way to Jerusalem. He appoints twelve apostles to share his mission of proclaiming the message, to exorcise, and to heal. Some students will see Molly as the little child(ren) in Mark's Gospel who represents both innocence and powerlessness in an adult world.

In a scene set during Thanksgiving dinner, Anna's grandfather and grandmother are present along with Anna and Molly. The dominate grandfather, who has achieved his wealth by hard work, along with his wife, meet with Anna privately and want to provide funds for a sitter for Molly. He hints that it is because of her poverty that she can't provide a private sitter for Molly. Anna says that she is not concerned about poverty, but with her independence, being her own person. The grandmother, from whom we will hear later in the film, sits, listens, and says nothing.

Some students will compare the grandfather to Jesus' adversaries in Mark's Gospel: priests, scribes, elders, Pharisees, Sadducees. They represent the dominate groups who perceive Jesus' preaching about a new lifestyle to threaten the status quo for which they stand. The grandmother is like the powerless widow who puts her last copper penny into the temple treasury. At the moment when she is least powerful, she is also most powerful, as we will see.

"The Good Mother" begins to fill in the blanks concerning Anna's previous marriage. The viewer is introduced to Brian, who takes Molly for a weekend. Also, the viewer meets Ursula, Anna's confidant, to whom Anna reveals the circumstances of her divorce, the fact that sex was "so nothing" between she and Brian during their seven-year marriage, and that Anna never felt erotic around Brian.

In the next scene Anna runs into Leo Cutter (Liam Neeson) in a laundromat. He confronts her because she has removed his clothes from a dryer. Leo invites Anna to Tommy's Grill for coffee. While she's tempted, she doesn't go. Later, looking at a bulletin board, she discovers a flyer with Leo's picture on it. From the flyer Anna sees that Leo is an artist and "safe." At Ursula's urging, she calls him.

Leo and Anna go to a blues bar. While walking home, Leo tells Anna that he changed his name from Lauren, that he is from Ireland, and that he is a sculptor. After arriving at Leo's apartment/studio, Anna explores his sculptures while he puts on some romantic music and turns down the lights. Making shadows on the wall, Leo teaches Anna to dance, they kiss, and they make love several times.

Their next date takes place in a restaurant. While they eat, they talk about intimacy. Back in Leo's place, they make love again. But Anna reveals to Leo that she is insecure. A series of scenes showing Leo and Anna together, erasing Anna's insecurity, follows: in a junk yard where Leo gets sculpture material; in Anna's apartment where he meets Molly; an outing of Leo, Anna, and Molly; in Anna's apartment where Leo and Molly play while Anna cooks after which Molly goes to bed and Leo and Anna make love; in Anna's apartment where Leo sneaks out before Molly gets up and rings the bell to pretend that he is just arriving; in the bathroom where Molly and Anna sit in the tub together while Leo sits on the floor and reads them a story.

Now, the necessary bonding is complete. Leo and Anna have bonded several times through sexual intercourse. Leo and Molly have bonded through play. The bonding is tested as Leo and Anna talk about commitment and passion while walking. At first they argue. Anna says that she is committed to Molly. Leo apologizes, they kiss, and make up. Back in Anna's apartment, they enjoy an evening of making love, only to have Molly join them in bed. Anna tells Leo, "Leo, I love you so much."

In contemporary films, the usual way to show the union of the person who needs to be saved with the person who can rescue him or her is through a sexual relationship. Mark's Gospel is weak in bonding. The Markan Jesus and his twelve followers never seem to form a unity. In fact, after Jesus is arrested, all of them, except Peter, run away. Later, even Peter abandons Jesus.

In "The Good Mother," the bonding begins to fall apart after Molly spends a month with Brian. From all appearances, all is well. Leo loads pieces of his sculptures into a truck headed for three days in New York, while Anna watches. He gives her a gift, which she puts in her apartment. She continues to work in the lab. Upon returning home from the grocery store, she finds Brian (James Naughton) waiting outside on her porch steps. He tells her that he's keeping Molly, that he has filed the necessary papers to do so, and that they will settle the custody suit in court. After a verbal fight between them in the street, Anna goes inside and calls Leo.

The next scene in the lawyer's office reveals what has happened, although the viewer never sees this. Leo, after being questioned by Anna's lawyer, Muth, explains that about a month ago he was babysitting Molly and decided to take a shower. Leo explains, "I got into the shower, and just as I finished Molly came in." He says that he had forgotten to get a towel, so he asked her to get one and hand it to him. As he was drying off, he says, he noticed her staring at him naked, even though she had seen him that way before. Leo states, "... When I'd finished she just said out of the blue, 'Is that your penis?' ... So, I just said, 'Yes, it is.'"

After clarifying a few of Leo's comments, the lawyer tells him to continue. Leo says,

I felt a wee bit uncomfortable about it, actually, but I'd seen how relaxed Anna was about things like that. And I didn't want to screw it up. I tried to seem natural and not cover it up or anything. Then she said, "Can I touch it?" And I didn't think about it for more than a second. I just said, "Sure." And she did.

The lawyer asks Leo why he had not told Anna about the incident. Leo says that he felt embarrassed, that he felt he had handled it OK, and that he didn't see it as a problem. After thinking a second, he adds that he thought Anna would have wanted him to be as relaxed and as natural with Molly as she was about her body.

The lawyer accuses Leo of misunderstanding the rules concerning sexual behavior. Anna informs him that the rules concerning nudity in her apartment are relaxed in comparison to most other people. In order to make a case for Anna, Muth (Jason Robards), the lawyer, proposes that he tell the court that Leo misunderstood Anna, but Anna says that he was only honoring her wishes. The lawyer gives the judge's perspective and suggests that he focus on the happiness of Molly and Anna, separate the sexual relationship out of his presentation, and say that Leo made a mistake. Anna is not comfortable blaming Leo. But by blaming Leo, Anna can get back Molly. Once both Anna and Leo are outside the lawyer's office, Leo apologizes to Anna for the mess she is in now.

Anna drives to the family summer home. Now, there is a road that takes her there directly--no need to cross the lake in a boat. She speaks to her grandmother, who is peeling apples, for a long time. The grandmother tells her that she understands happiness and that she regretted her marriage for the first fifteen years until Babe was born. She also tells Anna that Babe brought her happiness.

The grandfather arrives with a bucket of blueberries and discovers that Anna wants to borrow money to pay her lawyer. In a private conversation that the grandmother (Teresa Wright) can overhear, the grandfather (Ralph Bellamy) listens to Anna tell him that she needs money. Then, he begins to interrogate her. Anna explains that Brian (her former husband) has started a custody suit to get Molly. She needs money for a lawyer.

Now that he has the basic reason why Anna is asking for money, he steers their conversation toward the custody suit, probing Anna about it and the grounds Brian has for it. Anna tells him her story about Leo.

Now that he has the information he wants, the grandfather inquires if Anna has talked to a lawyer. Anna informs him that she needs four thousand dollars to cover her expenses. He asks her about what her chances are for keeping custody of Molly, and Anna responds that Brian has a reasonable chance of getting custody of her.

Attempting another probe, her grandfather asks about Leo, but Anna will tell him nothing, not even Leo's name. Finally, after several heated exchanges Anna says, "If you're not going to give me the money, why don't you just say so, and I'll figure out what to do."

However, the grandfather asks one more question. At this point the grandmother, who has been eavesdropping, enters the room, calming both of them. But the grandfather tells her that she does not need to concern herself with this. The grandmother, revealing the grandfather's name for the first time, makes herself clear, saying, "I'm talking to you, Frank." Frank explains that this business is between Anna and him. The grandmother urges him to help Anna.

Looking at Anna, the grandmother says, "I have money, too. You could ask me, Anna." But Frank, now revealing the grandmother's name for the first time, says, "That's not what your money is for, Eleanor." Eleanor retorts that it is for whatever she wishes. Looking at Anna again, she invites her to ask her for the money. Frank says that he will give Anna the money.

The up-to-now passive Eleanor has become the dominant Eleanor, the grandmother Anna came to adore. She tricks Frank into giving the money to Anna, and she demands to see him do it. He gets his checkbook out of a cabinet, writes a check, and hands it to Anna. After Anna's "Thank you," Eleanor congratulates Frank, who goes to take a nap after having been beaten by the two women.

After returning home, Anna meets a social worker and tells the story the lawyer told her to tell. Arrangements are made for a visitation with Molly, who is brought by Brian to Anna's apartment.

In the next scene Anna describes Molly and both Anna's and Molly's relationship with Leo to a Dr. Payne, a psychologist. Anna says that with Leo she saw no need for rules. She tells him that Leo and she had been naked around Molly. She explains how Leo had opened up her heart to her, and how their sex together was beautiful, and that Molly was part of their love.

Next, Anna contrasts the world Leo created with her to the world she had had with Brian. She states that she and Brian had stopped having sex a long time before they split up. She says she was frigid with him, but that changed with Leo. She adds that she thinks that it was good for Molly.

Then, getting to the point of the custody suit, Anna says that the night Molly came into Ann's room that she and Leo were making love. But she assures Dr. Payne that Molly didn't know. She says, "It was in that context that Leo let her touch him, because he misunderstood what the boundaries were." She says that what Leo did was a mistake, but she doesn't want to lose Molly.

The crisis takes on full steam in the court room, which, except for Anna, is full of men. Brian's lawyer is an African-American man, who, putting him under oath, questions him about what Molly told him. Brain says that Molly was very curious about his body in a way that seemed new and inappropriate to him. He narrates how, while he was shaving one time, Molly asked him if she could see his penis, and he said no. Then he says that she said, "Leo lets me see his penis. He let me touch it."

In the cross-examination, Brian reveals that he is not aware of the sex book Anna used with Molly nor of the anatomy taught in Molly's day care center.

Leo testifies. First, he mentions his dating of Anna and their sex life, his work, and the fact that he didn't move in with Anna. Then, he talks about Molly asking him to touch his penis. He mentions other occasions when Molly crawled into bed with him and Anna. Muth, Anna's lawyer, does not cross-examine Leo. In a scene outside the court room, Leo and Anna argue. Leo realizes that he has been used by Anna and her lawyer and that he has been blamed in terms of making a mistake with Molly.

Dr. Payne testifies that Molly's relationship with Anna is strong and that it will help Molly to move toward independence. He says that Molly is put at risk if she is removed from her mother.

Anna testifies that Molly enjoyed Leo, who was a stability in her life. She says that she was shocked at the incident involving Leo's nakedness. She blamed him and disapproves of his action. She testifies that she is willing not to see Leo again if that is one of the conditions the court puts on her regaining custody of Molly. In a cross-examination, she says that she disapproves of his previous behavior.

The court room scenes remind students of the trials in Mark's Gospel. Brian is a type of Judas, who betrays Jesus and hands him over to the Jewish authorities, who find him guilty of blasphemy. They hand him over to Pilate, who, like the judge, sentences him to death. In the all-male court room, the viewer recognizes that Anna doesn't have a chance to get custody of Molly. Likewise, Jesus didn't have a chance when confronted by the Jewish and Roman power of his day.

The bond between Leo and Anna begins to disintegrate as they discuss what to do now in a restaurant while waiting the judge's decision. Anna doesn't look at Leo, even when he tells her, "I love you."

In her lawyer's office, Muth tells Anna that she has lost custody of Molly. The decision is final. In an appeal, the decision is never re-versed Muth tells her. While Leo drives her home, they sit as far away as possible from each other. When he offers to take her inside, she tells him that she wants to be alone. He leaves.

Anna goes inside and lays on her bed and cries while her telephone rings. She goes to Molly's room and lays on her bed and cries. Leo visits, sees his gift of a painting thrown on the floor, and hears Anna say that her life is ruined. She tells him to leave her alone. He reminds her that he played the role of the criminal in court. She says that she has taken the rap, too. Anna throws a temper tantrum and Leo leaves without his keys to her apartment. She sinks to the floor in the kitchen and cries.

Anna as narrator now returns, saying, "I don't know how long I sat there, but I had a sense of returning to myself from a great distance." The setting is the family summer home. The viewer discovers that Molly, who is playing near the lakeshore, did not take Brian's winning of the custody hearing easily. Anna says that Molly took the outcome hard.

Anna continues to narrate how her lawyer called and told her to watch Molly, to see if she noticed signs of her being unhappy with her situation, and then he might try and reverse the decision. She says that she never called him, because what she wanted most wasn't to make use of Molly's misery, but to see it end. She says that she takes heart in know-ing that Molly is in a family of her own.

Next, Anna explains that all this is left of her relationship with Leo is a telephone conversation now and then.

Anna, rowing Molly out on the lake in a boat, paralleling a previous scene in which Babe took Anna out on the lake in a boat, explains that she sees Molly every second weekend and during school vacations. Sometimes, she says, the pain of the loss is terrible. She thinks of something that her grandmother said to her when losing Molly seemed unthinkable. Eleanor had said, "Everybody knows you're a good mother, Anna." And the film ends where it began: at a summer home on the lake.

The topic the film treats is sexual openness. How far can a per-son dispense with cultural mores and not cross over the line? Anna's and Leo's openness concerning sexual topics with Molly is contrasted to Brian's attitude of closedness. The fact that Brian wins custody of Molly testifies to the fact that in general society is not comfortable with speaking about sexual issues.

Some students see Leo as a type of Jesus. Leo was abandoned by Anna, much like Jesus was abandoned by his disciples. Leo was un-conventional, a sculptor by trade, like Jesus was an unconventional, itinerant preacher and a carpenter by trade. Both dared to risk. Leo lost his relationship with Anna and Molly; Jesus lost his life.

What makes Anna a type of Jesus, a tragic hero, is that she loses custody of Molly. She is abandoned in an all-male court room. Jesus is a tragic hero because he is abandoned by all his disciples to death. In Mark's Gospel, after Jesus is crucified and dies, he is buried. There are no post-resurrection appearances. The women go to the tomb, experience a young man sitting in it, and hear that Jesus has been raised. They leave and say nothing to anyone. Anna is a tragic heroine, who is still a "good mother," being somewhat raised to a new life without custody of Molly.

Ursula, Anna's confident, whom we meet only a couple of times in the film, is a type of Peter. She has a minor role in the story, but offers advice, which is usually wrong. In Mark's Gospel, Peter never under-stands the message that Jesus tries to teach him--namely that power is being powerless. Peter gets it wrong every time, until Jesus finally calls him a Satan because he judges by human standards instead of by God's way of seeing things.

Anna's lawyer resembles the Pharisees, who follow the oral law and societal laws. The best way to solve a problem, according to the Pharisees, is to eliminate it. The lawyer does the same; he eliminates Leo by blaming him for letting Molly touch his penis.

Both Frank and Eleanor, Anna's grandparents, appear to follow the custom of patriarchy. Frank is dominant and determines who does what and when it is done. This is somewhat reversed when Eleanor exercises her power and offers to give Anna the money she needs to cover her court costs. Matriarchy comes out on top in the end. From this point of view, the grandmother is like the poor widow in Mark's Gospel who gives to the Temple treasury out of her poverty.

The members of Anna's family are like the Markan disciples. In the first scene of the summer home on the lake, after everyone has arrived by boat, they break out in song: "We're here because we're here." They remind the viewer of Mark's portrayal of Jesus' disciples as stupid. They never understand what Jesus teaches. They argue about who is greatest. The want places of honor. They run away when Jesus is arrested.

And, finally, the summer home on the lake represents paradise and innocence. It is the place where Anna was taught by Babe. It is the place where Anna and Molly return. The lake is like the Jordan River. It isolates from the outside world, even after a road is built to the home. Once it is crossed, life is never the same on the other side. Ask Jesus of Nazareth, who crossed the Jordan River through baptism and was never again the same.

Exercises and Questions for Discussion

1. Choose the five major characters in "The Good Mother" and for each indicate whether you consider him or her to be good or evil. Explain why for each.

2. Outline the plot of the film by scene. For each scene indicate its importance to the whole story and what purpose it serves.

3. What do you think is the major truth which the movie attempts to communicate? Is this truth one that endures? Explain.

4. After reading the Gospel According to Mark in one sitting, choose the five major characters and indicate for each whether you consider him or her good or evil. Explain why.

5. Identify and compare three characters from "The Good Mother" with three characters from Mark's Gospel. Explain how each pair is alike and unlike.

6. Identify and compare two turns in the plot of "The Good Mother" with two turns in the plot of Mark's Gospel.

7. What do you think is the major truth which Mark's Gospel attempts to communicate? Is this truth one that endures? Explain.

8. Make a list of three questions which you have about "The Good Mother" and three questions which you have about Mark's Gospel.

9. Identify three issues, such as sexual openness in "The Good Mother," which need to be discussed today. Explain the importance of each and how each crosses societal lines.

10. How important is the role of the narrator in "The Good Mother"? Explain. How important is the role of the narrator in Mark's Gospel? Explain.

Teaching Mark's Gospel

Phenomenon

The majority of biblical scholars agree that the Gospel According to Mark is the oldest of the four canonical gospels, written around 70 C.E. It begins with a story about Jesus' baptism in the Jordan by John and quickly launches into Jesus' ministry in Galilee which consists of gathering a troupe of twelve apostles, healing people of unclean spirits (demons), physical ailments, and leprosy.

The Markan Jesus preaches two sermons, one consisting of several parables and the other called the eschatological discourse. Two cycles of stories each containing a feeding of a multitude and either walking on water or calming water complete the first half of the gospel. The pivot point of the story is the scene set while Jesus and his followers are making their way to the villages of Caesarea Philippi. The man of power and deed begins to teach a way of powerlessness and death.

The new theme is confirmed with the narrative of the transfiguration, a type of re-baptism of Jesus. Then, the story focuses on the meaning of being a powerless disciple and carrying one's cross in imitation of Jesus. After a triumphal entrance into Jerusalem, the Markan Jesus debates several issues with his adversaries, is arrested, and handed over to Pilate to be crucified. On the day after the Sabbath, some women discover that his tomb is empty, but they are told by a young man that he has been raised. The women leave in fear and tell no one--according to the original ending.

To help students understand the basic theme of the first half of Mark's Gospel and how the unknown author inverts it in the second half, "Phenomenon" (Touchstone Pictures, 1996) can be shown. The hero of the film, George Malley (John Travolta) is an ordinary man who lives in a run-down farm house, owns an old hound dog named Attila, and cultivates a small garden in his front yard. He works as a mechanic at the only auto-repair shop in a town called Harmon, California.

Malley's best friend, Nate Pope (Forest Whitaker), delivers a load of solar panels to his home as a birthday gift. Lace Pennamin (Kyra Sedgwick), a single mother of two--Al (David Gallagher) and Glory (Ashley Baccille)--makes wooden chairs and sells them at the auto-repair shop. She is the woman Malley has been trying to date. He invites her to his thirty-seventh birthday party to be held in the Elkhorn Bar, but she declines.

In the bar, all Malley's friends are present celebrating his birthday. As he escorts one of them to his car, Malley stands in the street and sees a bright ball of light in the sky. He hears a blast and sees the light explode. It knocks him over into the street. He recovers, stands up, and goes back into the bar inquiring of those there if they saw something "like an explosion and a flash" which Malley says "knocked me off my feet." No one saw or heard anything.

Malley proceeds to complete a chess game in a couple of moves and beat his friend and the man who delivered him thirty-seven years before: Doc (Robert Duvall). Astounded, Doc reveals that Malley had never beaten him before in chess. Malley has been changed by the light he saw in the sky.

At home in bed, Malley studies Spanish in order to be able to converse with the man who owns the garage where he works. He also makes a late-night call to Nate to tell him that he has solved a problem of a rabbit eating the vegetables in his garden, even though he buried the fence around it a foot and a half. He proves his solution, that the rabbit was in the garden when he put up the fence, by opening the gate and watching as it hops out.

The next day in the garage, Malley speaks fluent Spanish to the garage owner, and both the owner and another co-worker, who had been translating for Malley, are astounded by his expertise. Furthermore, while working under a car, he is able to draw a wrench to his hand without touching it, but only the viewer sees this event. After talking to Lace's kids, Al and Glory, waiting in her truck, he tries to talk to Lace, but she gets into the truck and drives away.

Back in the bar, Malley beats Doc at chess again and says, "I've been seeing things so clearly." He also reveals that he has been reading two to three books a day. Doc tells him to come in for a physical.

In successive scenes, Malley watches as the solar panels Nate had given him for his birthday are installed on his roof. From them he gets ideas for building experiments in his house. He visits Nate, bringing two of the chairs Lace made, and talks to him about the experiments he has been conducting using photosynthesis. Nate, who operates a short-wave radio, observes as Malley translates some Morse code which Nate cannot and hears Malley say that he's bored. Once he's decoded the message he's heard on the radio, Malley gives Nate a message to send.

Back at home, while reading a book, Malley notices that he has the ability to turn the pages of the book by waving his hand over them. Getting angry with his own extraordinary abilities and no way to explain them, he runs out of the house into the dark of night and looks up into the sky shouting, "Is somebody trying to tell me something? What?" Clearly, he thinks that he is having a religious experience.

One month later, Malley is in Doc's office finishing up a physical examination. Using Doc's fountain pen on his desk, he demonstrates his ability to move objects from afar. Doc calls his power telekinesis, saying, "I consider myself a rational man, a man of science. I feel like a child, George." But Doc promises to help Malley find out why he has this ability.

Back in the garage, Malley, using an old car, demonstrates how he has produced methane gas from pig manure and how a gallon of it can fuel the car for 90 miles. Meanwhile, Lace delivers more chairs, picks up one of the huge tomatoes that Malley has grown in his garden, but leaves as soon as he begins to talk to her.

Malley procedes to take a basket of tomatoes to Lace's home. After picking up her children at the entrance to the property in his tow truck, they stop to pick a bouquet of wild flowers while Malley tells the kids the biological name for each. Glory takes the ribbon out of her hair and ties it around the bouquet, replacing the wire tie Malley had around it. Malley finds Lace working on a chair and presents her with the basket of tomatoes and the flowers. They go for a walk and she tells him that she wants to keep her life simple without any complications that would come from a relationship with him.

Malley, approaching the edge of a gully, feels earth waves which precede an earthquake. He calls an official to report that an earthquake is going to happen, but can get no satisfaction because the official wants to know what instruments he used to measure the waves. While eating dinner, Lace, Malley, Al, and Glory laugh as Al shakes the table in a mock quake. Once Malley heads home, however, a real earthquake takes place. Lace quickly pushes her kids into her truck and drives to Malley's home, where she demands to know what is going on. He says, "What's happening is I don't know."

However, she spots all the chairs she's made and "sold" on

Malley's porch and in his house. He had told her that people were buying them. In anger she leaves, telling him that he didn't tell her the truth.

In Pope's house, Malley shows him how he decoded and diagramed the message they had heard previously on the radio. Malley hands Pope another message to send and demonstrates his telekinetic powers with a paper clip. Malley tells Pope that he is very confused.

In the next scene, Doc is called to a home where a man who speaks only Portuguese is sick. The doctor diagnoses it as food poisoning. He instructs a woman to call Malley, to tell him to stop by the library and get a book on speaking Portuguese, and to come immediately. Malley, who has returned to his home, hears the telephone ringing, but he is showing the phenomenal growth of his garden to Pope and ignores it.

Meanwhile, John Ringold (Jeffrey DeMunn), a seismologist from Berkeley, drives up and tells Malley that he is interested in his ability to predict earthquakes. Malley informs him that all he did was feel the ultra low frequency waves. Ringold invites Malley to come to Berkeley for some tests, as Malley shows him all his other experiments.

A man pulls into the driveway and tells Malley that Doc has sent him to bring Malley to the home of the Portuguese-speaking man. Malley is handed a book of Portuguese, which he reads, as Ringold accompanies them. Once Malley arrives, he converses with the man in Portuguese and discovers that they need to search for the man's grandson, Alberto, who also ate whatever the man ate. He is somewhere in the orchard.

As a group of searchers enter the orchard, Malley senses where the boy is. He feels the boy's stomach cramps, which drop Malley to the ground as he heads toward an old shed in the orchard. Using telekinesis, Malley draws back some of the debris piled against the shed to reveal a ladder. On the roof of the shed the boy is found.

Ringold, who has been observing all these events, sets up a meeting with Malley in Berkeley and leaves. Malley meets Alberto's mother, Michaela, whom he discovers is looking for work cleaning houses. Malley goes to Pope and asks him to hire her. Malley teaches Pope some Portuguese. However, what he records on a tape player for Pope to learn is not what he tells him it means. The sentences he records are words of love, not words about hiring a housekeeper.

Lace's daughter, Glory, is upset after reading a book and hearing a coyote howl outside her window. While Lace is comforting Glory, Al begins to talk about Malley, but Lace says that she doesn't want to talk about men. When Al asks, "Why do you hate him?" Lace responds, "Because I like him."

Back in the Elkhorn Bar, rumors spread about Malley. People

question his new abilities. Some ask him about how many books he reads and what's going to happen in the future. After becoming very frustrated with all their questions and his inability to answer them, he leaves his friends and walks out of the bar.

As he is leaving the Elkhorn, he spies Lace across the street. He goes to her and apologizes for lying about the chairs. He invites her to go to Berkeley with him for support, saying, "I'm scared. People are different now. I don't like it." She tells him that she will be at his shop on the appointed day by a certain time if she is going with him.

Michaela arrives at Pope's home and sees what a mess it is and how much he does need a housekeeper. They agree that she will come back to clean the next day. Before she leaves, Pope says in Portuguese what Malley had taught him. She is flattered. After she leaves, he goes to the radio and says, "I just met an angel from Portugal here in my house." Pope has fallen in love.

When Malley arrives home, he finds a team of FBI agents carrying away boxes of his experiments and papers. The leader of the team, Jack Cash, questions Malley about how he broke the code, which Malley discovers was a secret military training mission. He tries to explain, but they take him to their headquarters for questioning.

Malley is put through a battery of questions and then he is tested. When asked to name as many mammals as he can, he names a series of them in alphabetical order to the astonishment of the tester. When posed a question which challenges him to calculate the age of a person, he responds with his own questions requesting specifics, such as time zone, time of day, etc. He demonstrates his telekinetic ability to the tester with a pencil calling it a "collaboration, a partnership." Then, he explains saying, "We're all made of the same stuff. You know, energy. You know, the little pieces."

While Malley is being tested, Lace waits at the auto repair shop. She does not know what happened to him. Finally, he is released by the FBI. He says, "I want my life." Cash, the FBI agent, finds Ringold and tells him not to let Malley on the Berkeley campus and to cancel the meeting he had with Malley.

Malley heads to Lace's home, even though it is nighttime. After raising the window of her bedroom, he tells her, "I think I scared them," referring to the FBI. She says, "You scare me, too." He leaves and goes to the Elkhorn Bar to find Pope. He apologizes to Pope for all the problems that he has had with the FBI, who had arrested Pope also. In the bar, Malley tells Pope about the testing he has undergone with the FBI, how Ringold has canceled the meeting in Berkeley. Then, he tells others in the bar about ideas he has to renovate the bar's parking lot, to make the mail delivery more efficient, etc. Then, losing his temper, he says, "It (the light) was a mistake." Pointing to the mirror behind the bar, he uses telekinesis to break it.

Malley's life begins to take a downward spiral. His co-worker quits at the garage. Doc wants to do more tests, a CAT scan, and a blood test. Malley talks to Doc about making himself available at the upcoming book fair so that people can pose questions to him and he can answer them. He hopes that his will stop the rumors in town.

Back in Malley's garden, while he is rapidly hoeing his vegetables, he turns lose of the hoe and begins to loosen the soil with his bare hands. Suddenly he stops to listen to the wind softly whistling in the tree branches. He watches as the branches of the evergreens are moved by the wind. It is as if he is receiving a message from the breeze.

Lace's son, Al, brings home a piece of the mirror from the bar. Lace tells him, "Can't you just look inside and see who he is." She is referring to Malley, whom she is coming to love. In fact, she goes to Malley's home, where she finds him in his somewhat depressed mood. He tells her about what's been happening to him as best as he can, and that he's going to speak at the book fair.

In a touching scene, Lace helps him get himself ready. She dampens his hair and cuts it. Then, she smears shaving cream on his face and shaves him. After she is finished, Malley asks her, "You're running away? You're coming back?" She nods affirmatively.

The turning point of the film is the scene at the book fair. Malley shows up and tells the people that he'll answer their questions after he explains his "experiment of energy." They question him about the mirror in the bar and the light he saw. One man brings his son forward and asks Malley to lay his hands on him. As the crowd pushes in, Malley falls over a table of books in a faint and sees another blast of light in the sky.

Malley wakes up in the hospital, where he gets a CAT scan. But from his bed he can see the trees moved by the wind through the window. Doc, Lace, and Pope arrive. Doc explains to Malley that he has a tumor on his brain that has spread out like a hand over it. Instead of destroying the brain's function, it stimulates it. Doc tells him that he has more active use of his brain than anyone ever tested. The tumor explains his dizziness and the explosions of light he has seen. Malley responds by saying, "And its killing me." Doc explains that the tumor is in danger of prohibiting blood flow to the brain, adding, "Damn lousy scenario."

Then, Doc declares to Malley, "Somehow you got into my heart more than most. And for a man who has never been a father, I sure feel like I'm losing a son." Doc leaves the hospital room.

Pope steps forward with an offer to help Malley in any way he can. Malley tells him, "Next spring when you plan the South 40, I want you to use the new fertilizer. I want you to put corn in that field. And I know what you're thinking. You're thinking it's just too rough a crop, but it's not. Trust me on this."

Next, Malley talks to Lace, asking her how long he has to live. "Days or weeks--don't know," she says. Then, she adds, "I tried so hard not to love you." Malley: "How'd you make out?" Lace: "Terrible." Malley: "Would you love me the rest of my life?" Lace: "No. I'm going to love you for the rest of mine." She hugs him. Then, together they watch the rain through the window.

Making a cameo appearance as Dr. Wellin, Richard Kiley portrays a brain specialist who wants to perform surgery on Malley. He knows that there is little hope that Malley will survive the surgery, but he tells him it will be "an expedition, a voyage, into history" and that Malley "could be the greatest teacher." Wellin says, "I could present you to the world." Malley says, "But that's not me; that's my brain. I think I'm what everyone can be. I'm the possibility. The human spirit, that's the challenge, the voyage, the expedition." Then he denies permission for the operation.

Dr. Wellin runs into Doc in the local courthouse where he is attempting to get a court order declaring Malley incompetent so that he can perform the surgery. Doc heads to the Elkhorn Bar where all Malley's friends are gathered. Of course, they are talking about Malley, whom Doc defends saying that he "never changed." Losing his patience with them, he says, "He (Malley) wanted nothing from no one. Why do you have to tear him down."

Back in the hospital, Malley does not take the medicine he's given to make him sleep. Keeping it under his tongue, he removes the capsule and mixes its powder with some pudding, which he gives to the orderly. Once the orderly falls asleep, Malley puts on the orderly's clothes, slips by the guard, and leaves the hospital.

With Pope's help, Malley packs and prepares to leave. He goes to Lace's home, where he shows her kids how to fix their truck. While working, Al asks him, "You came here to die, didn't you?" Malley nods affirmatively as the kids run away. But Malley follows them carrying an apple. When he finds them, he says, "If we were to put this apple down and leave it, it would spoil in a few days. But if we took a bite of it, it would become part of us and we could take it with us forever." Glory takes a bite out of the apple. Then, Malley says, "Al, everything is on its way to somewhere--everything." Then, Al takes a big bite out of the apple.

Meanwhile, Jack Cash from the FBI arrives with a partner. Malley disappears, and Lace says that she hasn't seen him. When Cash examines the fixed truck with its hood still up and starts it with ease, Lace intuits that Cash knows Malley is there. So, she asks him what his first name is. When he responds with it, she says, "How would you want to die, Jack?" He can't answer the question, so he and his partner leave.

Lace finds Malley sitting under a tree and working on completing one of his journals. They sit close together and talk about how Lace knows how Malley feels. They kiss passionately, and the implication is that they make love, although no such scene is shown. Later, once the kids have fallen asleep and Malley and Lace are in bed together, he says, "It's happening. It's going to be OK." He closes his eyes and dies.

The next morning Ringold knocks on the door of Lace's home. She tells him, "George Malley passed away last night." She hands him the books and papers which Malley had instructed her to give him. Then, after Ringold leaves, she sits in a chair on the porch and weeps. She looks at the branches of the trees and notices that the wind is whistling. Her kids find her and bring her a cup of coffee. All of them embrace and watch the branches of the trees swayed by the wind.

In his South 40, Pope, who is picking ripe ears of corn, has stalks growing everywhere. Accompanied by Michaela and her son, Alberto, they get into his truck and drive down the road with corn on the right and the left sides. Pope has married Michaela, and she is pregnant. They arrive at the Elkhorn Bar and pass a sign as they enter: "Welcome to George Malley's Birthday Party." All of Malley's friends are in attendance: Lace and her kids--Glory and Al, with whom Doc is playing chess--, the men from the garage, etc. A picture of George Malley is enthroned on the bar, and in the background the words of "If I could change the world" are sung.

The phenomenon of "Phenomenon" is not only George Malley's new abilities triggered by his brain tumor, but the community he creates in his hometown, especially the family he forms with Lace, Glory, and Al. And it is in this way that the movie is like Mark's Gospel. In many ways, the film is Mark's Gospel retold in an American setting with adaptations made to an American culture.

Like Jesus, whom we meet for the first time in Mark's Gospel at his baptism by John the Baptist in the Jordan River when he was about thirty years old, we meet George Malley for the first time in the Elkhorn

Bar at his thirty-seventh birthday party. Like Jesus, who comes from the small town of Nazareth, Malley is a simple man, living in a small town, working in a auto-repair shop. Again, like Jesus, who lived his life doing good for others, Malley is known for his goodness in Harmon, California.

In Mark's Gospel, there are three important scenes in which Jesus of Nazareth is identified as God's Son. At his baptism, he hears the voice from the torn-apart heavens declare that he is God's Son. During his transfiguration, he hears the voice declare it again. And after he is crucified, the centurion, standing at the foot of the cross, declares Jesus to be the Son of God.

George Malley's baptism into his new life is his first experience of the blast of light when he falls over in the street after his birthday party. Like the dove, indicating the Holy Spirit, which descends upon Jesus after his baptism in the Jordan, Malley is illuminated by the light. Early Christians often referred to baptism as illumination. At the book fair, when Malley falls again and sees another blast of light, like Jesus, he has been transfigured, changed by the light. Like Mark's transfiguration scene serves as the point in the story where the plot is inverted, so Malley's experience of light sets the plot toward his ultimate death.

Furthermore, once he is in the hospital and has been diagnosed with the brain tumor, his three best friends--Doc, Pope, and Lace--declare not only their love for him but promise to stand by him throughout his suffering.

The first half of Mark's Gospel presents Jesus as a character who is powerful in word and deed. He heals the sick by touching them with his hand; he casts out demons with a few words; he teaches people a better way to live. George Malley is similarly presented. Possessing the power of telekinesis, Malley draws people to himself. With his super-human intelligence, he creates scientific experiments, learns languages in seconds, senses seismographic disturbances deep within the earth, and can find a lost boy using telepathy. He uses his power to help others. In fact, in an almost direct parallel with the scene in Mark's Gospel of Jesus healing a demonic boy, a man in "Phenomenon" brings his son to Malley and asks him to heal him by laying his hand on him.

But then Mark inverts the plot of his gospel. He is not interested in readers believing in Jesus because he works miracles and speaks powerful words. He wants people to believe because they experience the powerful powerlessness of Jesus on the cross. There is no reason to believe. Likewise, what had become fascination with Malley's telekinesis soon becomes fear. Malley's friends try to explain what's been going on and reduce his abilities to mere coincidences. They mock him and ridicule him. At this point in the movie, the viewer receives the information about Malley's brain tumor and that there is nothing anyone can do to help him. Malley is powerless before the tumor stretching over his brain. We learn that it will kill him.

At the book fair, as Malley attempts to alleviate people's fears by answering their questions, he is a man on trial. Made a public spectacle, he resembles Jesus in the scenes in Mark's Gospel when he stands both before the council and Pilate. The townspeople turn their backs on Malley, like Jesus' apostles abandon him in the Garden of Gethsemane and leave him to die all alone on the cross. However, in "Phenomenon" three of Malley's friends do stand by his side. The viewer should not miss the fact that there are three, a biblically sacred number signifying a theophany, the presence of God.

The three friends who stand by Malley's side represent those who have been touched and changed by him. Doc, who thought of Malley as his son, defends him to all in the bar, a type of church where the community gathers. Nate Pope is changed forever by the woman he marries at Malley's instigation and the fertilizer Malley created which Pope uses to produce an abundant crop of corn. Lace, who resisted for so long, has rediscovered love and the importance of relationships. Her children, who by sharing an apple with Malley, a type of Last Supper, have also eaten of his goodness.

Throughout the film, Malley is never abandoned by God, even though at times he thinks he is. The scenes of the wind swaying the branches of trees and the whistling sound that can be heard is a sign of the divine presence. Just as it is with Malley, so it is with Lace and her children after he dies. The Spirit permeates the whole earth and everything and everyone on it. Malley's personal spirit flows from and is mingled with that Spirit.

Once Jesus of Nazareth is beaten, crucified, and dies, he is buried. On the third day some women go to his tomb and hear a young man seated therein declare that he has been raised from the dead. They go away and tell no one. Likewise, Malley is beaten by tests administered by the FBI, he is crucified by Dr. Mellin who wants to reduce him to his brain, and he dies. After he is buried, Malley's friends believe that is still present to them in some way. He lives in their lives in the manner in which he affected them. So, as the movie ends, the viewer sees Malley's smiling face in a photograph sitting on the bar. Remembering that the bar is a type of church, it is not too far-fetched to say that the community has been altered forever by the presence of one George Malley, who has left it enough of his spirit to still celebrate his birthday.

Exercises and Questions for Discussion

1. Choose the five major characters in "Phenomenon" and for each indicate whether you consider him or her to be good or evil. Explain why for each.

2. Outline the plot of the film by scene. For each scene indicate its importance to the whole story and what purpose it serves.

3. What do you think is the major truth which the movie attempts to communicate? Is this truth one that endures? Explain.

4. After reading the Gospel According to Mark in one sitting, choose the five major characters and indicate for each whether you consider him or her good or evil. Explain why.

5. Identify and compare three characters from "Phenomenon" with three characters from Mark's Gospel. Explain how each pair is alike and unlike.

6. Identify and compare the turn in the plot of "Phenomenon" with the turn in the plot of Mark's Gospel.

7. What do you think is the major truth which Mark's Gospel attempts to communicate? Is this truth one that endures? Explain.

8. Make a list of three questions which you have about "Phenomenon" and three questions which you have about Mark's Gospel.

9. What is the phenomenon of "Phenomenon"?

Teaching Mark's Gospel

Sommersby

Mark's Gospel presents the reader with a hidden hero in the person of Jesus of Nazareth. Biblical scholars call this uniquely Markan theme the "messianic secret," since everyone in Mark's Gospel who shouldn't know who Jesus is (demons, unclean spirits) does know, and everyone who should know (apostles) never figures it out. Likewise, "Sommersby" (Warner Brothers, 1993) presents the viewer with a hidden hero, John Robert Sommersby (Richard Gere), who is not the same person he was six years before he went off to fight in the Civil War. Furthermore, the viewer is left to determine whether or not Jack Sommersby, who returned to his hometown, is the same man who had left it, just as the reader is left at the end of Mark's Gospel to determine who Jesus of Nazareth was.

Also at work in Mark's Gospel is what scholars refer to as the inside-outside theme. Those who should be inside Jesus' circle of followers, such as his disciples, end up outside at the end of the story, and those who should be outside, such as tax collectors, prostitutes, lepers, end up inside at the end of the story. In "Sommersby," the members of Jack's family, especially his wife, Laurel, who should know who he is, are never completely convinced, while the townsfolk, those outside his family, believe him to be who he claims to be.

As the film begins, the viewer watches a man pile rocks over the dead body of another man on the top of a hill. When he is finished, he runs down the hill quickly, stopping at a stream to wash his hands. The camera follows him as he journeys through snow and mountains and over roads. He, draped in a blanket, meets a troop of union soldiers, dressed in their blue uniforms, which informs the viewer that the setting is post-Civil War. The as-yet-unidentified man walks through a cemetery marked only with crosses, through a town in which people are rebuilding, through a hanging scene of two black men, and through a field to his home, a cotton plantation. In the course of his travels, he removes his blanket to reveal his Confederate gray uniform and he wraps a handkerchief around one hand.

As he approaches the outskirts of his home, a maimed man working in the field recognizes him as Jack Sommersby and begins to welcome him home as a local war hero. As word spreads among the hometown folk, a crowd gathers to welcome home Sommersby and escort him to his two-story, brick, white-columned porch, southern plantation home. Meanwhile, his wife, Laurel (Jodie Foster), who has been working in the field, prepares herself and her son, Robert, for Jack's arrival by changing clothes and taking a photo of a bearded Jack Sommersby out of a drawer of her bureau.

Readers of Mark's Gospel can't help but see the similarities in heros. The crowd of townsfolk welcoming home Sommersby is much like the crowd who appears so frequently in Mark's Gospel. The author of the gospel uses the word so frequently that the reader senses that the crowd takes on a persona of its own. Furthermore, the narrator of Mark's Gospel portrays Jesus' hometown crowd as being astounded by his return and ability to teach. Unlike Jesus, who ultimately was rejected and could do no deed of power in his hometown, Sommersby will be accepted and will bring about one great deed of power.

The crowd makes a second major appearance in Mark's Gospel when it welcomes Jesus to Jerusalem with cloaks and branches and singing, while he rides on a colt. Later in the story, the crowd will call for his death, much like the crowd in Sommersby will watch a hidden hero sentenced to hang by the neck until he is dead.

Furthermore, the author of Mark's Gospel ends many of his individual stories of healing and exorcism by referring to the amazement of the crowd. Throughout "Sommersby," the crowd will be amazed at the change that has taken place in Jack, who was known before the war as a bitter man, one who had alienated himself from his wife and slept in a separate bedroom.

As Sommersby approaches his wife and son, whom he hasn't seen for six years, Jethro, the old dog, growls at him until he extends his hand with the handkerchief tied around it. Robert meets his father, and then Jack and Laurel embrace. He has come home, but there is tension in the air.

During a welcome-home party on the lawn in front of the Sommersby home, Jack tells people from his hometown about being captured during the Civil War and spending five years in prison. When a black family, led by a man named Joseph, comes to welcome home Jack, they remain on the periphery of the celebration, creating tension between white and black. Afterward, one man asks Sommersby, "What's the matter?" Adding, "You're not acting like yourself," leads the viewer to question Jack's identity.

Throughout Mark's Gospel, the apostles question Jesus' identity, wondering who he is who stills the sea, who he is who heals the afflicted, who he is who walks on water. Meanwhile, the demons and the unclean spirits are constantly shouting out that they recognize Jesus of Nazareth as the Son of God.

Once the welcome-home party ends, Jack and Laurel enter their war-stripped home, and Laurel tells him how the Yankees came and took their silver, carpets, and anything else they could carry away. She, however, was able to save a brooch by "sitting on it." As they walk up the stairs, the viewer discovers that before Jack left they had been sleeping in separate rooms. As Laurel is undressing and preparing for bed, Jack appears in her room and asks her to shave his beard. He tells her that he promised himself that if he made it home after the war, that he would get rid of it. They move to the kitchen, where, while she shaves Jack's face with a straight razor, stopping periodically to position the razor on his neck, Laurel reveals that Jack wasn't as kind in the past as he is now. Once finished with the shave, she asks, "Who is this man sitting in my kitchen?"

The "shaving of the beard" scene is a way to portray a change of life in the journey of a man. It indicates that he has taken a new path and is not the same person he was before. It is similar to the baptism of Jesus by John the Baptist in the Jordan River in Mark's Gospel. After he is baptized, Jesus goes to the desert for forty days, defeats evil, and prepares for his ministry. He is not the same person as he was before he was baptized. Now, he is Spirit-filled, a man of powerful deeds and words. A voice from heaven confirms his divine status. The voice will be heard again during his transfiguration, a type of re-baptism. At that time, it will indicate a change in paths from power to powerlessness and death on a cross.

A character the viewer had met in the homecoming scene now reappears with a name. Oren (Bill Pullman) talks to Laurel about Jack coming back. Through their dialogue, the viewer learns that Oren had intended to marry Laurel if Jack hadn't returned. Oren reveals that Jack had abused Laurel in the past.

Robert emerges to discover that Jethro, the old dog, is dead.

When they were ascending the stairs after the homecoming party, Jack had asked Laurel what she had done with the handkerchief he had wrapped around his hand. She told him that she had burned it because it was so filthy. He reminded her that she had given it to him before he left. The viewer concludes that without the handkerchief the old dog doesn't recognize Jack. Oren buries the dog for Robert and prays over the grave.

Jack rides away from his house on a horse to check on the state of his plantation. He finds the outbuildings in shambles and the fields dry and hard and overgrown with weeds. He says that the land is tired and no cotton will grow in his fields.

Oren and Jack talk about his coming home and who Laurel wanted--Oren, who reminds Jack that before the war he left often. The tension between Oren and Jack mounts as Laurel tells Jack that she had promised Oren that she would marry him next year if Jack hadn't come home by then. Jack discovers that Oren had never kissed Laurel, thus effectively removing Oren as a contender for Laurel's support.

Jack goes to his bedroom, where he is putting on a shirt embroidered with the initials "J.S." as Laurel enters the room. He reminds her that she made it for him before the war, but it was too small and wouldn't fit. Now, it fits. She pulls it off of him and invites him to her bed, in which they make love. Before they do so, Jack tells her, "I don't remember how I was with you, how to be."

The conflict between Oren and Jack is now established in the film, much like the conflict between Jesus and his apostles' lack of faith in him is etched throughout Mark's Gospel. Also, the bonding between Jack and Laurel through intercourse will be questioned as to its effectiveness later in the film, much like Jesus' bonding with his apostles (their call and Jesus' last meal with them) will be questioned at the end of the gospel when all of them abandon him.

Immediately following Jack's bonding with Laurel is the scene of his bonding with Robert. Robert is sweeping the porch when Jack arrives at the front door driving a horse and buggy. After Jack invites Robert to go to town with him, he hands over the reigns to Robert and lets him drive the wagon, even though Robert makes it clear that Laurel would never let him drive.

While in town, Jack goes to the boot shop to be measured by the cobbler for a new pair of boots. The man has a wooden model of the right foot of his customers hanging on the wall. As he finds Jack's model, he places it under his foot to discover that it is two sizes smaller. The subject of having one's foot shrink two sizes in six years is quickly dismissed by Jack for another topic.

In the next scene of the film, a town meeting is in progress. Jack is standing in the center of the townsfolk and talking about "the future." He thinks that the way they can recover economically after the Civil War is to plant tobacco instead of cotton. He offers each of them a parcel of land, tools, and the opportunity to buy the land with the money they make from their future harvest. He ask them how long they have been sharecroppers and how good his offer must now sound. And he offers the same opportunity to both white and black townsfolk.

Oren says that tobacco seed is expensive and that Jack has no cash to purchase it. Sommersby, looking at Laurel, says, "We're all sittin' on a little somethin'," a reference to the ruby brooch that Laurel had hidden from the Union soldiers. She offers the brooch to Jack and, thus, indicates that she is supporting his plan. The only way to purchase tobacco seed is for all the townsfolk to bring their jewelry, watches, silver sets, and other valuables to Jack, who will exchange them for cash and buy tobacco seed in a nearby town. As all the treasures are collected, Joseph (a black man), who brings his own treasured piece of carved ivory, says, "You will be comin' back, Mr. Jack, won't you?" Robert contributes his own knife, like the poor widow in Mark's Gospel who gives everything she has to live on, and Jack heads off with a wagon full of the townsfolk's wealth. The people have supported Jack's plan, much like Jesus' apostles seem to support his ministry in Mark's Gospel.

The people of Vinehill, the local town, go to work clearing the fields of rocks, marking out plots, getting the earth ready for planting, and weeding. In a Sunday scene, Oren, dressed in clerical black, is found preaching about trees bearing fruit and how one can tell a tree by its fruit, a passage found in Matthew's Gospel and Luke's Gospel, but not in Mark's Gospel. The closest the author of Mark's Gospel comes to a saying about trees is the scene where Jesus curses a fig tree for not having any fruit on it. In a manner of speaking, "Sommersby" declares that Oren is cursing Jack, who has not yet returned with the tobacco seed and some people are wondering if he, indeed, will ever return.

However, their fears are abated when Sommersby shows up with a puppy for Robert. After delivering the puppy, he goes to Laurel and tells her that he had to go to Virginia for the seed. After they make love, the camera shows the whole town at work planting tobacco seeds, covering the seed beds with straw and burlap. More love-making between Jack and Laurel follows and the seeds grow. While the viewer doesn't catch it immediately, the love-making scenes interspersed with the seed-planting scenes are intended to show that both tobacco and human seeds are being planted and are growing. Later in the film, the viewer will discover that Laurel is pregnant.

Meanwhile, there is a series of several family-bonding scenes in "Sommersby" interspersed with tobacco-cultivating scenes. Jack reads to Robert from Homer while Laurel sews. Fields are plowed and prepared. Laurel washes Jack's back as he sits in a bathtub. The tobacco seedlings are transplanted by the townsfolk into huge fields. When the plants don't begin growing, fertilizer is poured on them. Laurel tells Jack that she used to be rich and sad, but now she is poor and happy. But she asks Jack about reading Homer and how he never used to read him. He says that the schoolteacher with whom he was in prison gave him his copy when he died. Months pass, the tobacco plants grow tall and blossom. While breaking off the blooms, Laurel faints. The viewer learns that the seed planted in her, like the seed planted in the ground, has become fruitful.

The family-bonding scenes in "Sommersby" contrast to the lack of bonding between Jesus, his family, and his disciples. Unique to Mark's Gospel is the fact that Jesus' own family--his mother and brothers (and sisters)--think that he is out of his mind and they attempt to take him home. He informs them that they are outside his circle of followers. Likewise, his apostles, who never understand who Jesus is, end up outside his circle by abandoning him and running away when he is arrested by the crowd. Those who are left in the circle are all societal outcasts: tax collectors, prostitutes, the deformed.

The fruitful tobacco crop faces a crisis. Hogworms are attacking the precious leaves. Meanwhile, another crisis develops. Three travelers arrive looking for work on Jack Sommersby's plantation. The fact that there are three of them indicates that something significant is being revealed. As he is speaking to them, one draws a knife. Jack takes it away and uses it to force the three men to continue on. While Jack pauses at a pool of water to wash his face, Laurel, who has watched all this take place from the porch, asks Jack about the men. Jack does not respond to her, but says the current crisis of worms must be dealt with.

Help comes in the person of Oren, who is first shown cutting the grass with the scythe in the cemetery next to the church. He notices a tombstone with the name Sayer on it. He goes to Jack and shows him how to keep the worms off of the tobacco by pouring a type of liquid around the base of the plants. When Jack asks about how Oren knew about this procedure, Oren tricks him by referring to Sayer, who, Oren says, owns land by the church. Jack says that he will have to thank him. The viewer, who knows that Sayer is dead, later discovers that Sayer was Jack's best friend.

Oren goes to Laurel and tells her that he has helped her work the land for six years. He also tells her that he talked to the three drifters, who informed him that the man claiming to be Jack Sommersby isn't Jack Sommersby. One of them was with Jack at Wilson Creek "when his chest got tore up" and Jack has no scars. Oren tells Laurel that Jack didn't know that Sayer, his best friend, was dead. In a direct approach, he tells her that she has known all along that Jack isn't Jack, that she's living in mortal sin, and that she and her child will be confined to everlasting damnation. Oren says that the hogworm invasion of the tobacco is a sign of the rottenness of the place, a reference to Oren's sermon about good and bad trees and their fruit.

This conversation gets Laurel to doubt Jack's identity more than ever. As she begins to look through his desk while he is sitting in a chair in the corner of his study, he surprises her by asking, "Who do you think I am? Do you love me. I love you." Laurel spies a handgun in the drawer of the desk, draws it, points it at Jack, and tells him to get out of the house. He says that he is not leaving: "I'm home, and I am not going to leave again." She says, "You are not my husband." He says, "May God strike me dead if I am not."

In the next scene the camera focuses on a burning cross planted in the front yard of the Sommersby home and a gang of Knights of the White Carnelian or the Ku Klux Klan on horses. Jack and Laurel rush to the scene. Jack goes to the cross while Laurel stops on the porch and Robert watches from an upstairs window. One KKK member declares, "We are God's vengeance." The body of Joseph, the freed black man, has been beaten and dropped in front of Jack, whom a KKK member states is a teacher. Jack recognizes Oren, who has a wooden leg, by noticing the brace on his boot in the saddle stirrup. The KKK informs Jack that he has transgressed by selling land to a black man. Jack defends the black man's right to own land. The KKK rides off and Jack and Laurel assist Joseph. Once again, the viewer is left with the question of Jack's identity.

The divisiveness and the unevenness of human dignity between white and black fostered by the KKK is similar to both the division between Jew and Gentile and Judaism and Jesus in Mark's Gospel. Jews considered Gentiles unclean and outside of their social circles. Judaism had great difficulty with the egalitarianism of Jesus, who erased boundaries and attempted to include everyone in his circle of followers. Just as the raising of tobacco brought the citizens of Vinehill together as one community, so the preaching and table fellowship of Jesus brought the citizens of God's reign together as one community in Mark's Gospel.

A series of "family" scenes follow the KKK episode. Jack reads Homer to Robert as he begins to fall asleep, while Laurel strokes Jack's hair. The part of the Trojan War that Jack reads is important as he states that the Trojans knew the victory would be theirs. Such a line is ironic, since the Trojans ultimately lost the war to Oddeseus and his soldiers who hid themselves in a wooden horse in order to get into Troy. The irony is that Sommersby will ultimately lose his life.

In biblical language, this part of the story serves as a "prophecy-fulfillment" scene. It is similar to Jesus' three predictions concerning his suffering, death, and resurrection in Mark's Gospel. The "prophecy" serves to deepen interest in the story and keep the viewer watching or the reader reading to see if and how it is fulfilled.

While Jack is at work in his barn, Oren arrives and accuses him of killing Jethro, the old dog. In a monologue, Oren asks Jack who he is. Then, he picks up a shovel and tries to kill Jack with it. As the fight progresses, Jack gets caught with a rope around his neck as Oren attempts to strangle him. In the midst of their fight Robert arrives to announce that Laurel's baby is on the way. The fight is abruptly ended, and Jack runs to Laurel's bedroom where she is holding their new baby girl named Rachel after Laurel's mother.

Just as the fruit of Laurel's womb emerges into the world, so does the tobacco crop. It is a huge crop, ready to be harvested. Before that begins, Jack runs through the field, weaving in and out of rows, celebrating his bounty. All of the townsfolk participate in the harvest and the tobacco is hung to dry and cure, preparing it for sale.

In the old dilapidated church building, whose steeple is partially missing, Rachel is baptized. Just as Jack, Laurel, and Rachel are leaving the church, a federal marshal and his deputy greet them on horseback. The marshal states that he has a warrant for the arrest of John Robert Sommersby for the death of a Charles Coughlin.

This scene is the turning point of the film. It initiates the crisis of the identity of Jack Sommersby and begins the process of turning the story from one of success into one of tragedy. It is similar in function to the scene set along the way to Caesarea Philippi in Mark's Gospel. The Markan Jesus asks his disciples to identify him. Peter declares that Jesus is the Messiah, and the reader thinks that for the first time in the story Peter has got one answer right. However, the Markan Jesus immediately verbalizes his first prediction of his suffering, death, and resurrection and Peter rebukes him for such talk. Jesus, then, calls Peter a Satan because he is judging according to human standards instead of God's standards. After this, the author of the gospel changes his story line. The Jesus of powerful deeds and words in the first half of the gospel becomes the Jesus who teaches the way of powerlessness in the second half--all the way to the cross.

Before he is taken to Nashville for trial, Laurel visits Jack in jail and asks him if he killed Coughlin. Jack declares, "No, I did not." Afterwards, he is found on horseback between the federal marshal and his deputy on their way to Nashville. A large crowd of townsfolk gather around the three men. Jack promises them that he will return, much like the Markan Jesus speaks about the coming of the Son of Man. The people promise Jack that they will support him as a large group of them join the procession with him to Nashville. The viewer can't help but recall Jesus' triumphal entry into Jerusalem in Mark's Gospel.

Judge Barry Conrad Isaac (James Earl Jones), a black man, enters his courtroom while the assembly emits groans of shock. The first witness for the prosecution states that he saw Jack hit Coughlin and then kill him, identifying Jack as Jack Sommersby. The second witness states that he saw a man lying on the ground who said, "Don't shoot, Sommersby." But Sommersby killed him. The third witness identifies Jack Sommersby's signature in a Grand Hotel registration book and on bank mortgage papers. Court is adjourned.

While Laurel is sitting alone in the courtroom, Oren finds her and tells her that Jack will hang unless she accepts his offer, which the viewer doesn't get to hear.

Laurel visits Jack in jail and asks him to tell her who he is. Jack: "Do you really want to know?" Laurel: "Yes." Jack: "Are you sure?" Laurel: "Yes." Jack: "I'm Jack Sommersby. Pleased to meet you." Laurel walks away, calling him a stubborn fool and saying, "I'm not going to let you do this."

She seeks out Oren in his hotel room to inform him that she accepts his offer.

The sequence of scenes showing Oren finding Laurel in the courtroom, her visit with Jack, and her seeing Oren in his hotel room is called intercalating in biblical terminology. It means that one part of the story is told, another story or scene interrupts it, and the original story resumes. It is a technique that the author of Mark's Gospel uses several times, such as in beginning the story of Jarius' daughter, interrupting it with the story of the woman with the hemorrhage, and then competing the original story.

Back in the courtroom, the defense presents its case by calling Laurel as its first witness. She identifies the signatures from the hotel register and the bank note as Jack's. When asked to point him out to the court, she declares, "My husband is not in this room." The defendant is declared to be an imposter. Laurel says she knew him to be an imposter from "the little things," such as he looked different, he didn't remember some things, the dog didn't recognize him, he didn't talk about his father who was an important person in his life. Especially, she said, she knew Jack wasn't her husband from the way he was intimate with her.

When asked why she continued to act as if Jack were her husband, she said that everyone wanted Jack to be alive and to be home. So, it was easier to accept him as Jack Sommersby. Then, she narrated the signs that gave away his identity, such as the shoemaker discovering that his foot was two sizes smaller than it was before and the identity given by the drifters who had come looking for work during the hogworm infestation of the tobacco crop. Finally, when shown one of the promissory notes for land in exchange for working it that Jack had given to all those who contributed their valuables in order to buy the tobacco seed, Laurel says that the signature on it is not Jack's signature and that he had made up the story about hurting his hand.

The identity of Jack Sommersby continues to be questioned through the second witness, Matthew Fulsom, a farmer owning 2,000 acres of land in Clark County. He identifies Jack as Horace Townsend, a school teacher who collected $1,200 from people in the area to built a new school house and ran off with the money. Fulsom says that there is a story that Townsend went south where he got a woman pregnant, joined the army, and then deserted. At this point, Jack's attorney asks the judge to rule a mistrial since Jack is not who he claims to be. However, Jack objects, saying, "Without my name I don't think I have a life."

Jack dismisses his lawyer and the judge permits Jack to continue his own defense as Robert smiles. Jacks asks Fulsom if they have ever met, and Fulsom says no. Jack declares that Fulsom was one of the members of the KKK who burned a cross in his front yard and that he doesn't want Jack to sell land to a black man. When Fulsom begins to berate black people, the judge (remember, he is a black man) first sentences him to thirty days in jail, then, after Fulsom talks back to the judge, to sixty days in jail for contempt of court.

After Fulsom is removed from the courtroom, Jack asks members from the community of Vinehill to swear to the judge who he is. All of them say he is Jack Sommersby. The judge accepts their group testimony and agrees with Jack that there is no reason to call each one to the witness stand.

However, Laurel is called to the witness stand. Jack questions her about believing that he is her husband. She says that she accepted him as her husband because she was lonesome and wanted a father for her son. She says, "Jack Sommersby never said a kind word to me in his life."

And that's how she knows Jack is not her husband.

The judge interrupts to tell Jack, "You proceed at your own jeopardy," as Jack will end up incriminating himself if he continues in his line of questioning. But he does continue, telling Laurel that if he is not Jack Sommersby, then the paper contracts for land that he signed are not legal and none of the townsfolk who have them will get any land, that her children will be bastards, and that she is a thief-lover. Jack accuses Laurel and Oren of being in league. Laurel admits that she promised Oren that things would be the way they were before Jack came home if he helped her get Jack acquitted. Jack emphasizes his own integrity and asks Laurel to identify him. She says that he is her husband. Immediately, the judge tells Jack that he has argued to his own guilt by establishing his identity. He will die for having killed Coughlin.

The twists and turns of the trial scenes echo Jesus' trial scenes in Mark's Gospel. In the trial before the council, the issue is Jesus' identity. Peter denies knowing Jesus. The issue in Jesus' trial before Pilate is again his identity. In both trials, the Markan Jesus argues to his own guilt as the Messiah and the King of the Jews. Thus, like Sommersby, in establishing his identity he prepares for his own death.

Before Laurel goes to visit Jack in prison for the last time, the camera focuses on the tobacco being sold at market. A buyer places a card on top of the Vinehill crop and the scene cuts to Laurel telling Jack that they got twelve cents per hundred weight when they had hoped for eight or ten at best. Laurel tells Jack that the crop brought in over $10,000. They celebrate. And Jack asks about the kids and tells Laurel to tell Robert that his dad never killed anyone.

Laurel asks about Horace Townsend. Jack tells her that he knew Townsend and that they had spent four years locked up in a cell together. He declares that Townsend is dead but that he didn't kill him; he got stabbed when he killed Coughlin. Jack buried him on a hill under some rocks. This last statement sends the viewer back to the beginning scene of the movie and interprets what happened at that time.

Again, Laurel doubts Jack's identity. He says that if he is Townsend, then they have no home. He says that he will not be Horace Townsend again. "Being your husband is the only thing I've ever done that I'm proud of," Jack tells Laurel.

Now, preparing for his hanging, Jack changes shirts, putting on the one Laurel made for him years ago with the letters "J.S." embroidered on it. He asks Laurel to be with him as he is hung. She tells him that she always loved him as he gives her his wedding ring. The guards enter the cell, tie Jack's hands behind his back, and lead him to the gallows.

At the gallows the sentence of the death penalty is read while the camera scans the crowd to show most of its members weeping for Jack. The minister from Vinehill begins a reading from Psalm 91, which speaks of God protecting, delivering, and showing salvation to those who call upon him, while Jack scans the crowd looking for Laurel, who works her way through the throng to the front. When he can't see her, Jack shouts, "Laurel," who shouts back, "Jack, I'm here." The hood and rope are placed over his head and the trap door swings open. Jack Sommersby hangs.

Jack's death is paralleled by the crucifixion scene of Jesus in Mark's Gospel. After he is nailed to the cross, he is taunted by those passing by and by the Jewish authorities. After he dies, the pagan, Roman centurion declares, "Truly this man was God's Son." This is the third time that the reader has "heard" Jesus be declared to be God's Son. The first was the voice from heaven at his baptism. The second was the same voice from heaven during his transfiguration. In both cases only God knows who Jesus is. Now, a human being identifies Jesus as God's Son. And it is important to note the irony that it is a pagan and a Roman--not one of Jesus' apostles!

The sound of the trap door flying open in the film moves to soft music and panoramas of Vinehill. A new steeple is being placed on the church. Jack's home is getting a fresh coat of paint. Falling-down fences are being repaired. And Laurel approaches John Robert Sommersby's tombstone on the top of a hill with a bouquet of flowers. The dates on the tombstone, 1831-1867, under Jack's name, indicate that he was but thirty-six years old. The words "Beloved husband" appear below the dates. As the camera again begins to scan the town, the movie ends.

John Robert Sommersby lives on in Vinehill. He lives through the new steeple on the church, the fresh paint, and the repaired fences. He gave his life in exchange for the life of the town. In a way similar to the announcement of the resurrection of Jesus in Mark's Gospel, in which there are no post-resurrection appearances, Sommersby is declared to be alive and well.

Jack Sommersby is a tragic hero best compared to the Markan Jesus, another tragic hero. In both the film and the gospel the question is one of identity. Is each man who he claims to be? The viewer of "Sommersby" is left to answer the question for himself or herself. Evidence can be produced for either a yes or a no answer. Likewise, the reader is left to answer the question in Mark's Gospel. Because he or she has access to privileged information by getting to know what many of the characters in the story don't know and getting to "see" what many of the characters in the gospel never see, he or she must decide for himself or herself if Jesus is God's Son. Evidence can be produced for either a yes or a no answer.

Laurel is a type of Peter. One minute she believes that Jack is her husband and one minute she doubts. Likewise, Peter in Mark's Gospel at one minute believes and one minute doubts. Just when the reader thinks Peter has finally figured out who Jesus is, Jesus names him Satan. Then, Peter denies ever knowing Jesus three times. He disappears from the story and, after Jesus' death and the announcement of his resurrection, is never seen again.

There is little doubt that Oren is a type of Judas. The director of the film, Jon Amiel, certainly makes a statement about ministers through Oren, who appears usually dressed in the black clothes of a preacher, who preaches one sermon in the church, and who tends the church cemetery. After working for Laurel for six years during Jack's absence, his plans for marrying Laurel are upset when Sommersby comes home. He seeks out proof that Jack is not Jack and attempts to help Laurel secure Jack's life by proving that Jack isn't Sommersby which will free Laurel to marry him. Like Mark's Judas, who disappears from the story once he turns Jesus over to the crowd, Oren disappears from the story after Jack accuses him of being in league with Laurel to say that he wasn't who he claimed to be.

Exercises and Questions for Discussion

1. Choose the five major characters in "Sommersby" and for each indicate whether you consider him or her to be good or evil. Explain why for each.

2. Outline the plot of the film by scene. For each scene indicate its importance to the whole story and what purpose it serves.

3. What do you think is the major truth which the movie attempts to communicate? Is this truth one that endures? Explain.

4. After reading the Gospel According to Mark in one sitting, choose the five major characters and indicate for each whether you consider him or her good or evil. Explain why.

5. Identify and compare three characters from "Sommersby" with three characters from Mark's Gospel. Explain how each pair is alike and unlike.

6. Identify and compare two turns in the plot of "Sommersby" with two turns in the plot of Mark's Gospel.

7. What do you think is the major truth which Mark's Gospel attempts to communicate? Is this truth one that endures? Explain.

8. Make a list of three questions which you have about "Sommersby" and three questions which you have about Mark's Gospel.

9. Identify at least two sections in Mark's Gospel where the author employs the technique of intercalating. Explain how the literary technique works to elucidate the stories.

Teaching Mark's Gospel

The Shawshank Redemption

"The Shawshank Redemption" (Castle Rock Entertainment, 1994) can be used to illustrate the inside-outside theme which is incorporated throughout Mark's Gospel, considered by biblical scholars to be the earliest narrative of the ministry of Jesus of Nazareth. The author of the oldest gospel, written around 70 C.E., employs the subtle inside-outside theme in many scenes to make his readers aware that those people who think that they are insiders may discover, like the apostles did, that they are really outsiders. Those who should be included in Jesus' inner circle--his mother, family, apostles, etc.--are portrayed as being outside of it, and those who should be outside--tax collectors, prostitutes, the deformed, etc.--are found to be inside of it.

The astute reader must read Mark's Gospel very carefully in order to discern the inside-outside theme. Sometimes Jesus is portrayed as being inside a house, in a boat, or in a geographical area with people a devout Jew of the early first century common era would not have associated, while the people with whom he should have been sharing a meal, a boat trip, or a plot of earth are nowhere to be seen. The inside-outside theme reaches a crescendo as Jesus dies on a cross, abandoned by all.

"The Shawshank Redemption" is a story about a man falsely accused of killing his wife and her golf-pro lover. He is tried in court, found guilty, and sent to Shawshank Prison, located in the state of Maine, to serve two life sentences. There, after a struggle to be accepted, he becomes a leader of inmates. After serving 19 years of his sentence, he escapes from the prison in an elaborate and well-planned scenario, but only after he has transformed the inside of the prison walls by awakening in hardened criminals a humanity most of the world thought they had lost. Furthermore, he imparts to his special friend a hope, a dream of freedom, which materializes on a beach in Mexico.

Andy Dufresne (Tim Robbins) enters Shawshank Prison in 1947 with another group of prisoners on a bus, which pulls into the prison yard and is greeted by inmates lining both sides of the chain-linked fence. As they examine the new inmates, those who have made Shawshank their home place bets on who will and who will not survive the rigors of prison life. The narrator of the film, Ellis Boyd "Red" Redding (Morgan Freeman), says that he didn't think much of Andy when he first saw him.

After a brief orientation by Warden Norton (Bob Gunton), Dufresne is initiated into prison life. He is sprayed with water from a fire hose, after which a white powder is thrown onto his wet skin to delouse him. He is given prison clothes, shoes, and a Bible and is marched naked to his cell. Thus begins his new life as a prisoner within Shawshank's walls.

Dufresne escapes from Shawshank in 1966. After spending nineteen years within the prison's walls, he crawls through a tunnel and a large sewer pipe to freedom outside the prison's walls.

The setting of "The Shawshank Redemption" presents the teacher the opportunity to help students understand the use of the inside-outside theme in Mark's Gospel. First, the film illustrates the environmental difference between inside the prison's dull gray walls and barbed-wire-topped gray chain-linked fence and outside the physical enclosure where trees grow, rivers flow, and people come and go in freedom.

Second, the film locates the inside-outside theme in the lives of two characters: Brooks Hadlin (James Whitmore) and Ellis Boyd Redding. Hadlin, who has been the prison librarian since 1912 and who has never had a helper, is assigned an assistant--Andy Dufresne. Shortly thereafter, the prison board decides that Hadlin is ready for parole. Once he finds out that he is being paroled, Hadlin grabs a fellow inmate and friend named Heywood (William Sadler), puts a knife to his throat, and threatens to kill him in order to stay in prison. Brought to the scene of the attack in the library, Dufresne talks Brooks into putting down the knife.

In the prison exercise yard, Red explains the inside-outside dilemma, saying, "Brooks is institutionalized. Man been in here fifty years. In here he is an important man, an educated man. Outside he's nothing." Red continues,

> These walls are funny. At first you hate them, then you get used to them. Enough time passes and you get so that you depend on them. That's institutionalized. They send you here for life, and that's exactly what they take--the part that counts anyway.

Before he exits the prison, Hanlin sets free his pet crow named Jake, who had fallen out of his nest as a baby and had been fed and raised by Hanlin. Standing at the window and letting the crow fly through the bars, Hanlin tells Jake, "You're free." The setting free of the crow is not only of a sign of the setting free of Hanlin, which takes place immediately, but it is also a sign of what happens to one who passes from the inside to the outside. Later in the movie, in a letter to his friends in Shawshank, Hanlin tells them that the goes to the park and feeds the birds in the hope of one day seeing Jake, but that day never comes.

Hanlin, dressed in a brown suit, white shirt and tie, and wearing a brown 1950s-style dress hat, walks through the prison gate carrying a brown suitcase. He rides a bus to a town and crosses a street while almost getting hit by a car. He cannot cope with the fastness of the outside world. He checks into his room, provided by the parole board, at a half-way boarding house and goes to work in a grocery store as a bag boy. At night, he tosses and turns, unable to sleep. In his letter to his friends in Shawshank, he writes about his desire to get a gun, rob the grocery store, and be sent back to prison. He decides "not to stay," which the viewer comes to understand means suicide. After climbing up on a small table and carving "Brooks was here" on an exposed ceiling rafter, he ties a rope around the beam, kicks away the table, and hangs himself. In Shawshank, as Red is reading Hadlin's letter, he says that Hanlin should have died in Shawshank.

Hadlin's inability to live outside the prison is set in contrast with Red's ability to do so. At first, Red is not sure of himself. "I don't think I could make it on the outside," he tells Dufresne in an extended dialogue between the two of them following Andy's two-month stint in the hole for bringing some of the "outside"--music--into the prison. "I've been here most of my life," says Red. "I'm an institutional man now, just like Brooks was."

Dufresne offers hope to Red that he can change and live outside Shawshank. Andy tells him, "You underestimate yourself. It comes down to a simple choice: Get busy living or get busy dying." While he has to struggle, Red's opportunity to get busy doing one or the other comes when he is paroled. He represents the hope of freedom and the ability to live outside. Earlier in the film, describing Dufresne's first years in Shawshank, Red had said, "Andy kept to himself, trying to adapt to life on the inside." Andy did adapt to life on the inside, but he never abandoned hope for life again on the outside. He represents the ability of people to adapt to the situation in which they find themselves--but not permanently.

Dressed in a brown suit, white shirt and tie, wearing a 1950s-style brown hat, and carrying a brown suitcase, just like Hadlin before him, Red rides the bus to town, checks into the same half-way house room, and is employed in the same grocery store. What is different is that he does not commit suicide, but he learns how to live on the outside. Once he had said, "Prison life consists of routine and more routine," but he discovers that routine can be changed.

In Mark's Gospel, the reader is bombarded with the inside-outside theme. It seems to roll out of control throughout the story as Jesus of Nazareth declares that his family is outside while his inner circle of apostles, tax collectors, prostitutes, lepers, and the deformed are inside. But as the inside-outside theme picks up speed, even those who are declared to be insiders abandon the hero once he is arrested and, in the story, are never rehabilitated. Such a negative portrayal of Jesus' gang prompted the authors of Matthew's Gospel and Luke's Gospel later to write their own account of what took place in an attempt to reorganize what became known as the Christian movement. Students should be alerted to pay attention in Mark's Gospel to the physical settings, such as Jesus with people in a house, in a boat, or in a deserted place, in order to grasp fully the inside-outside theme.

Warden Norton further illustrates the inside-outside theme in Mark's Gospel, especially when he instigates what Red called his "inside-out program." After putting inmates to work outside prison walls in community service projects, Norton began skimming money off of the top of what the prisoners were paid for the work they did. Also, other contractors, who couldn't compete on bids with Norton's labor force, bribed him to bid higher than they so that they would get the jobs. Dufresne, with his background in banking, was put in charge of keeping Norton's books and preparing direct-mail deposits to banks outside the prison in order to launder Norton's money.

In a scene involving only Red and Andy reshelving books in the library, Dufresne tells Red about the "river of dirty money" running through Shawshank and how he has funneled it into different banks under the name of Randall Stevens, a fictitious person who had a birth certificate, a driver's license, and a Social Security number. He was "a phantom" of Andy's imagination. Red tells Andy that he is "a Rembrandt." Andy replies, "On the outside I was an honest man, straight as an arrow. I had to come to prison to be a crook."

After taking Norton's ledger and escaping from Shawshank, Dufresne, pretending to be Randall Stevens, goes to Main National Bank and withdraws the money Norton had been depositing there. Andy had the right identification, Social Security number, and his signature matched that on file at the bank. He tells the banker that he is going abroad and receives a cashier's check closing the account. Red continues the story saying, "Mr. Stevens visited nearly a dozen banks in the Portland area that morning. All totaled, he blew town with better than $370,000 of lord Norton's money--severance pay for nineteen years."

Exercises and Questions for Discussion

1. In what ways does the film illustrate the inside-outside theme found in Mark's Gospel?

2. What do you think is the major truth which the movie attempts to communicate? Is this truth one that endures? Explain.

3. How do the characters in the film, especially that of Andy Dufresne, Brooks Hadlin, and Ellis Boyd Redding illustrate the Markan inside-outside theme? Explain.

4. Compare and contrast life inside Shawshank Prison to life outside of it. What do you discover?

5. In the film, Andy Dufresne states that he had to come to Shawshank prison to become a crook. After he escapes, he takes the money he had laundered for Warden Norton with him to Mexico, essentially stealing that for which other inmates had worked and implying that he had earned it by spending nineteen years in prison for a crime he didn't commit. Evaluate the morality of Dufresne's action.

Teaching Matthew's Gospel

Being There

In scholarly circles, it is generally accepted that the author of Matthew's Gospel borrowed both material from Mark's Gospel and from another source to which the author of Luke's Gospel also had access. This source shared by Matthew and Luke is called Q (from the German "Quelle," meaning "source"). Also, the author of Matthew's Gospel has some unique material in his narrative that is found in no other story in the Christian Bible (New Testament). Biblical scholars call this special material "M."

Matthew's author writes in irony. He uses words to communicate his message by not employing their literal meaning. Matthew's irony is difficult to detect because we usually "hear" irony by noting it in the tone of voice of a speaker. Because we are dealing with a written text, the irony is not only difficult to "hear," but the reader may understand the text literally and miss the message of the author. In other words, what the author writes literally often is not what he means. He also uses hyperbole, extravagant exaggeration, with an ironic tone to communicate his message.

For example, he portrays Jesus as declaring that if a person's eye or right hand causes one to sin, he or she should gouge it out or cut it off and throw it away. That can't be taken literally; otherwise, most of humankind would be walking around without right hands and blind. The exaggeration is employed to insist that people avoid sin, which the author of Matthew's Gospel understands to be any action which divides the community, the church.

Ironic hyperbole can be missed easily because of the differences between the author's culture and our own. When the Matthean Jesus instructs his disciples to give away their cloaks as well as their coats when they are sued, we can miss the fact that the person would be left standing naked in court, a far worse offense from a Jewish perspective than simply and freely giving away an extra set of clothes from our walk-in closets.

Matthew's Gospel has no over-arching plot, like Mark's Gospel does. However, this author manages to keep his story together by using several major themes, the principal of which is righteousness. For Matthew, righteousness means "doing God's will." But it is more than merely following the Law as found in the Torah. It implies going beyond the Law to the principles upon which the Law is based. The author never tells the reader what acts or behavior indicates who is righteous and who is not because he believes that no one can judge except God and the Son of Man when he returns. All that people can do is to watch the weeds and the wheat grow together until the harvest.

Discipleship is a call to righteousness. Before the author begins to narrate the sequence of Jesus' suffering and death, he tells the story of the judgment of the nations and reveals the criterion for righteousness-- taking care of the needs of others because they are needy. In other words, those who hear God's word and act on it are the righteous. They do the right thing because it is the right thing to do--and for no other reason, not even seeing Jesus in those who are needy.

In order to teach his Jewish audience this new form of righteous- ness, Matthew portrays Jesus as a type of Moses through his gospel. As an infant, Jesus is taken by his parents to Egypt, where Moses was born and raised. Just as Moses led the Hebrews out of Egyptian slavery, so Jesus is called forth from Egypt to Israel to lead his people to a higher righteousness. Moses is credited with having written the five books of the Pentateuch (Genesis, Exodus, Leviticus, Numbers, Deuteronomy), so Jesus gives five sermons. Moses received the Law on Mount Sinai, so Jesus delivers his most important discourses from a mountain.

In order to help students understand the irony in Matthew's Gospel and the author's use of hyperbole and righteousness, the film "Being There" (Warner Brothers, 1979), based upon the novel of the same name by Jerzy Kosinski, can be used. While the film is a comedy, it is one of hyperbolic irony. Only the viewer understands what none of the characters comprehend when in dialogue with each other. Thus, the viewer is forced to another level of discourse, namely, what the characters say is not what they mean.

The film begins with a TV. In rapid succession the viewer sees and hears an orchestra, cartoons, and then "snow." The camera gives a panorama of the room in which a man gets out of bed and brushes his hair. Then, the camera moves to the garden--it is winter--where the same man is watering plants. We see him dusting off an old car that has four flat tires, then sitting at a table where he, Chance Gardener (Peter Sellers), watches the TV. Louise, the maid, enters the room and announces that the old man has died and that she covered him up with a sheet. Chance, while watching Sesame Street and Captain Kangaroo on TV, asks Louise if she has seen the garden. He says that it feels like it may snow. Louise castigates Chance for not caring about the old dead man.

In the next scene, Chance views the "old man," who is dead in bed. He uncovers his face, touches his head, and, sitting on the edge of the bed, turns on the TV, which shows an ad for a posture-pedic mattress. The viewer notices the irony of the mattress ad and the dead man on the bed! Then, Chance goes to work in the garden. Louise emerges from the house and tells Chance that she is leaving and that he needs to find a lady. Then, she declares that he will always be a little boy. After Louise leaves, Chance walks into the kitchen and sees that everything is covered with white sheets. He uncovers the TV and turns it on.

Two people enter the front door, hear the TV on in the kitchen, and proceed to investigate. What the viewer has suspected is confirmed through the dialogue between Thomas Franklin and Sally Hayes, lawyers, who are attempting to settle the old man's estate: Chance is the gardener. Officially, Chance doesn't exist. There is no mention of him in any of the old man's records, yet he has been living in the house since he was a child. He is not related to the old man. He was never allowed outside the perimeters of the house. He has never been in a car, he can't write, and he can't cook or prepare food for himself. Chance successively shows the two lawyers the garden, the garage with the old car in it, and his room.

Franklin tells him that they need some proof of him living there, and Chance states that they have him. Later, Chance explains to Franklin that the TVs in his room, in the kitchen, and in the garden were gifts from the old man. He also tells him that he was allowed to go to the attic and wear any of the old man's clothes.

Next, Franklin asks Chance what kind of claim he is going to make against the deceased's estate. Chance states, "The garden is a healthy one, Thomas. I have no claim." When Franklin asks him if he would be willing to sign a paper saying he has no claim, Chance reveals that he cannot read or write. Next, Franklin informs Chance that the house is being closed and that he will have to be out in one day.

As they are preparing to leave, Field asks Chance about any medical or dental records that he might have to prove his identity. He says that he has no doctor or dentist. So, Chance prepares to leave the only world he has known, but first he watches TV, then goes to the attic and finds a suitcase. Bringing it to his room, he packs it with his clothes while continuing to watch TV. As he walks out the door dressed in a long black, double-breasted overcoat with a gray bowler hat and carrying his suitcase in one hand and an umbrella in the other, the theme from "2001: A Space Odyssey" is heard in the background. Chance is beginning a journey into the world, which for him will be like a trip into outer space.

In his first encounter walking down a Washington, D.C., street, he discovers a new world: slums, kids playing basketball, a gang, a statue, and he examines a tree. He asks the gang, "Can you please tell me where I can find a garden to work in?" The gang's leader thinks he has been sent by a rival gang, so he gives him a message to deliver to Raphael. In front of the White House, he tells a police officer, "That tree is very sick; it needs care." The officer says that he will report it.

Next, Chance walks down the median of Pennsylvania Avenue between four lanes of traffic toward the Capitol, stopping in front of a store camera to play with his own image on a TV screen. He pulls a TV remote control from his pocket and attempts to use it to change the channel, but, of course, it won't work. As he is attempting to make the remote work, he steps into the parking area along the street and a limousine backs into him. A chauffeur who isn't driving rushes out of the car and asks if he is OK. Chance explains that his leg is very sore.

Out of the limousine emerges Eve Rand (Shirley MacLaine), who offers to take Chance to the hospital. After inviting him to get into the limousine, Chance tells her that he has never ridden in a car. On their way to the hospital, Eve asks Chance about how he is feeling. He tells her that he is still not feeling any better. She suggests that he accompany her to her house, and she tells him that she will take care of him there. He agrees to her suggestion. Then, she offers him a drink, which he interprets as water, but she understands to be alcohol. She tells him about her sick husband, who is attended by doctors and nurses at home. He asks if he can watch TV.

Eve asks him his name. He replies, "Chance the gardener." She says, "Chauncey Gardener," then asks if he is related to the Gardeners she and her husband know. He says he's not related, as he notices that he has lost the TV remote control before the limousine hit him.

On the fringes of the Rand estate, two men open large iron gates to permit the limousine onto the property, while Chance continues to watch TV. Making its way over a winding road through a well-groomed forest, the limousine pulls up to the front door of the Rand mansion where many servants stand ready to assist. Five chauffeurs help get Chance into a wheel chair and lift it up the steps to the front door of the house. Once inside, Eve tells the servant pushing Chance's wheel chair to take him to the third floor guest suite and Doctor Allenby will look at his leg.

The servant pushes Chance in the wheel chair into the elevator. Chance tells him that he has never been in an elevator. Then, he asks if it has a TV.

In the next scene, Dr. Allenby, finishing up an examination of Chance, inoculates him in the hip and asks him if he is planning on making any sort of claim against the Rands. Chance informs him that that is what Thomas Franklin had asked him. So, Allenby concludes that Chance wishes to handle his being hit by the car claim through his attorneys. Chance declares that there is no need for a claim, because he doesn't know what one looks like. Walking toward a TV, Chance takes the remote and turns it on. Allenby asks Chance to stay in the Rands' home for a day or two so he can keep an eye on Chance's leg. Chance says yes, then asks, "Does this house have a garden?" Allenby answers that it has many gardens. Before he leaves Chance's room, Allenby orders an x-ray of his leg.

Meanwhile, Eve visits Ben Rand, her husband, who is being attended by doctors and nurses in his own private, fully-equipped hospital room in their home. She tells Ben that the man her limousine driver hit is named Chance Gardener. Ben calls him Chauncey Gardener. Eve explains what happened to Chance and tells Ben that he is reasonable. Ben, making a pun based on Chance's name, states that he would like to meet a reasonable man for a chance. He suggests that Eve invite Chance to join them for dinner.

Eve and Dr. Allenby talk about Chance. The doctor informs Eve that he has asked Chance to stay for a couple of days. Eve agrees that that is a good idea. She tells Allenby that she thinks Chance is different and that he is "very intense." Allenby says that he thinks Chance has quite a sense of humor.

Next, Chance arrives in his wheel chair, dressed in a dark suit, vest, coat, and tie, wearing long black socks and only his boxer shorts. He visits Ben, who is in bed. Ben welcomes "Mr. Gardener" to Rand Memorial Hospital. Chance says that he feels very good in that room of the Rand home. Ben explains that the whole room has extra oxygen pumped into it. He also tells Chance that he is suffering from aplastic anemia; he doesn't have enough red blood cells. It's usually a young person's disease, but the irony is that he is an old man with it. Then, Ben invites Chance to dinner. Chance says that he is hungry.

Dinner is held in a formal dining room at a long table with only four people seated at one end: Ben at the end, Chance to his right, and Eve and Robert to his left. Standing behind them are ten servants, who proceed to serve dinner to the four, course by course.

During the dinner conversation, Chance tells Ben, "My house was shut down." Ben: "You mean your business was shut down." Chance: "Yes, shut down and closed by the attorneys." Ben goes into a triad about the businessman being at the mercy of kid lawyers. Allenby, who has been listening to their conversation, adds that the lawyers will legislate the medical profession right out of existence. Ben says that it is a shame. Then, turning to Chance, Ben asks him about his plans. Chance responds, "Well, I would like to work in your garden," meaning the flowers and the trees on the estate. Eve, who has been quiet until this moment, says she knows exactly what he means: "Isn't it wonderful to be with the trees and the flowers like that?" Ben states that he never had much feel for it. Chance says, "I'm a very good gardener." Eve says that it is a pleasant way to forget one's troubles. Chance agrees.

Ben now turns the conversation by using the gardening metaphor, asking rhetorically, "Isn't that what any business man is--a gardener?" Then, he continues,

> He works on flinty soil to make it productive with the labor of his own hands. He waters it with the sweat of his own brow. Makes a thing of value for his family and the community. Yes, indeed, Chauncey, a productive businessman is a laborer in the vineyard.

Chance, who understands Ben's garden metaphor literally, says that he knows exactly what Ben means. "The garden that I left was such a place. I don't have that anymore. All I have left is the room upstairs."

Now, Ben takes Chance's literal statement about "the room upstairs"--meaning the suite he has in the Rand home--to refer to heaven. Ben tells Chance that he has his health and that he has to fight. He states, "I don't want to hear anymore from you about that room upstairs. That's where I'm going too damn soon." Chance, who thinks Ben is also referring to his physical room, states, "It's a very pleasant room, Ben." Ben responds, "I'm sure it is. That's what they say anyway."

After dinner, they retire to the billiard/smoking room, where Ben, sitting in his wheel chair opposite Chance, smokes a cigar while Allenby plays pool. Ben tells Chance that he has been thinking about starting a financial assistant fund for businessmen, and he asks Chance for his opinion. Chance, attempting to figure out how to light his cigar, answers that he has no opinion because he hasn't understood a word Ben spoke to him. But Ben concludes that Chance is just reluctant to speak. Ben tells Chance, "You work on the idea, watch it, fertilize it." Continuing to use the gardening metaphor, Ben says, "I'm sure you'll sprout some thoughts in a few days."

On the way to his room for the night, Chance meets Eve in the hall. She tells him that she is glad he is staying for a few days because he has lifted Ben's spirits. Then Chance says that he sees that Ben is very ill because he has seen illness before in the person of the old man. Chance is speaking about the old man for whom he had served as gardener. As he heads toward his room, he asks Eve if she is going to leave and close the house when Ben dies.

Some secret service agents come to the Rand home to prepare it for a visit from the president, who is due to arrive shortly. Chance walks out the front door where the doorman asks him if he wants a car. Chance says yes. But then Dr. Allenby appears on the scene and checks Chance's leg and tells him that the president will arrive at ten that morning. Chance asks him how he will know when it's ten o'clock. The viewer learns that Chance can't tell time. He leaves the limousine, which has arrived, and goes back into the house. He tells Allenby that he knows about the president's arrival and that Ben has invited him to meet the president. By this point in the film, the viewer learns that Chance continually uses the phrase, "I understand," when, in fact, he doesn't.

The president arrives with a full police escort, while in Ben's room Chance uses a bed control to try to turn on the TV. Ben arrives dressed in a suit with some make-up on his face. Ben tells Chance that nobody likes a dying man because nobody knows what death is.

Ben and Chance proceed to the library to meet the president. Ben gets out of his wheel chair and prepares to walk to the library as he tells Chance that he wants to meet the president "on his own two feet" and fills in Chance on how he has used his wealth. He says that wealth is power, but it shouldn't be used to make a president. He has tried to remain honest to himself. Meanwhile, Allenby, the doctor, investigates Chance's room.

Chance is presented to the president, who is called Bobby. The president asks Ben if he has read the president's speech. Ben answers that it is pretty good. He adds that he thinks it is very dangerous to play around with temporary measures during a slow economic time.

Turning to Chance, the president asks him if he thinks growth can be stimulated through temporary incentives. Chance, recognizing the gardening metaphor and taking it literally, answers, "As long as the roots are not severed, all is well and all will be well in the garden." The president asks, "In the garden?" Chance explains, "Yes. In the garden, growth has its season. First comes Spring and Summer, but then we have

Fall and Winter. And then we get Spring and Summer again."

Now, seeing that the president is puzzled, Ben interprets what he thinks Chance means. "I think what our insightful young friend is saying is that we welcome the inevitable seasons of nature, but we're upset by the seasons of our economy." Not having understood what Ben meant, Chance affirms that there will be growth in the Spring. Still puzzled, the president says that Chance's optimistic statement is refreshing. Ben applauds and the president tells Chance that he admires his good, solid sense. The irony, of course, in the president's words is that Chance has no solid sense. He's speaking about a physical garden and not the economy.

The issue that keeps developing is Chance Gardener's identity. The president orders a background check on him. Meanwhile, while Ben and Chance are walking back to Ben's room, Ben tells Chance that he knows that Chance doesn't play games with words to protect himself. Of course, the viewer concludes that Chance is playing a game with words.

Next, Ben asks Chance about his plan for financial assistance to businessmen. He tells Chance that he thinks that he is the man to take charge of the plan. Ben tells him that he knows that he will not act on the spur of the moment and that he can wait for Chance's decision concerning the plan. Then, Chance expresses his sorrow about Ben's illness.

Later in the day, while touring the green house and garden with Eve, who explains what type of flowers are planted where in the garden and points out the gardener's house, she leads Chance to the greenhouse and asks him about his past. He tells her, "I like to watch the young plants grow. Young plants do much better if a person helps them." Eve tells him that the president was very taken with him. She also recalls the previous night's conversation about the old man who died and tells Chance the he must have been very close to him. Eve is talking about emotional closeness, but Chance understands her to mean physical closeness.

She continues by asking about Louise and if Chance was close to her. Chance, again understanding physical closeness, says that he liked her very much and that she was the old man's maid. Eve says she thought Louise was someone Chance was romantically involved with or his sister. Chance informs her that Louise used to bring him his meals, and that she was very kind to him.

That evening, Chance and Allenby watch the president on TV in one room, while Ben and Eve watch it in their bedroom. In the course of the speech, the president says, "Chauncey Gardener, Mr. Rand's close friend and advisor, was at the meeting this morning." He says that he found Mr. Gardener to be an intuitive man. Then he says that he will quote Chance: "As long as the roots of industry remain firmly planted in the national soil, the economic prospects are undoubtedly sound." Of course, the viewer knows that Chance said nothing like that.

The president urges viewers not to fear the inevitable chill and storms of autumn and winter but to anticipate the rapid growth of springtime and to await the rewards of summer. He urges all to learn to accept and appreciate the times when the trees are bare as well as the times when they pick fruit.

During the president's speech, Ben has an attack. The next morning, Chance comforts Eve in the hall. Allenby walks up to them, joining in the conversation. A secretary announces that Sidney Courtney, the financial editor of *The Washington Post* wants to talk to Chance on the telephone. As Chance walks away to take the call, Eve tells Allenby that he is a kind and sensitive man. However, while talking on the telephone to Courtney, Chance becomes preoccupied with a demonstration of physical exercises on the TV in the secretary's office and ends up hanging up on Courtney.

Before he can leave the office, however, another call comes for Chance. This time it is the producer of the Gary Burns show who wants him to make an appearance on the show to fill in for the vice-president, who has had to cancel. Meanwhile, the president's men can't find any information on Chance Gardener and neither can Courtney of *The Washington Post.*

On the Gary Burns TV show, watched by Ben and Eve Rand, Allenby, Franklin, Louise, and Chance in his limousine as he is being brought back to the Rand estate after earlier having taped the show, Burns states that it is surprising to find a man like him working so intimately with the president, and yet somehow managing to remain relatively unknown. Chance says yes. Burns continues by saying that Chance's anonymity will certainly be a thing of the past from now on. Chance merely says that is good.

Finally, Burns gets to heart of the matter, stating that he assumes that since the president quoted Chance that Chance is inclined to agree with the president's view of the economy. Chance asks about which view. Burns explains that the president compared the economy to a garden and that after a period of decline a time of growth would naturally follow. Recognizing the garden metaphor, Chance states, "Yes, it is possible for everything to grow strong, and there is plenty of room for new trees and new flowers of all kinds." Continuing to use the metaphor, Burns asks Chance if he is saying that this is just another season in the garden. Chance affirms Burn's statement.

Chance continues by saying how a garden needs a lot of care and a lot of love, and how things grow if one gives one's garden a lot of love. He adds that some things must whither, some trees die, and fresh, young saplings take their place. Chance, of course, is talking about a physical garden, but Burns, who thinks he is talking about the economy, asks him about the bad seasons. Chance answers that what is needed is a very good gardener. He says that he agrees with the president, that the garden needs a lot of care, and that it is a good garden and it's trees are healthy. Burns concludes that Chance is referring to the president as the gardener and asks him if he thinks the president is a good gardener. Chance says, "Some plants do well in the sun and other grow better in the shade." Burns comments, "Sounds as if we need a lot of gardening?" Chance: "We certainly do." Then Chance continues to talk about how the garden can be flooded in one part and dry in the other. He says that it is the responsibility of the gardener.

When Burns asks Chance what sort of gardener he is, Chance replies that he is a very serious gardener. Burns says that he is sure that he is. When Chance arrives back at the Rand residence, he receives a standing ovation from the servants at the front door.

Because of his illness, Ben cannot attend a formal reception, so he sends Chance as Eve's escort, telling him that he has the gift of being natural, which is a great talent. Of course, Chance is being natural. He's talking about nature. Then, commenting on the Burns' TV show, Ben tells Chance that the entire country was listening to him.

On their way to their rooms, Eve gives Chance a goodnight kiss --her first attempt to seduce him. Meanwhile Thomas Franklin and Sally Hayes try to figure out who Chance Gardener is. *The Washington Post* can't find anything. The president's men can't find anything. All his clothes are out of date, his suits were made in 1928, and his underwear came from a factory destroyed in 1948. He carries no identification, no wallet, no credit cards, and has no driver's license.

Some of the best irony appears in short scenes interspersed throughout this section of the film. The president and his wife are in bed. She wants to make love, but he is impotent. After several attempts to satisfy his wife, he gives up in frustration. His impotence is a reflection of his presidency and stands in sharp contrast to Chance Gardener, who has supplied him with not only the metaphor of gardening for life, but has surpassed his influence through his appearance on TV.

While "Sesame Street" is on TV and the viewer hears, "You are my friend; you're special to me," Eve visits Chance in his room. She asks him if he has seen the morning paper and the good reviews he got the previous evening. He tells her that he doesn't read newspapers. Sitting on the edge of his bed, she asks him if he minds her being there. Chance says no. However, as she touches his face with her hands, rubs his head, and passionately kisses him, he has no idea that she is attempting to seduce him.

After she kisses him and throws herself at him, figuring that she is getting nowhere, she tells him that she thinks he is strong, and she is grateful. She says that she would have opened up to Chance at the slightest touch. She is talking about opening up to him for sex, but he understands her to be talking about flowers, saying, "I'm glad you didn't open, Eve." Meanwhile, the doctor talks to Franklin, and the viewer knows that Allenby is learning about Chance.

Arriving at the formal reception, Chance is questioned by reporters concerning any response he would like to make to the articles in the morning's newspapers. He tells them that he does not read newspapers, but he does watch TV. They think he places more credibility in TV than in newspapers, when, in fact, he can't read.

Inside, Chance talks to Vladimer, a Russian ambassador. The diplomat, referring to ideologies, says that they are not so far from each other. Chance, looking towards the floor, says that they are not so far and that their chairs are almost touching. He leads the ambassador to believe that he speaks Russian and he gets a book offer, even though he keeps saying that he can't write, that he can't read, and that he likes to watch TV. Those to whom he speaks concludes that he doesn't have time to write or read, when, in fact, he can't.

Finally, a senator attending the gathering tells three other people, one of whom is Eve, that he has heard that Chance speaks eight languages and holds a degree in medicine as well as law. Later in the evening, Chance gets propositioned by a homosexual, but has no idea of what is going on. He tells the man that he likes to watch, referring to television, but the man thinks Chance means watching others have sex. Meanwhile, the president receives information that sixteen countries have investigated Chance Gardener and all of them report that his files have been erased.

On their way home in the limousine after the reception, Eve tells Chance that she feels close to him and safe. She also tells him that her husband, Ben, understands her feelings for Chance and accepts them. Chance replies, "Ben is very wise." As they are taking the elevator to their rooms, Eve says that it is very difficult for her to say goodnight to him and to leave him. Chance says that it is very hard for him, too.

Allenby arrives in Ben's room. Ben has been busy dictating some final directions concerning the selling of stocks. Allenby wants to tell Ben what he knows about Chance, but before he can, Ben tells Allenby that there's something about him that he trusts, that Chance makes him feel good, and that the thought of dying has been much easier for him since Chance has been around. Meanwhile, in Chance's room, Eve enters while the TV shows two people kissing in a soap opera. Chance kisses Eve while he watches TV, imitating what he sees and telling her that he likes to watch. Eve, embarrassed by his remark and thinking that he is referring to sex, asks him about this. Chance replies that he just likes to watch. Eve thinks she knows what he means, saying that he likes to watch her. Chance says, "It's very good, Eve."

Eve continues to kiss him, but Chance gets rigid. Unlacing her housecoat, Eve slips it off to reveal her negligee underneath. She tells Chance that she is a little shy. Chance, watching TV, nods affirmatively. While eve plays with her gown in an attempt to seduce Chance, he merely sits on the bed and continues to watch TV. She rolls onto a bear rug on the floor and plays with his foot and leg, but he changes channels. She watches as he moves to the middle of his bed and imitates the exercises he sees on TV.

The next day, while standing on the porch together, Eve tells Chance that he uncoils her wants and that desire flows within her. She adds that he sets her free. She alone, however, feels her sexual excitement. Chance has no clue as to what she is talking about.

Ben refuses any more shots from his doctor. After summoning Chance to his bedside, Chance asks him if he is going to die. Ben responds that he is close to death. He tells Chance that he hopes that he will stay there with Eve and take care of her. He tells him that Eve cares for him. He says, "She's a delicate flower." Chance, recognizing the gardening metaphor, says, "A flower. Yes, Ben." Then, saying that there is so much left to do, Ben dies.

Allenby, who has been standing near Ben's bed and listening to the conversation, says that Ben is gone. Chance responds that he has seen this before and that it happens to old people. As the doctor is touching Ben's head, Chance asks him if he will be leaving. He says yes. Chance tells him that Eve is staying and that she will not close up the house. Allenby remarks about how close Chance has come to Eve. Chance declares that he loves Eve very much. Allenby asks, "And you really are a gardener, aren't you?" Chance replies, "I am a gardener." Chance says that he will tell Eve about Ben. Then, using the line that Chance has used multiple times, Allenby says, "I understand. I understand?"

During Ben's funeral and burial scene, the pall bearers, while escorting the casket to a mausoleum on the Rand property, discuss politics and the possibility of Chance Gardener as a candidate for president. The mausoleum is shaped in the form of a triangle with an eye at the top. It is meant to resemble the icon found on the back of a dollar bill.

The president states that he knows that Ben wanted his funeral kept small and quiet. But while Ben is being carried to his last resting place, he will read from his quotes.

As the pall bearers proceed, the president reads, "I have no use for those on welfare, no patience whatsoever. But if I am to be honest with myself, I must admit that they have no use for me either."

Continuing, the president reads, "I do not regret having political differences with men that I respect. I do regret, however, that our philosophies kept us apart."

Meanwhile, Chance slips away from the funeral and walks through the woods of the estate around a lake, stopping to fix a fallen-over sapling. Then, Chance begins to walk across the lake, stopping to dip in his umbrella up to his hand. The president, who has continued reading some of Ben Rand's words, states, "Life is a state of mind."

As the film ends, the viewer is left with at least two questions: Who is Chance Gardener? Do people see in another what they want to see in another, ignoring what is really there?

Chance has no last name except "Gardener," which is given to him by Eve and is descriptive of what he does, not his family name. The irony continues as he answers the telephone and hears, "Are you there," and responds, "Yes." When asked by Thomas Franklin, one of the lawyers, if he had a claim on the estate of the "old man," he answers by telling him that it had a "healthy garden." When asked if he would "like a car" to be driven in, Chance replies, "Oh, yes," meaning he would like to have one as his own. The Russian ambassador tells him, "We are not so far apart," a reference to economic ideology, but Chance understands him to be talking about the proximity of their chairs.

Throughout the movie, Chance says, "I understand," when in fact he understands nothing. Meanwhile, those engaged in conversation with him think he is profound. He cannot read or write. The only thing he can do is take care of a garden. Through the dialogue, the viewer learns that Chance is in fact a very simple man. Only the maid, who cared for him for years, and the doctor realize that he is nothing other than a gardener. Even his name, Chance, is full of irony, in that it is by chance that everything happens to him.

Eve Rand is also an ironic character. She names Chance Chauncey Gardener and falls in love with him. She is sexually aroused by Chance, who doesn't understand what sex is all about. Eve thinks that he purposely cured her of her sexual inhibitions, when in reality he hadn't the slightest idea of what was really going on. She feels close to him and safe in his presence, when he hasn't a clue as to what she wants from him. In one scene, she offered him "a drink" after he says he is thirsty. She is offering him alcohol; he is requesting water. The viewer is actively engaged in this hyperbolic irony, sorting it out and being amused by it as it unfolds.

Eve's husband, the dying Ben Rand, also thinks that Chance is brilliant. Ben is a successful businessman and very intelligent. He is a maker of presidents and a presidential advisor. Chance, who knows nothing about politics or government, tells his parable of the garden, and Ben feels safe leaving his wife and his business to Chance after he dies. He says that he gains strength from what he concluded was Chance's strength.

The doctor, Robert Allenby, at first meeting Chance thinks he is humorous. He tells him the inoculation will not hurt, but it does. When he finally discovers who Chance really is, he does not tell Ben, thus permitting him to die in peace. However, using Chance's favorite line, once he discovers Chance's identity, Allenby declares, "I understand, I understand." In this scene, the irony is reversed, as the doctor, who knows who Chance is, does not understand the way that Chance does.

The president, who thinks that Chance is profound, quotes Chance's garden parable in one of his speeches. The irony is that in a public speech, the president refers to a man who can't read or write. He is absolutely sure that there is much more to Chance Gardener than what he hears and sees on the surface, and he is determined to find out what that is. But not one member of the president's staff can find out anything about Chance, except the age of his clothes, thinking that the FBI or the CIA has destroyed his files.

The lawyers, Thomas Franklin and Sally Hayes, at first think that Chance is trying to get part of the estate of the "old man" who dies at the beginning of the film. They discover that he is slow to understand, until they see him on TV. After watching him on TV, they think, even though he is still talking about gardening, he is really a mastermind who just played dumb during their first encounter with him. However, after investigations, they return to their original understanding that Chance was only the gardener. However, by then, the myth surrounding Chance Gardener has taken on a life of its own.

The journalist, Sidney Courtney, in an ironic twist, announces on TV that Chance never existed before, meaning he had not made his insights known. In fact, Chance didn't exist in any records any place. He was a nobody, who acknowledged that all he did was watch TV and garden. Courtney thinks that Chance is being secretive in not divulging more of his insights when Chance tells him to ask his questions of Ben Rand. Chance is being honest, but Courtney thinks he is hiding something.

Once the viewer understands the irony of the characters in "Being There," a move can be made to Matthew's Gospel whose author is rich in hyperbolic irony. After opening with a lengthy genealogy, the author tells the reader that there are three sets of fourteen generations each. Most readers have a tendency to believe the author. However, upon close examination, the last set contains only thirteen.

Also in the genealogy, the reader will notice that there are only the names of men, since in Judaism's primitive biology it was understood that one man gave birth to the next man by sewing his seed in the womb of his wife-incubator. Thus, genealogies are traced from one man to another. But there are five woman in Matthew's genealogy. Upon close inspection, the reader discovers that all of them contaminate the blood line: a prostitute, a whorehouse owner, a Gentile, a concubine, and a woman discovered to be pregnant outside of marriage. The reader is left to determine what the author intends by all this; he never says.

The first character to whom the reader is introduced is Joseph, who is not the physical father of Jesus if God is Jesus' Father. Therefore, the genealogy falls apart if Joseph isn't Jesus' dad. Joseph accepts pregnant Mary as his wife even though the Law says that she ought to be stoned to death because she is used property. After a journey to and from Egypt and settling with his family in Nazareth, Joseph disappears from the story. He is called just or righteous by Matthew, but the reader is left wondering how one can be righteous when he broke the very law that governed righteousness.

Jesus is presented as an ironic character in Matthew's Gospel. He speaks with authority, like Moses. He performs great deeds and miracles, like Moses. He gives long speeches, like Moses. He teaches the way of righteousness, like Moses, yet he seems to constantly break the very Law Moses received from God. He is declared to be the Son of God, yet he cannot save himself from death. He dies so that other people might live.

Jesus and Chance, the only righteous person in "Being There," are a lot alike as characters. Both view the world through lenses which are different from the way their society sees it. The Matthean Jesus teaches people to do the right thing because it is the right thing to do. Chance does the right thing because he knows no other way. Jesus has a vision of what society can become, while Chance's vision is that of what the garden can become. Both characters influence many people through the stories they tell.

Matthew's Peter can be a study in irony, especially if he is compared to Mark's Peter. The author of Mark's Gospel portrayed Peter as a disciple who never figured out who Jesus was. When the going got tough, Peter denied knowing Jesus three times and then abandoned him to the cross, where Jesus suffered and died alone. Matthew presents Peter as the rock of the church who has access to divine revelation. Peter walks on water with Jesus and confesses him to be the Son of the living God. But despite his profession of faith and his insistence that he would never deny his teacher, Peter ends up betraying Jesus three times and weeping bitterly in repentance. The irony is that such a man became a leader of the fledgling Christian church.

Matthew presents the group he calls Pharisees as a collective ironic. The Pharisees awaited a Messiah, but couldn't see him when he stood in front of them. They attempt to achieve their own righteousness, rather than trust God to make them so. Matthew calls them hypocrites, because who they are on the outside does not reflect who they are on the inside. There is no harmony in them.

The irony of Jesus' disciples according to Matthew is that they are witnesses to his deeds and they doubt him all along the way. They are slow to comprehend, so Jesus has to explain his teaching, especially his parables, to them. While they do desert Jesus after he is arrested, they are rehabilitated at the end of the gospel and commissioned to spread the good news throughout the world.

Pilate is portrayed by Matthew as a character full of irony. He has access to divine revelation through his wife, who has a dream telling her to tell Pilate not to have anything to do with Jesus. Pilate recognizes the jealously of the Pharisees and those others who want Jesus sentenced to death and believes that Jesus is innocent. He washes his hands of the whole affair, a sign of his ironically guiltless state, and hands Jesus over to crucifixion. The one who is really innocent stands before Pilate, but the governor fails to recognize him.

And the most ironic of all Matthew's character is Judas. As one of Jesus' disciples, he is among the inner circle who betrays his master for money. After his dastardly deed, the irony of his character reaches a high point as he regrets what he's done, attempts to undo it by returning the money, and, finding no way out of the mess he has created, betrays himself by committing suicide. He is contrasted to Peter, who even though he betrays Jesus, finds that he can repent and be rehabilitated. Peter's irony leads to hope; Judas' irony leads to despair.

"Being There" reminds the viewer that what is on the surface is not always reality. People "understood" Chance in the manner they wanted, much like people can "read" Matthew's Gospel from the perspective they desire. Neither the way Chance was understood or the way Matthew's Gospel is read may be a correct understanding or a correct reading. Chance Gardener brings about a lot of good for the people surrounding him despite all their misunderstanding of his simple talk about gardening. Likewise in Matthew's Gospel, Jesus teaches about a new way of living, a higher righteousness to those tax collectors, prostitutes, lepers--all the societal outcasts--who listen to him, while the elite and knowledgeable hear him as a threat to their power and position. By dying he shows that there are values worth the sacrifice of one's life. Both Chance and Jesus teach that God is found exactly where most people wouldn't have thought to have looked--in a garden and on a cross.

Exercises and Questions for Discussion

1. Irony can be defined as the use of words to express something other than and especially the opposite of the literal meaning. What is the irony of each of the following characters in "Being There": Chance Gardener, Eve Rand, Ben Rand, Robert Allenby (the doctor), the president (Bobby), Thomas Franklin (lawyer), Sally Hayes (lawyer), and Sidney Courtney (journalist).

2. Outline the plot of the film by scene. For each scene indicate its importance to the whole story and what purpose it serves.

3. What do you think is the major truth which the movie attempts to communicate? Is this truth one that endures? Explain.

4. After reading the Gospel According to Matthew in one sitting, identify the irony found in each of the following characters: Joseph, Jesus, Peter, Pharisees, Disciples/Apostles, Pilate, and Judas.

5. Identify five stories in Matthew's Gospel that illustrate the author's use of irony. Explain how each of the five stories is illustrative of irony.

6. Identify and compare three characters from "Being There" with three characters from Matthew's Gospel. Explain how each pair is alike and unlike.

7. What do you think is the major truth which Matthew's Gospel attempts to communicate? Is this truth one that endures? Explain.

8. At the beginning of "Being There," before she leaves the "old man's" house, Louise tells Chance that he needs to get a lady. How is her "prophecy" fulfilled at the end of the film?

9. What do you think is the meaning of the last scene of "Being There" as Chance Gardener walks across the water?

Teaching Matthew's Gospel

Willow

Biblical scholars call attention to the use of Moses-imagery by the anonymous author of Matthew's Gospel. Like Moses, who by Pharaoh's command was supposed to be thrown into the river and drowned but was hidden by his mother, the Matthean Jesus, whose life is placed in jeopardy by King Herod, is rescued by his mother and father and taken to Egypt.

Again, like Moses, who leaves Egypt and then returns to lead his people from slavery to freedom, Jesus returns from Egypt to lead his people from the slavery of sin to freedom as children of God.

The author of Matthew's Gospel keeps Moses in mind as he portrays Jesus delivering five great sermons which are meant to parallel the Torah, the first five books of the Hebrew Bible. Jesus is the new lawgiver, like Moses, who joins Jesus and Elijah, the archetype of prophets, for a scene presenting Jesus as the transfigured image of those two Hebrew Bible personages.

Moses leads the twelve tribes of Israel out of captivity to the Sea of Reeds, which parts and permits them to cross. Jesus crosses the Jordan River through his baptism by John and chooses twelve men to serve as his apostles, thus beginning his ministry. When the people need food in the desert, Moses intercedes with God, who sends manna and quail. When Jesus' followers have nothing to eat in a deserted place, he fills thousands of them with a few loaves and fish.

Moses leads his people toward the promised land, while Jesus speaks about the kingdom of God. Moses dies before the people enter the promised land, but Jesus demonstrates that death is not the end. He passes through death to new life, revealing that while people cannot yet experience the kingdom of God fully, they can experience it now. In other words, the prophet like himself, whom Moses had foretold that God would raise up, is Jesus of Nazareth for the author of Matthew's Gospel.

In order to help students understand the Moses-typology employed by the author of Matthew's Gospel, the film "Willow" (RCA/Columbia Pictures, 1988) can be shown. The viewer recognizes that the state of the people before Jesus is similar to the state of the world in "Willow," as these words flash on the screen:

> It is a time of dread. Seers have foretold the birth of a child who will bring about the downfall of the powerful Queen Bavmorda. Seizing all pregnant women in the realm, the evil queen vows to destroy the child when it is born.

The film portrays a time when women rule the world and men are their servants (a contemporary statement about male dominance). The child whose birth will bring about the end of evil, personified as Bavmorda, is a girl named Elora Danon (Ruth and Kate Greenfield). As soon as she is born, her mother asks the midwife to save her life. She obliges by smuggling the child out of Bavmorda's castle in a basket, just as the evil queen orders the mother's death. Taking Elora Danon over the mountains, through the snow, and through a forest, she protects her from wild dogs by sending her floating down a river in a basket, a Moses-typology which no viewer will miss. The dogs attack the midwife and kill her, as the baby floats to freedom and a new life.

Stopping at a bank, the basket is seen by two children--a boy and girl--who run to get their father, Willow Ufgood (Warwick Davis), who is plowing his field with an implement attached to a pig. He follows his children to the river and, seeing her, explains to his children that she is another kind of human being, one who is much bigger than they are. They are midgets. While Willow leaves the river to meet someone he hears coming toward his field, his wife, Kaia, first joins him and then follows the children to the river. She picks up Elora Danon and takes her to their home, where she washes the baby and notices the sign on the baby's arm.

Willow and his children go into their village to attend a carnival, consisting of games, music, dancing, and magic tricks, in preparation for High Aldwin's choosing of an apprentice to succeed him as town sorcerer. Willow, a magician, demonstrates how he can make a pig disappear, but is disgraced when the pig wanders out from under the table.

High Aldwin (Billy Barty), a taller member of the community who is dressed in a conical hat and wears a long white beard, looks over three candidates for the position of apprentice. He says, "Magic is the bloodstream of the universe. Forget all you know or think you know. All that you require is your intuition." Holding up his hand, he asks the candidates, "Now, the power to control the world is in which finger?" All three pick the wrong finger, and Aldwin states, "No apprentice this year."

Just as Aldwin is finishing, wild dogs attack the village. The people flee and hide behind anything they can find. The men kill one of the dogs with their spears after noticing that it had been looking for a baby in a cradle. Willow grabs his two children and rushes home to Kaia, who has Elora Danon in her arms.

At a town meeting, all present talk about finding the culprit who caused the wild-dog attack. High Aldwin calls forward Willow, who is holding Elora Danon. He shows Aldwin the baby and explains how she came to be in his home. Aldwin declares, "This child is special. This child must be taken beyond the boundaries of our village--all the way across the great river to the Dikini crossroads." The mayor suggests that since Willow found her, he should be the one to take her to the crossroads.

Aldwin asks him, "Do you have any love for this child?" Willow responds, "Yes, yes, I do." Then, Aldwin tells him, "Willow Ufgood, the safety of this village depends upon you." Then, Aldwin asks for volunteers to accompany Willow on his journey. While they are preparing to leave, Aldwin says to him, "What's your problem, son?" Willow asks, "What do you mean?" Aldwin: "When I held up my fingers, what was your first impulse?" Willow: "Pick my own finger." Then, Aldwin reveals, "That was the correct answer. You lack faith in yourself. More than anyone in the village, you have the potential to be a great sorcerer. Now, when you're out there, listen to your own heart."

Aldwin gives Willow some magic acorns and explains that anything he throws them at will turn to stone, adding, "You have much to learn, young Ufgood." Before he leaves, his children ask him if he's afraid of fairies and trolls. After telling them that he's not and saying good-bye to them and his wife, who gives him a braid of her hair for good luck, he and his party begin their journey, as Aldwin says, "Good faith people, the outerworld is no place for an Ufgood. Give the baby to the first Dikini you see. Then hurry home."

Throwing a rock into the air and watching it turn into a white bird, Aldwin says, "Go in the direction the bird is flying." But the bird heads back toward the village, so Aldwin says, "Ignore the bird. Follow the river." And so the journey begins, and the party walks through the woods and past a waterfall. Willow carries Elora Danon papoose-style on his back.

Queen Bavmorda, clothed in a floor-length black dress and

matching veil, receives the news of the dead midwife from her daughter, Sorsha (Joanne Whalley), who wears undergarments of black with a silver armor cover and carries a quiver of arrows on her back. Then, General Kael (Pat Roach) makes a grand entrance into the throne room. He, too, is dressed in black clothes from head to foot, but wears a skeleton's face on his helmet. Viewers familiar with the "Star Wars" trilogy will recognize the similarity between Kael and Darth Vader. After reporting on a castle that he and his men have destroyed, Queen Bavmorda gives Kael an order to find the baby.

Kael asks, "The baby of the prophecy? The one who will destroy you?" Bavmorda states, "I need that baby alive. I must perform the ritual that will exile the child's spirit into oblivion. Find her." With that, Sorsha and Kael leave, but one of Bavmorda's counselors has his own prophecy to deliver to Bavmorda: "I read the signs. One day I fear your daughter will betray you." However, Bavmorda says, "I trust her loyalty more than I trust yours."

Meanwhile, Willow and company hide in the woods when they see men on horseback looking for Elora Danon. Their journey continues through the woods. They cross ravines. They make camp. And, finally, they come to the crossroads, where they see skeletons in cages hanging from trees. They build a fire and hear a shrieking voice, discovering that one man in a cage, Madmardigan (Val Kilmer) is alive and asking for water. He, a Dikini, tells them that if they let him out, he'll help the baby. However, none of the party believes him. All decide to head home, since they have reached the crossroad, and leave Willow with Migosh, one of his companions, and Elora Danon in the camp.

The next morning, a rider goes through the crossroad, but doesn't stop. Madmardigan tells Willow, "I'm the greatest swordsman that ever lived." A second rider goes by. Madmardigan, faking tears, asks for water, just as an army approaches. Willow, standing on the ground, tries to get someone's attention, but no one sees him. However, one soldier recognizes Madmardigan, but won't let him out. The army passes on. Madmardigan, trying to persuade Willow to release him, says that no one will take care of the baby and no one will care for her as well as he will. Willow and Migosh set free Madmardigan, who takes Elora Danon and heads off while Willow asks Migosh, "Did we do the right thing," and he responds, "Absolutely."

For all practical purposes, Willow's task is complete and his journey ended, except for the return trip home. While heading toward his village, an owl with Brownies, people about six inches tall, on its back flies by carrying Elora Danon in a basket in its beak and saying, "I stole the baby." An army of Brownies attacks Willow and Migosh, tie both of them up with rope, and drag them to a bright, Tinkerbell-like light which fazes into the shadowy figure of a woman, who first discloses Elora Danon's name and then says, "She is very special. My Brownies have been searching for her ever since we heard she was born. Elora Danon has chosen you to be her guardian. Elora Danon knows you have the courage to help us."

The woman instructs Willow to take her magic wand to Raziel, a sorceress who will help him. She adds,

> Elora Danon must survive. She must fulfill her destiny and bring about the downfall of Queen Bavmorda whose powers are growing like an evil plague. Unless she is stopped, Bavmorda will control the lives of your village, your children, everyone. All creatures of good heart need your help, Willow. The choice is yours.

And with that she disappears, and Willow is entrusted with a new mission.

First, Willow sends Migosh home. Then, carrying Elora Danon and accompanied by two of the Brownies, he continues the journey, learning from the Brownies than Raziel has been exiled to an island by Bavmorda. While in the midst of a heavy rain, they come to a village and enter a bar where Willow finds Madmardigan dressed in woman's clothes. He's been having an affair with another man's wife and is trying to escape. But in the midst of that scene, Sorsha appears with some of her army and asks for Elora Danon, whom Madmardigan has taken into his arms. A fight erupts, but Madmardigan escapes with the baby into a wagon and Willow, with the Brownies in his pack, jumps from the second story of the bar into the wagon's bed as Sorsha's troops give chase.

Repeatedly, Madmardigan, Willow, and the Brownies knock Sorsha's troops off the speeding wagon. After escaping into the woods, Willow tells Madmardigan that he needs his help. Madmardigan says that Willow and the Brownies can follow him to the lake. While Kael reports to Bavmorda that the army has not yet found the baby and she declares, "Find the child. Time is running out," Willow and company make camp. Willow informs Madmardigan about Elora Danon's status as "a great sorcerer." Using the magic wand he has managed to hold onto, he recites a spell and places himself on a branch of a tall tree. The next day, after crossing a valley and making a stop near a waterfall, Willow tells Madmardigan, "She's Elora Danon, future princess of Terra Lee."

Once they reach the lake, Willow finds a boat, entrusts the care of Elora Danon to Madmardigan, and begins to row to the island to find Raziel. When he gets to the shore, he finds the beach strewn with skeletons and skulls. He shouts, "Raziel," and a rat on a tree branch asks, "Who are you?" Raziel explains that one of Bavmorda's spells transformed her into a rat. Willow gives the wand to Raziel, who says, "Then the prophecy is true. The princess has been born. Take me to her."

Willow takes Raziel (the rat) to the mainland where she tells him to use the magic wand and turn her back into her original form, but Willow can't remember the spell. As Willow is struggling to remember the words, Sorsha arrives with her army and captures Madmardigan and Willow and takes them with Elora Danon and Raziel as prisoners. As they walk through the snow-covered mountains, Raziel keeps urging Willow to remember the spell.

In camp for the night, Willow and Madmardigan share a cage while Raziel is housed in a rat-sized cell. Madmardigan frees Raziel, and Willow attempts to change her to her former self, but ends up turning her into a crow. The Brownies, who had escaped at the lake, arrive and free Madmardigan and Willow, who searches the tents until he finds Elora Danon with Sorsha, who is asleep.

After indicating where Elora Danon is, Madmardigan goes into the tent to get her. But he has been sprinkled with Brownie dust and falls in love with her immediately. He walks to her bedside and leans over to kiss her just as she wakes up. He tells her that he loves her. Soldiers entering the tent interrupt them. Willow has been caught, but Madmardigan knocks out a tent pole, kills some of the soldiers, and instructs Willow to grab Elora Danon and to get on a shield, which they use to slide down the snow-covered mountain.

Madmardigan falls off of the shield, but Willow and the baby slide right into a home. Raziel (crow) arrives and announces that Kael and soldiers are coming. When Kael and Sorsha appear, the villagers hide Willow, Madmardigan, and Elora Danon in the basement of a home. Sorsha carefully searches the hiding place and finds them, just as Madmardigan grabs her as a hostage. Using Sorsha as a human shield, Madmardigan, Willow, and the baby escape by stealing some of the army's horses. Raziel follows on wing, and sympathizers to their cause attack the soldiers.

As they travel to lower ground on their journey to Terra Lee, Sorsha tells Madmardigan what he said in her tent the night before. She jumps off the horse they are on and tries to escape, but he catches her. During her second attempt, she runs away successfully and Madmardigan and Willow flee to Terra Lee.

When they arrive at Terra Lee castle, no one is there. Queen Bavmorda has put a curse on the palace and turned its inhabitants into stone. Raziel, the crow, wants Willow to transform her into a human, but ends up turning her into a goat instead. Madmardigan finds a supply of swords, armor, bows, and spears in the castle, which he uses to prepare for the imminent attack by Sorsha, Kael, and Bavmorda's army. Madmardigan just gets the old gates shut and prepares to defend the castle when the soldiers arrive.

However, Bavmorda's army will not be defeated. After cutting down a tree to use a battering ram, they break down the gate. Madmardigan's traps of crossbows and other weapons kill some of Bavmorda's troops, but not enough, as they overrun Terra Lee. To make matters worse, a two-headed beast emerges from the moat. While each head breathes fire and eats soldiers, Willow fights a troll and Sorsha watches Madmardigan fight her own troops and then the beast which he kills. Sorsha manages to find him in the foray and kisses him.

Meanwhile, Kael finds the baby, grabs her, and races through the ranks of soldiers on horseback. Madmardigan and Willow follow him to Bavmorda's castle where the drawbridge is being pulled up. After getting the baby from Kael, Bavmorda learns that Sorsha, her daughter, has turned against her and has aligned herself with Madmardigan. Thus, the prophecy made by Bavmorda's assistant early in the film is fulfilled. Spotting the army below her castle walls, Bavmorda casts a spell on it and turns Madmardigan and the rest of the troops into a herd of pigs. In order to protect himself from Bavmorda's spell, Willow holds the magic wand and casts his own spell.

Bavmorda prepares the baby for the ritual which will send her enemy to oblivion. First, she summons thunder and lightning through an opening in the roof to the stone altar below it. Elora Danon is wrapped in a black blanket as Bavmorda engages in other ritual preparations, such as cutting a lock of the baby's hair, putting it into a goblet, and pouring it into a potion.

Using his magic wand, Willow turns Raziel into several animals, successively, until he finally returns her to human form. Raziel immediately returns the army from its pig form to human form. But no one can figure out a way to get into Bavmorda's castle.

In a meeting between Willow, Madmardigan, Sorsha, and Raziel, Willow says that he has an idea of how to get into the castle. Raziel says, "If the baby dies, all hope for the future is lost. I'm going to find her." Willow declares, "Me, too." As Willow and Raziel walk toward the castle to enact Willow's plan, Raziel says, "Willow, all these years I have wanted to face Bavmorda. It is you that have made this possible. Whatever happens I shall always admire you. Your children will come to remember this day."

After approaching the wall of the castle, Willow and Raziel tell Kael and some soldiers patrolling the wall to surrender and to give them the baby. This serves only to antagonize the powerful Kael, who orders the drawbridge lowered and soldiers to go out and kill the two weak people standing below. But as several of Bavmorda's soldiers emerge, Willow's plan begins to unfold. The mercenary army that had helped them escape Sorsha once before now emerges from under tents. They attack and defeat Bavmorda's soldiers and storm her castle. Meanwhile, she continues to prepare for her ritual.

Sorsha, Willow, and Raziel make their way into the castle to Bavmorda's chamber. Reaching the room, Sorsha, who is attacked by several soldiers guarding Bavmorda, manages to kill them. But Bavmorda uses her magic and hurls Sorsha toward a set of spikes embedded in the wall. Raziel exercises her own power and stops Sorsha from being killed. Raziel proclaims that Elora Danon will be queen, as the battle between the two armies rages outside.

Bavmorda hurls fire toward Raziel, who counters with snow. Then, Raziel, using the wand Willow had entrusted to her, throws Bavmorda against the wall, and then they fight to get control of the wand. Meanwhile, Willow attempts to steal Elora Danon, who is near the altar in the room, and outside Madmardigan fights Kael, hits him with his sword, and kills him before rushing into the castle.

The two women continue to fight for the wand: evil Bavmorda verses good Raziel. When it looks like Bavmorda has won, Willow grabs the baby and tries to escape, but Bavmorda stops him by causing the door to her chamber to close. He takes one of his magic acorns and throws it at her, hitting her arm, which begins to turn to stone. But her magic is more powerful, and she reverses the action. Willow takes the baby and makes her disappear, like he had made the pig disappear during the carnival in his village. At that moment, lightning strikes Bavmorda, who is turned into a cloud of red dust and sent forever into oblivion. Raziel, who has been lying on the floor, recovers. And Willow produces Elora Danon from behind a table where he had hidden her.

The castle exterior has been transformed from black to white. Raziel gives Willow a book of magic saying, "You are on your way to becoming a great sorcerer." Sorsha, who had been dressed in black, wears a white dress. She holds Elora Danon while Madmardigan stands near the two of them. Willow says good-bye to the baby and entrusts her care to Madmardigan and Sorsha.

Riding home on a small horse, Willow enters his village triumphantly. All come out to greet him, including his wife and children. Demonstrating that he is a great sorcerer, he takes an apple from his bag, tosses it into the air, and watches the crowd's amazement as it is transformed into a white bird. His journey is ended, but it has just begun.

The Book of Exodus begins with a genealogy of the sons of Israel and traces generation after generation to Moses. In order to explain Jesus' lineage, the author of Matthew's Gospel provides a genealogy at the very beginning of his narrative. By naming personages from the Hebrew Bible, Matthew gives Jesus of Nazareth a history. While Willow Ufgood has no genealogy, the film depicts him as having a history which consists of not only having a wife and children, but includes his desire to be a great sorcerer.

The Hebrew Bible Book of Exodus explains Moses' miraculous escape from Pharaoh's orders, that all male babies be killed by drowning them in the river, by portraying Moses' mother putting him in a basket and sending him down the river. In Matthew's Gospel, while there is no basket-on-the-river scene, Joseph and Mary take Jesus to Egypt to flee the order of King Herod that babies born in Bethlehem be killed. In "Willow" the midwife whisks Elora Danon away from death at the hands of Queen Bavmorda and places her on a clump of sod and sends her down the river to save her.

In Exodus, the Pharaoh's daughter finds the baby in the basket floating in the reeds, adopts him, and raises him. In Matthew's Gospel, Jesus is escorted to Egypt by his parents and from there he emerges as the savior of all people. Jesus is the adopted son of Joseph and Mary; his true origin is God. In "Willow," Ufgood's children discover the baby on the river's bank. Even though Willow is at first reluctant to take her, his wife adopts her, and, finally, Willow agrees to escort Elora Danon to her rightful place in the world.

Moses is a special child to Pharaoh's daughter, who has no children of her own. However, he is more special to the Hebrews, who are awaiting a deliverer to be sent by God. Jesus is the only child of Mary and Joseph, the child who has been promised, the one who is God present and saving people. Repeatedly, Elora Danon is declared to be a special child, the one who would defeat all evil. Even Queen Bavmorda knows the specialness of Elora Danon. That is why the queen wants to destroy her.

Pharaoh learns of Moses' plan to lead the Hebrew slaves out of Egypt and attempts to stop him at every move. After seeing the signs Moses works, Pharaoh is glad to see Moses go, but, after repenting of his decision, leads his army in pursuit of the slaves. His army suffers the fate that he had imposed on all male babies: It is drowned in the Sea of Reeds. Herod learns of the birth of a new king--a threat to his throne--through magi, who refuse to obey his orders and slip away in the darkness of the night after finding the baby and acknowledging his greatness. Likewise, Sorsha, Queen Bavmorda's daughter, at first pledges her loyalty to her mother, but, after experiencing the love of Madmardigan, she transfers her loyalty to the opposing forces and, ultimately, becomes the baby's guardian. Queen Bavmorda is destroyed by the power of her own magic.

In Exodus, once Moses accepts his call from God to lead the Hebrews out of slavery, they reject him when, because of his demand that Pharaoh let the people go, the king of Egypt demands more work from the slaves. Jesus is rejected by his own people, even though in Matthew's Gospel he is portrayed as seeking them first. Likewise, Elora Danon is rejected by the very people she has come to help--the Dikini.

Rejection by one group leads either to conversion by the group or to acceptance by another group. We see this in Exodus, as the Hebrews rally around Moses and make their escape. We see this in Matthew's Gospel as Jesus is accepted by the Gentiles, who proclaim him to be God's Messiah, the Anointed One. In "Willow," Elora Danon is accepted by the Brownies and, after a while, by Madmardigan and Sorsha.

What aids conversion or acceptance is some kind of experience of the divine. Moses discovers God in a burning bush whose flames do not consume and in a voice which has no discernible source. The author of Matthew's Gospel employs the literary technique of dreams to portray divine intervention. Joseph has a dream to take Mary as his wife, to take Jesus and Mary to Egypt, and to bring them home again. Jesus, in a dream-like trance, is transfigured on a mountain. He glows with light. The leader of the Brownies, a Tinker-Bell-like character, appears as light and convinces Willow that his mission of delivering Elora Danon to her rightful place in history is not yet complete. And before the light, High Aldwin, while not being the best of sorcerers, knows the specialness of the child, Elora Danon, when she is placed before him.

One of the most obvious parallels between Exodus, Matthew's Gospel, and "Willow," is the power of good overcoming evil. In Exodus, Moses (and God) represents the force of good and Pharaoh (and the Egyptian gods) represents the power of evil. In Matthew's Gospel, Jesus stands as a sign of the good God, whom he calls "Father," and any who oppose him, especially Pilate (and the Pharisees) represent evil. In "Willow," Ufgood and Elora Danon (along with all who help them) stand for good, while Queen Bavmorda and her army commander, Kael, represent evil.

Moses' God triumphs over the king of Egypt. Jesus, who is put to death, is raised to life by God. And in "Willow," both Bavmorda and Kael suffer death, while Elora Danon reigns as princess of Terra Lee. The forces of evil, no matter how powerful, cannot overcome the forces of good, no matter how weak they may at first appear to be.

Both Exodus and Matthew's Gospel were written for a patriarchal society. Therefore, the main characters are men. The viewer can contrast this fact to "Willow," a film prepared for a culture in which men and women are considered to be equal. In "Willow," the main characters are women: Elora Danon, Raziel, and Queen Bavmorda. Because she is a baby, Elora Danon does not engage in the final battle, but she is the reason for it. In the last fight, Raziel and Bavmorda struggle for power, signified by the magic wand, while Willow, a small man, can only stand and watch.

If there are male heros, they are Willow and Madmardigan. But Willow's role is to see that Elora Danon gets to Terra Lee, and Madmardigan's role, like that of John the Baptist, is to prepare the way for Elora Danon to claim Terra Lee as her home.

As Moses journeys with the Hebrews through the desert, so Jesus makes his way to Jerusalem, and Willow carries Elora Danon to Terra Lee. Ultimately, the Israelites enter the promised land; Jesus is hailed as king upon his entrance to Jerusalem, put to death on a cross, and raised to new life in the kingdom of heaven; and Elora Danon is hailed as princess of Terra Lee. Journey is a metaphor serving as the basic plot for all three stories.

Exercises and Questions for Discussion

1. What themes from Matthew's Gospel can you find in "Willow"? Identify at least five themes and explain them.

2. Make a list of three comparisons of characters between "Willow" and Matthew's Gospel.

3. In "Willow" who has power? Explain. In Matthew's Gospel, who has power? Explain.

4. What do you think is the real issue with which "Willow" deals? What do you think is the real issue with which Matthew's Gospel deals? Explain.

5. What are signs of the divine presence in "Willow"? What are signs of the divine presence in Matthew's Gospel?

6. Do you agree with the way the problem is solved in "Willow"? Explain. Do you agree with the way the problem is solved in Matthew's Gospel? Explain.

7. Compare and contrast the matriarchal culture found in "Willow" to the patriarchal culture found in Matthew's Gospel. What do you discover?

8. What do you think is the major truth which the movie attempts to communicate? Is this truth one that endures? Explain.

9. What do you think is the major truth which Matthew's Gospel attempts to communicate? Is this truth one that endures? Explain.

10. In "Willow," why do you think that it is important for Madmardigan and Sorsha to fall in love? Explain.

11. Both "Willow" and Matthew's Gospel portray good as conquering evil. Does good always triumph over evil? Explain and give examples to support your answer.

Teaching Luke's Gospel

Witness

In scholarly circles, it is generally accepted that the author of Luke's Gospel is also the author of the Acts of the Apostles. Scholars also accept the theory that the author borrowed both material from Mark's Gospel and from another source to which the author of Matthew's Gospel also had access. This source shared by Luke and Matthew is called Q (from the German "Quelle," meaning "source"). Also, the author of Luke's Gospel has some unique material in his narrative that is found in no other story in the Christian Bible (New Testament) referred to as "L."

While one of Luke's major themes is that Judaism gives birth to Christianity (the gospel begins and ends in the Temple in Jerusalem) and another major theme is that Christian life is a journey (the author devotes ten chapters to Jesus' journey to Jerusalem), the presupposition supporting the narrative is the role of witnessing.

The witness, who is guided by the Holy Spirit, observes or hears the word of God and testifies about or practices it.. In Luke's Gospel, Jesus is portrayed as a witness, whose innocence is attested by Herod, Pilate, one of the co-crucified criminals, and the centurion at the foot of the cross. The Lukan Jesus is a model of discipleship as witnessing; he prays before every major decision he makes, he eats meals with the outcast of society (tax collectors, prostitutes, lepers, etc.), declaring that God's reign has arrived.

The word "witness" is the English translation of the Greek word "martyr," a person who voluntarily suffers death as the penalty for witnessing to and refusing to renounce his or her faith or principles. The author of Luke's Gospel portrays Jesus as the primordial witness, the model of one who hears and practices the word of God all the way to the cross, through death, and beyond into the realm of the resurrection.

Students can gain a good understanding of Luke's Gospel by watching the film "Witness" (Paramount Pictures Corp., 1985), a story illustrating what happens when the city of Philadelphia meets the Amish, who live in the Pennsylvania countryside. Not only do the two worlds collide, like the emerging Christian world of Luke's Gospel late in the first century and the Roman Empire, but they enrich each other, teaching lessons easily forgotten in the isolation each provides. The viewer should pay close attention to the names of the characters in "Witness," since most of them refer to Hebrew Bible (Old Testament) personalities upon whom the characterizations are based, much like Luke creates characters from Hebrew Bible types.

"Witness" begins in an Amish wheat field with children and adults seemingly walking out of nowhere. They seem to emerge from a world long past by technology and forgotten. The viewer knows they are Amish by the black hats and beards worn by the men and the long black dresses and bonnets worn by the women. A horse and buggy alerts us that we are in the countryside of the state of Pennsylvania in 1984. A wake is taking place for a man named Jacob Lapp, who was married to a woman named Rachel Lapp (Kelly McGillis), in whom another man named Daniel Hackmeiner (Alexander Godunov) is interested. Daniel extends his sympathy to Rachel, assuring her that Jacob will walk with God. A post-funeral dinner allows the viewer to get steeped in the Amish community.

The wheat fields, the horses, the wagons, and the hay-making give way to focus on one horse and buggy leaving the country, traveling over a highway, stopping at a traffic light, and bringing Rachel Lapp and her son, Samuel (Lukas Haas), to a train station in Strasburg, Pennsylvania. They are on their way to Baltimore to visit family. The slow pace of the horse and buggy are contrasted with the swiftness of the train. The viewer has left the country and moved to the city.

At the railroad station, Daniel, who has accompanied Rachel and Samuel, tells Samuel that he'll see many things in the city. Eli Lapp, Rachel's father-in-law, who has also accompanied them to the train station, states, "You be careful out there among the English."

In the Philadelphia train station, where Rachel and Samuel encounter a three-hour delay, Samuel discovers a world he has never known. First, there is the water fountain. Then, seeing a man in a black hat and thinking that he is a fellow Amishman, Samuel is disappointed when he discovers that the man is a Jew. He sees the famous statue in the train station of an angel holding a dead man, showing brotherly love, the meaning of the word "Philadelphia." While in the restroom, Samuel witnesses two men kill a third man, an undercover narcotics agent. They rob him and then check the stalls to be sure no one has seen what they did. Samuel escapes notice by slipping under the stalls and standing on one of the toilets. During his first trip to the city, he has witnessed a murder.

John Book (Harrison Ford), a Philadelphia cop, investigates the crime and interrogates Rachel and Samuel, who tells him about the two black men who killed the white man. Speaking to Samuel, Book informs him that the dead man was a policeman and that it is his job to find out what happened. He asks Samuel to tell him everything he saw in the bathroom. Then, after Samuel tells Book what he knows, Book tells Rachel and Samuel that they cannot continue their trip to Baltimore until he has completed his investigation. So, riding in the police car, they pass by a bar to see if Samuel recognizes a man named T-Bone, but the boy declares that he isn't the man. Book takes them to the home of his sister, Elaine, for the night. The next day they are found in the police station where a line-up takes place, but Samuel identifies no one.

Before the line-up, Rachel asks Book about when they can leave. Book answers that he is trying to get the investigation over with as quickly as possible. Then Book tells Rachel, "Samuel is probably going to have to come back and testify. I'm sorry." Rachel responds, saying, "No, you're not. You're glad because you have a witness." Rachel tells Book that she doesn't like her son spending time with a man "who carries a gun and goes around whacking people."

In a meal-eating scene, the Amish pray quietly before slowly and meticulously eating their food. They are contrasted with Book, who, literally, stuffs the food into his mouth. He does not know how to eat, but will learn from the Amish later in the film. Since the Lukan Jesus spends a lot of time eating with different people, a mode of bonding, it would be wise to point out the importance of this scene and the later one since students seem to miss the contrast.

Back in the police station Samuel looks over mug shots of various criminals, but can identify no one. While Book answers a telephone call, Samuel explores the world of the police station by talking to people and walking around it. He comes upon a trophy case and spots the photo of the black man he saw kill the white man in the restroom in the train station. He points him out to Book, who identifies him as McFee (Danny Glover). Book then meets with Paul Schaefer (Josef Somner), another police officer, who tells Book that McFee is on vacation in Florida. Schaefer leads Book to believe that the murder was an inside job. In other words, someone else in the police department is also involved.

The viewer doesn't immediately discover who that someone else is. However, McFee engages Book in a shoot-out in a parking garage. Book is hit by one of McFee's bullets as McFee flees the scene.

Borrowing his sister's car, Book takes Rachel and Samuel from his sister's house and proceeds to take them to their home. He stops for a moment and calls his partner, Eldon Carter (Brent Jennings), and tells him to destroy all the paperwork on the case, "to watch his back," and that Schaefer is involved in "this thing" too. Meanwhile, those who are engaged in illegal drug traffic--McFee, Schaefer, and another man named Fergie (Angus MacInnes)--find Book's car hidden in his sister's garage, but he has taken Rachel and Samuel back home to their Amish country home.

Before leaving the car, Rachel asks Book if he will come back to take Samuel to trial. Book responds that there will be no trial. After they get out of the car, he drives a short distance down the road, faints from loss of blood, and drives the car into a birdhouse pole. Rachel runs toward the car, opens the door, sees the blood on Book's clothes, and says, "My God, why didn't you get to a hospital?" Book, who is semi-conscious, answers, "Gunshot wound. They have to make a report. And if they make a report, they find me. And if they find me, they find the boy."

Rachel's father-in-law, Eli, who refers to Book as "the English," arrives at the car with a horse and wagon, asking, "Is the English dead? He looks dead." He helps Rachel haul Book into their guestroom in their home, where an Amish medicine man arrives, examines Book's side, determines where the bullet entered and exited, and states that Book should be taken to a hospital. Rachel says that he must stay there. Eli asks, "What if he dies?" Rachel says, "Then we must pray that he doesn't die. But if he does, then we must find a way so no one knows." Eli, who doesn't yet understand the danger Samuel is in, says, "But Rachel, this is a man's life. We hold it in our hands." Rachel says, "I know that. God help me, I know that, Eli. But I tell you that if he is found, the people who did this to him will come get Samuel."

The medicine man instructs Rachel to make a poultice of milk and linseed oil for Book's wound. He will brew tea and send it over with his wife. Before he leaves, he tells Eli that he will have to speak to the elders about this. Eli says, "As you see fit."

Rachel keeps vigil at Book's bedside, washing his wound, holding his hand, and helping him through stages of delirium. At one time she thinks he is dead, but he moves a little, and she is comforted that he is still alive. Later, Book opens his eyes. Meanwhile, Eli, in a contrast of the means of transportation, pulls Book's car into his barn with his horse.

In Philadelphia at the police station, Schaefer, who is after Book because Book knows that Schaefer is behind the murder of the undercover narcotics agent in the train station, calls the sheriff of Lancaster County for help in finding the Lapps. The sheriff tells Schaefer that there are many Lapps in his county and they have no telephones. Meanwhile, Book, who is as out of place as a fish out of water, by his very presence in an Amish home causes a disturbance among the Amish elders, who debate as to how long he can remain with them. Rachel tells Book that they are happy that he is going to live. She adds, "We didn't know what we were going to do with you if you died."

Another scene contrasting the difference in the point of view between Book and the Amish follows. Samuel, who finds Book's gun in a dresser drawer, takes it out to look at it. Seeing him with it, Book takes it away from him, saying, "This is a loaded gun. This is very, very dangerous. Never ever touch a loaded gun. I'm taking the bullets out. Now its safe." To the Amish, the gun is a sign of violence. Rachel walks into the room, takes the gun away from the boy, barely touching it and treating it as if it were contaminated or unclean, and gives it back to Book telling him that as long as he is there she will insist that he respect her ways. Book agrees. And handing her the gun, he tells her to put it somewhere safe where Samuel won't find it. She puts it in a cabinet and the bullets in a flour canister in the kitchen.

Eli, who is sitting in the kitchen, teaches Samuel that the gun was made to take life, which, as he explains to Samuel, the Amish believe is wrong for human beings to do. Eli says that only God can take a life. Then, he explains: "Many times wars have come and people have said to us, 'You must fight. You must kill. It is the only way to preserve the good.' That, Samuel, there is never only one way. Remember that."

Then, Eli asks Samuel, who is sitting on the old man's lap, "Would you kill another man?" Samuel answers, "I would only kill a bad man." Eli asks, "Only the bad man, I see. And you know this bad man by sight? You are able to look into the heart and see this badness." Samuel replies, "I can see what they do. I have seen it." Eli says, "And having seen you become one of them. Don't you understand?"

Next, Eli explains to Samuel that the Amish are a people set apart; they have "come out from among" the English. He tells Samuel that the Amish are non-violent, but Samuel has been a witness to the English violence.

As Book heals and grows stronger, Rachel offers him some of the clothes of her dead husband to wear. The clothes have no buttons, which Rachel explains are signs of being proud and vain. Next, Book accompanies Eli to the town of Strasburg, where the closest phone is located which Book can use to call his partner, Carter. But before he goes, he gets the gun from the cabinet and retrieves the bullets from the flour canister. In town, tourists gawk at the Amish and some taunt them. Once he gets Carter on the line, Book tells him not to come to get him but to make some telephone calls in further investigation of what is taking place in the police force.

Back home, Rachel takes care of domestic chores. Book puts the gun back in the cabinet and gives her the bullets. Samuel begins to teach him about the Amish water wheel, the silo, and some kittens. In the barn, Book tries to start his car, but the battery is dead. Meanwhile, Eli pops up through a door in the barn's floor from the level below and tells Book that he can help milk the cows the next morning. At 4:30 a.m., Eli awakens him, takes him to the barn, gives him a stool, and tells him to get busy milking by hand. After the milking, they sit down to eat breakfast and Rachel teaches Book how to eat.

Daniel meets Book and tells him that he has come to see Rachel. Daniel is the man interested in Rachel. He courts her by simply sitting in the porch swing with her. Book observes this strange courting procedure while he works on repairing the birdhouse he had broken when his car ran into it. Later, after Daniel leaves, Rachel brings Book a glass of lemonade, which he drinks in one gulp, still not having learned how to drink properly. Rachel tells Book that Daniel is like a son to Eli.

Then, they work on Book's car, turning on the radio and dancing in the barn. Rachel tells him that he's invited to a barn-raising. They continue to dance around the barn to the music on the radio. Eli enters and sees them and is upset with Rachel. He asks her, "Rachel, what is it with you? Is this the ordinal?" Rachel answers, "I have done nothing against the rule of the ordinal." Eli states, "Nothing. You bring this man to our house with his gun of the hand. You bring fear to this house, fear of English with guns coming after ...." Rachel interrupts him, saying, "I've committed no sin." Eli: "Maybe. Maybe not yet."

Eli tells Rachel that some are talking about having her shunned. Rachel says that it is only gossip. Eli warns her,

> Do not take it lightly. They can do it. They can do it just like that. You know what it means, shunning? I cannot sit at table with you. I cannot take a thing from your hand. I cannot go to worship with you. O child, do not go so far.

Rachel: "I'm not a child." Eli: "But your are acting like one." Rachel: "I'll be the judge of that." Eli: "No, they will be the judge of that and so will I, if you shame me." Rachel: "You shame yourself."

Eldon Carter, Book's partner, who is serving now as a double agent, is questioned by Schaefer during their hunt for Book. Schaefer tells him that the police are like the Amish, a club with their own rules. He says that John has broken the rules, just as has Carter. The viewer concludes that Schaefer now must kill Carter, which is confirmed later in the film.

A bonding scene between the Amish community and Book ensues through the use of a barn-raising. Before beginning work, Daniel asks Book if his wound is better. Book tells him that it is just about healed. Daniel then says that Book can go home. A woman serves the men lemonade. Daniel and Book drink from the same glass, but Book does not gulp down his glass of liquid, like he did once before. He has learned to drink properly and savor every drop; he is becoming Amish. During lunch, Book demonstrates that he has learned how to eat properly. After lunch, while the men continue the barn-raising, Rachel joins other women in a quilting circle and hears about the gossip circulating about her and Book.

After all return home, Book, sitting in the porch swing, eyes Rachel bathing inside the house. He goes to her, but the opportunity for a sexual bonding scene is not taken. There is no love-making because if they bonded, either he would have to stay or she would have to leave. Their worlds are too different and cannot be brought together. The next morning, Book finds Rachel gathering eggs in the hen house. He says, "Rachel, if we'd made love last night, I'd have to stay or you'd have to leave."

Back in Strasburg, tourists taking pictures of the Amish infuriate Book, who, after making a telephone call, discovers that Carter is dead "in the line of duty." Book calls Schaefer and lets him know that he knows what's going on and that he's coming to get him. Before he can finish, Schaefer hangs up on Book. Now, Book is the only clean cop left; he is all alone.

The conflict between the world of the Amish and the world of the English now intensifies. The picture-taking tourists further infuriate Book, who defends Daniel, with whom he has traveled to town, and beats up a young punk. Eli tells Book that violence is not the Amish way, but Book replies that it is his way. As two members of the young gang approach Book, he bloodies their noses and knocks them to the ground.

Back in their home, Samuel plays with a toy that Book made him. Looking through the window, Rachel sees Book and Eli putting up the repaired birdhouse. After sending Samuel to bed, Rachel speaks to

Eli, who is coming into the house, asking him if Book is leaving. Eli tells her that he leaves the next morning and that he is going back to his work where he belongs. Rachel goes out to Book, who is finishing the bird-house. She removes her white cap, one of the signs of her Amish heritage. She's willing to leave her people. They embrace and kiss passionately.

Meanwhile, Schaefer, McFee, and Fergie find out where Book is hiding. The next morning before Book can leave they arrive in a car, which comes over the road on the horizon, stops momentarily, and backs down a little so it cannot be seen from the Lapp farmhouse. The three heavily armed men get out of it and proceed to walk toward the Lapp home. They invade the Lapp home, scaring Rachel and looking for Book. The men stop Eli, who's carrying two pails of fresh milk. Eli yells, "Book," as one of the men slaps Eli to the ground. Book, while fleeing to his car in the garage is told by Samuel, who is in the area, that he doesn't have his gun. Book sends Samuel to Daniel so that he won't get hurt.

After opening the barn door, Book tries to start his car, but the battery is too low to turn over the engine. Fergie finds Book and shoots at him. He misses. Book leads Fergie through the barn to the grain silo.

Book climbs into the grain silo into which Fergie follows. Releasing some of the grain, Book buries him, takes his riffle, and uses it to kill McFee, who has also made his way to the silo. While all this violence is taking place, Eli, who has Schaefer's gun keeping him at bay, secretly sees Samuel and motions to him with his hand. The viewer is prone to think that he wants Samuel to get Book's gun, but instead Samuel goes to the bell and begins to ring it, calling the whole community to come to Rachel's house.

Now, only Schaefer and Book are left. Schaefer has taken Rachel as a hostage. Book asks him, "What are you going to do, Paul? You going to kill me, shoot me, shoot him (Eli), shoot him (Samuel), the women, me? It's over. Enough." Book takes the rifle away from Schaefer as a huge community of the unarmed Amish are gathered around them. Schaefer slumps down in repentance. Meanwhile, police cars arrive to take Schaefer away. Rachel and Samuel watch from a window in their home.

Dressed in city clothes again, Book prepares to leave the Amish community. On the bank of a stream, he says good-bye to Samuel. Then, he says good-bye to Rachel, who turns away from him but does look back at him. After saying good-by to Eli, who is coming out of the barn, the old man tells him, "You be careful out among them English." In some ways, Book has become Amish and found a deeper meaning to life with them in the country, but their worlds cannot mix. He must return to the city. On his way back to the city he is no more than started when he meets Daniel walking down the road and heading toward Rachel's house. The viewer concludes that Daniel will marry Rachel, and the worlds of the Amish and Book will remain forever separated.

"Witness" presents the theme of witnessing from a variety of perspectives. First, Samuel Lapp witnesses the murder of the under-cover narcotics agent in the train station and is forever changed. Second, John Book witnesses the Amish way of life in the country and is healed physically, emotionally, and spiritually. Third, Eli witnesses the sincerity of John Book and comes to accept him to some degree as a member of the Amish community. Fourth, Rachel Lapp witnesses the forbidden love Book has for her, the rumors created by members of her community, and her need to remain true to her Amish roots. Fifth, in the midst of the violence which Book's world brings to their non-violent world, the whole Amish community witnesses to the power of a peaceful way of life. Sixth, Rachel and Samuel Lapp witness to the deliverance from death which Book ultimately gives to them.

In relating Luke's Gospel to "Witness," students can come to understand the various dimensions of the meaning of the word "witness" through a study of the characters. Samuel, who struggles to understand the differences between the non-violent world in which he lives and the violence he witnesses in the other world, can be compared to Jesus' disciples, who struggle with how to integrate their Lord's teaching with the historical Roman oppression and domination in which they find themselves.

Book, the hardened Philadelphia cop, and Eli, the hardened Amish elder, are examples of how witnessing brings about conversion. They can be likened to the sinful woman who is forgiven because she loves much, the parable of the barren fig tree, the three parables about the lost sheep, the lost coin, and the lost son, and Zacchaeus, the tax collector who repents and gives half of his possessions to the poor. While Book and Eli cannot live each other's lives, they come to understand better the way each lives and to recognize that they are human brothers.

Rachel can be compared to the many women in Luke's Gospel. They are portrayed as disciples who support Jesus out of their own means and follow their itinerant Lord. Rachel, even though she flirts with another way of life, remains faithful to her Amish roots. Mary, the pregnant-out-of-wedlock mother of Jesus, remains true to her Jewish roots. Rachel, a strong woman, is also like the widow in the parable of the unjust judge in Luke's Gospel; she does not stop until she gets what she needs. She is also like the widow who gave her last two copper coins to the Temple treasury in Luke's Gospel; Rachel devoted herself totally to saving Book's life and teaching him another way to live.

The use of such biblical names as Eli, Samuel, Rachel, and John in "Witness" should not be lost on the viewer. Eli, the Hebrew Bible (Old Testament) priest at Shiloh, accepts Samuel, the son of Elkanah and once-barren Hannah, as his student and educates him in the ways of God, especially teaching him how to listen to God's call. Once he comes of age, he replaces Eli as priest and anoints both Saul and David as king of Israel. In "Witness," Eli, the wise elder, teaches Samuel the ways of God, especially the path of non-violence.

Biblical Rachel is Jacob's first wife, who gives birth to Joseph and dies after giving birth to Benjamin. Joseph, after he is sold into Egyptian slavery by his brothers, becomes governor of Egypt and saves the world from famine. Benjamin, the smallest of Israel's tribes, gives birth to Saul, Israel's first king. In the Christian Bible (New Testament) Paul claims that he is a descendent of the tribe of Benjamin. The Rachel of "Witness" is like the biblical Rachel insofar as she has given birth to Samuel, a little boy who becomes a great witness.

Finally, John Book bears the name of both the man who baptized Jesus and the traditional author of the fourth gospel. Like John the Baptist, John Book "baptizes" the Amish into the world of Philadelphia and violence. Then, he leaves. Unlike John the Baptist in the gospels, John Book is not killed. Like John, the traditional author of John's Gospel and the three letters of John, John Book tells a story of love, even as he is loved by the Amish community.

The Amish community can be compared to either the crowds who surround Jesus in Luke's Gospel at various times, to the smaller group of Jesus' disciples, and to the ideal community in the Acts of the Apostles. The Amish stand together firmly; otherwise, they know that they will fall apart individually. Even though Peter denies Jesus three times, Luke does not narrate, like the author of Mark's Gospel and the author of Matthew's Gospel, that all of the disciples run away when Jesus is arrested. In fact, at the end of Luke's Gospel, Jesus' disciples are found gathered together in Jerusalem expecting a post-resurrection appearance of Jesus. When he arrives, he teaches them and reminds them that they are witnesses to his suffering, death, and resurrection. They are sent to the nations to proclaim repentance and the forgiveness of sins. Then, Jesus, who has come from another world, like Book, withdraws from his followers and ascends into the heavens, like Book, who leaves the world of the Amish to return to Philadelphia.

Exercises and Questions for Discussion

1. Choose five characters from the movie "Witness" and identify what he or she witnessed and how that affected his or her life.

2. Outline the plot of the film by scene. For each scene indicate its importance to the whole story and what purpose it serves.

3. What do you think is the major truth which the movie attempts to communicate? Is this truth one that endures? Explain.

4. After reading the Gospel According to Luke in one sitting, identify what each of the following characters witness and how it affects his or her life: Zechariah and Elizabeth, Mary, Jesus, Peter, Pharisees, Disciples/Apostles, Pilate, and Judas.

5. Identify five stories in Luke's Gospel that illustrate the author's stress on the importance of witnessing. Explain how each of the five stories is illustrative of witnessing.

6. Identify and compare three characters from "Witness" with three characters from Luke's Gospel. Explain how each pair is alike and unlike.

7. What do you think is the major truth which Luke's Gospel attempts to communicate? Is this truth one that endures? Explain.

8. Why do you think John Book leaves the Amish community after he defeats his enemies? In other words, why doesn't he stay with the Amish, marry Rachel, and live happily ever after?

Teaching John's Gospel

Jeremiah Johnson

The Gospel According to John, written near the end of the first century common era, is unlike the synoptic gospels (Mark, Matthew, Luke) in that it does not tell a similar story about Jesus of Nazareth. In fact, the final editor of the gospel is more interested in telling the reader that Jesus is the eternal Word of God become flesh. He who lived in the world above came to the world below to show people how to get to the world above.

Two literary techniques are used quite frequently in John's Gospel. First, the author uses signs. A sign is something which represents or stands for something else. At the end of the account of the wedding feast at Cana, during which water becomes wine, the reader is told that that was Jesus' first sign. It is the reader's responsibility to determine what the sign represents.

Second, the author uses double-entendre, a word or phrase that can have at least, and sometimes more than, two meanings. For example, the Johannine Jesus speaks to a crowd about eating his flesh and drinking his blood. One meaning of the phrase "eating flesh and drinking blood" is cannibalism. Another meaning implies eating the bread and drinking the wine of eucharist. The reader must determine what the Jo-hannine Jesus intends, and he or she does so based on whether or not he or she believes that Jesus is God's Son.

In order to help students understand the function of signs and how double-entendres work, the film "Jeremiah Johnson" (Warner Bros., 1972), may be shown. A minimal amount of dialogue occurs in the film. Thus, the viewer must determine what each scene means as he or she reads the signs. When dialogue does occur, it often contains double-entendres, words which the viewer can understand to have at least two meanings. Sometimes, because the meaning intended does not become clear until later in the film, the viewer must keep all possible meanings in mind.

"Jeremiah Johnson," based on the novel *Mountain Man* by Vardis Fisher (New York: Simon & Schuster, Inc., 1965), opens with a scene of Indians and one man, Jeremiah Johnson (Robert Redford), in a boat crossing a river, a sign of a new beginning, a new life. A narrator tells the viewer, "His name was Jeremiah Johnson, and they say he wanted to be a mountain man. Nobody knows from whereabouts he came from, but don't seem to matter much." The viewer, by interpreting the signs of the clothes worn by Johnson concludes that he was a sailor (pants) or an ex-soldier of the Mexican War (cap).

The viewer concludes that the setting is the Rocky Mountains in the mid-1800s. The narrator tells the viewer that Johnson was looking for a Hawkin gun and that he bought himself "a good horse and traps and other truck that went with being a mountain man and said good-bye to whatever life was down there below." Meanwhile, scenes show Johnson buying a horse for himself and a mule upon which to pack his gear.

Then, the viewer hears this song: "Jeremiah Johnson made his way into the mountains bettin' on forgettin' all the troubles that he knew. The trail was wide and narrow. The eagle or the sparrow showed the path he was to follow as it flew." Then, the song moves into a description of the life of a mountain man. The vocalist sings, "A mountain man's a lonely man and he leaves a life behind. It ought to have been different, but you often times will find that a story doesn't always go the way you had in mind. Jeremiah's story was that kind." Meanwhile, Johnson begins to grow a beard, the sign of his new life as a mountain man.

There follows a sequence of scenes in which there is no dialogue and the viewer must determine the meaning of the signs in each. First, Johnson misses a shot at an antelope. Second, in a snow-surrounded stream he desperately tries to catch a fish with his hands, while an Indian, whom we find out later is called Paints His Shirt Red, on horseback sees him and Johnson sees the string of fish the Indian has, but the Indian leaves. Third, Johnson attempts to get a fire started under a tree. Just as it begins to burn, the wind blows and a large clump of snow falls out of the tree and puts it out. Fourth, Johnson comes upon a frozen man, sitting upright on a hillside and holding a 50-calibre Hawkin rifle. From the note he pinned to himself before he died, the viewer learns that the man was named Hatchet Jack and, as he states in the note, he gave his rifle to anyone finding him. Fifth, using the Hawkin rifle--one item the narrator had told us Johnson wanted--Johnson makes a kill for food, but his horse dies in the snow. He has to walk, leading his pack mule through the snow-covered mountains. By watching the signs, the reader concludes that Jeremiah Johnson is a miserable failure as a mountain man.

While fumbling around, Johnson encounters Bear Claw (Will Geer), an old trapper, a sage, and a teacher. His first words to Johnson, "Don't come any farther, pilgrim," indicate not only his cautious approach to one from "down there" (meaning the world outside of the mountains), but also contain the double-entendre "pilgrim," which can refer to one who crossed the ocean in the Mayflower or one who is on a pilgrimage, a journey.

Bear Claw is dressed in light-colored animal skins with a white fur hat, and he rides a white horse. Johns meets him in an open area where everything is covered in snow. There is little doubt that the viewer who knows the Bible, especially the Book of Daniel and the Book of Revelation, and is familiar with the description of the transfiguration and resurrection scenes in the synoptics, will recognize who Bear Claw represents. After teasing Johnson for disturbing his hunt and seeing that Johnson has not been a successful hunter, he reveals that he traps grizzly bears and that the land has been trapped out, except for "grizz," for twenty-five years. Then, Bear Claw invites Johnson to join him for some food and warmth in his cabin, and Johnson accepts.

In a series of scenes, Bear Claw is depicted as a teacher, who instructs Johnson in the fundamentals of mountain-man life. He shows him how to sew gloves out of bear skin. Then, he teaches him about trapping, respect for nature, Indians, how to sharpen knives, how to make a bed in the snow, and how to kill elk. After a short discussion about loneliness in the mountains, Bear Claw asks Johnson about why he came to the mountains. Johnson says that he wanted to be different. Bear Claw says that many come to the mountains to be different, to get from the mountains something they couldn't get below, and it always comes to nothing. Then, he adds, "Can't cheat the mountain, pilgrim. Mountain's got it." The viewer must determine what it is that the mountain has and what Johnson wants.

Once Bear Claw has taught Johnson everything he needs to know in order to survive, Bear Claw says, "You learn well, pilgrim. Go far. Time you ain't burnt alive or scalped." They separate. Immediately a sequence of scenes shows Johnson setting up his own camp, successfully killing food, successfully trapping, trading with Indians and smoking a peace pipe, and respecting nature. He has learned well, the viewer concludes, by contrasting the signs in these scenes with the signs in the series of scenes before showing him a failure.

Johnson comes upon a homestead and meets a crazy woman (Allyn Ann McLerie) who is running around dead bodies. By observing the signs, the viewer concludes that the family has been attacked by Indians and all of the members have been scalped. With an economy of words, Johnson tells her that he is her friend and that they have graves to dig. After digging graves and burying the dead, Johnson discovers a mute child, about eight-years-old, still alive in the cabin. He fixes a meal and shares it with the woman and the boy. Then, as Johnson is preparing to leave, the woman makes him take the boy with him. Johnson names the boy "Caleb," which a biblical reader will notice was one of the men Joshua, Moses' successor, sent to reconnoitre the land of Canaan. Unlike the other men with him, who didn't think that the Israelites could defeat their enemies on the other side of the Jordan, Caleb trusted unreservedly in God when God brought Israel into the promised land. As Johnson rides away, the woman remains.

In the next scene, Johnson has descended from the snowy mountains and meets Del Grue (Stefan Gierasch), dressed in dark brown skins in a desert-like setting. Johnson finds Grue, a bald-headed man, buried in sand up to his head. He learns that the Crow Indians stole Grue's horses, pelts, rifle, and put him in the ground to die. After tracking the Indians and finding their camp during the darkness of night, Johnson wants merely to retrieve Grue's belongings without incident, but Grue wakes up the Indians and he and Johnson have to kill them. Johnson gets very angry at Grue, who scalps the Indians and tells Johnson that he sells the scalps to the English.

Back on the trail together, they run into Flathead Indians, but before they can tell to which tribe they belong Grue switches the Crow scalps from his horse to Johnson's horse. That way, if the Indians were Crow, Johnson would be their enemy and Grue would be free. But as it turns out, the Flathead praise Johnson as a hero for having killed and scalped some of their enemy.

By this point the viewer should be suspicious of Del Grue. He represents evil. He appears in the desert. Whatever he does ends up putting people at risk. His word means nothing. And he is willing to do anything to save his own scalp. He is Johnson's tempter.

All travel to the Flathead Indian camp. In the tent of the chief, who is named Two-Tongues Lebeaux, the viewer discovers that the Flathead are Christians and that Two-Tongues Lebeaux learned French from missionaries from France. The chief offers Johnson two ponies, and Johnson offers the chief a gift in return. Grue says to Johnson that the Indian chief is trying to honor him by giving him a gift. He explains that if the chief cannot give him a better gift, the chief will consider it an insult.

In order to top Johnson's gift, the chief offers the hero his daughter, who is named Swan. Grue tells Johnson, who is not too thrilled about having a squaw, that if he turns down this gift, the Indians will kill both of them. Clearly, Grue is worried only about saving his own life.

Following an Indian wedding ceremony, Johnson, Swan, and Caleb leave the camp with Grue, who goes his own separate way from them, telling them that he will see them in the fall. What follows are scenes showing Johnson, Swan, and Caleb traveling on horseback through the mountains while a vocalist sings this song: "The way that you wonder is the way that you choose. The day that you tarry is the day that you loose. Sunshine or thunder a man will always wander where the fair wind blows."

In a succession of scenes, the viewer recognizes that not one of the three people in the party can communicate with each other. Johnson knows only English and no Flathead. Swan knows only Flathead and no English. And Caleb doesn't speak.

Before undressing for bed and preparing for her wedding night, Swan prays. Johnson observes, but he does not sleep with her. In other words, there is no sexual bonding scene. The next day, Swan teaches Johnson how to kill a prairie chicken quietly. Johnson is still learning how to survive.

All is now ready for a house-building scene. Upon approaching the ideal location, Johnson says, "This will do: river in front, cliffs behind, good water, not much wind. This will be a good place to live." The viewer will notice that they have crossed a river, a sign that their lives are changing. A sequence follows in which they fashion a log cabin out of nothing but the trees they cut and the logs they move. The three of them-- Jeremiah, Swan, Caleb--work together as a team, growing as a family, and the viewer watches their love grow for each other. Jeremiah Johnson, the pilgrim mountain man, has become a settled family man.

One day while watching an eagle, a sign of transcendence and a sign of Johnson's call to the life of an itinerant mountain man, float on the wind currents, Johnson is reminded of his life's work. But the three settlers move into their newly completed house as a family. Swan makes Johnson a coat out of skins to keep him warm in the wind, he says, and to keep the rain from getting him wet.

While wearing the coat and hunting buffalo, he is attacked by coyotes, which he kills. But he is wounded. After returning, Swan bathes his wounds and demonstrates her love for him. She asks him to shave off his beard, the original sign of his change of life. He does so. His un-shaven face now represents his status as a family man, which is demon-strated in successive scenes of Johnson showing Caleb how to set traps and cut trees, all three playing a game of Indian ball, and Swan planting flowers near their home. Jeremiah, Swan, and Caleb have become a family.

One day soldiers arrive under the command of Lieutenant Mour-eaux with a missionary named Rev. Linquist. At first Johnson is startled by having English spoken. Moureaux informs Johnson that they have three wagons of settlers broken down in the snow and ice on Feather Mason. Linquist says that they have to get the settlers out before they freeze or the Indians get them. When Johnson seems not too enthusiastic about leaving Swan and Caleb, Linquist, sniveling with his handkerchief-in-hand, adds, "These are Christian families, Johnson. Christian women and children starving. You mean to tell me that you intend to let those people die!" Reluctantly, Johnson agrees to lead them through the passes to rescue the settlers.

However, to get to one pass, they must pass through a Crow Indian burial ground. When eying the scaffolds with dead bodies wrapped in skins, Johnson tells Linquist that they can't go through there. Johnson explains that it is a Crow burial ground and that it is sacred. Johnson says that they will have to turn around and head east. Linquist asks about the distance, and Johnson says that it is about twenty miles. Linquist, who is not pleased with the prospect of riding another twenty miles, reminds Johnson that people are waiting for them, and that they are freezing and hungry and scared. Johnson: "Crow don't even come here except with medicine men and bearing parties." Linquist: "But we are not Crows."

After Linquist asks Johnson what would happen if they pass through the burial ground, Johnson says that he doesn't know, but he does know that this is big medicine and that the Indians guard the place with spirits. Linquist asks, "You don't believe that?" Johnson replies, "It doesn't matter; they do." Linquist: "You've been up here too long, Johnson, believing in this." Linquist asks about the possibility of finding his own way through the mountains, but Johnson tells him that he will get lost. Then Linquist declares that he is riding through.

Linquist, an ironic Christian missionary, is not so much worried about the wagons and families stuck in the mountains, but about himself and his reputation. He's another Del Grue in disguise. He has tempted Johnson to break the unspoken covenant Johnson entered into with the Crow Indians not to desecrate their burial ground. Once Johnson gets the missionary and the soldiers to the stranded families and their wagons, he rides back through the Crow burial ground, stopping to look at the skeletons, and all he can feel is a sense of death. His ears begin to ring and he cannot understand why the Indians have not retaliated for his trespassing. Then, the burial ground becomes a sign and a double entendre of what has taken place in his home. Swan and Caleb are dead.

Johnson rides as fast as he can through the burial ground to his home, where he finds that Caleb and Swan have been killed by the Crow Indians. He determines that they are responsible for their deaths by examining the arrows they have left behind. At this moment, Johnson is most human. His family is gone because he violated the burial ground and helped the soldiers get to the wagons to save some Christians. Swan and Caleb are signs not only of Johnson's love and change of life from a mountain man to a family man, but their deaths stand in sharp contrast to the lives saved by the missionary and the soldiers. Johnson has regained his status as a mountain man, but at what a price--the deaths of those he loved and his own loneliness.

While slumping down in mourning in his home, Johnson's horse walks up the door, a sign of his mountain-man call and his lonely life (a man and his horse). He gathers the bodies of Swan and Caleb, wraps them in skins, and puts them in the center of the cabin, which he sets on fire. He watches as it burns to the ground. The home, a sign of his family life, is gone. Now, he returns to his status as a mountain man and begins again to grow his beard, a sign of his change of life.

Johnson has come to understand that he must fight to protect the life he has chosen. And so he begins a journey of revenge. He tracks the Crow Indians who killed Swan and Caleb. Finding four of them, he manages to kill three. The one who escapes is finally caught by Johnson, but the Indian sings a dirge pleading for his life and Johnson recognizes the uselessness of revenge.

The viewer sees that Johnson has been wounded in the back. He lies down on the ground with the three dead bodies of the Indians he had killed. This action is a sign of his own death to himself and the revenge that he had taken on the Indians. It is also a sign of his repentance. While he is experiencing death, a vocalist sings: "An Indian said if you search in vain for what you cannot find. He said you found out in pain running down the time. The Indian didn't scream it. He said it in a song. And, he's never been known to be wrong."

Now the film begins a series of scenes which parallel exactly the reverse of the sequence at the beginning of the film. Beginning at the now burned-down home to which Johnson has ridden, he sees a flying eagle, a sign of transcendence and a sign of his own call to return to the mountains. A juxtaposition of shots of Johnson and the mountains and the Indians confirms that he is being called back to a mountain-man life.

But the Crow want revenge on Johnson for killing their three braves. A brave approaches as Johnson fishes and Johnson kills him even as he is wounded in the eye, which he bathes in the river, a sign of washing, baptism, purification. The next brave, hidden in a snow bank, lunges at Johnson, who kills him but gets his hand wounded in the process. Finally, in what has been a long series of silent scenes, Johnson lets out a big cry, a yell of despair, the cosmic cry of one who has been crucified symbolically.

In the next scene, Johnson again meets Del Grue, who now has hair growing on his head. Grue tells Johnson that he decided that when he dies that he would like to leave some hair to be remembered on some Indian's lodge pole. After Johnson asks him where he is headed, Grue says that both of them will end up in hell. Evil comes in many disguises, as Johnson and the viewer has now learned.

After pitching camp together, Johnson tells Grue about Swan and Caleb. A Crow Indian comes out of the darkness of night to attack Johnson, who kills him. Grue tells Johnson that he is lucky they are Crows because Apache send fifty men at once. Then Grue says that most Indian tribes measure their greatness by the might of their enemies. Then, Grue tempts Johnson to leave his life in the mountains, recommending that he get out of the mountains and move to a town. All Johnson says is, "I've been to a town."

The next morning they separate while passing through the desert. Grue says that he is heading to a place to trap beaver. Johnson says that he may head to Canada. Immediately a series of scenes shows Johnson killing more Indians who attack him. Each attack results in the brave's death and Johnson's death and resurrection. One Indian stabs Johnson with a spear in the stomach, but he draws his gun and kills him. He pulls the spear out of his chest and lays it on the ground near the dead Indian.

Johnson travels back to the place where he encountered the crazy woman, whose family had been murdered by Indians. He finds a new family establishing a homestead there. The new settler, whose last name is Qualen, tells him that she is dead. Johnson heads toward the shack where Qualen has hidden his family but stops when he sees a pile of bones, skulls, beads, and shells arranged in front of a big stone. Qualen tells Johnson that it is for him. Johnson at first thinks it is a tomb stone, but Qualen interprets its significance for him, saying, "It ain't a grave like the others. More like a statue or monument. Some say you're dead on account of this. Others say you never will be on account of this."

Now back in the high country, Johnson again meets Bear Claw, dressed in white skins and a white fur cap and riding through a mist of snow on a white horse. Jeremiah has been cooking a rabbit on a spit. Bear Claw says, "You come far, pilgrim." Johnson replies, "Feels like far." Bear Claw: "Were it worth the trouble?" Johnson: "Weren't no trouble." Bear Claw informs Johnson that an avalanche took his cabin and his mule and he is still hunting "grizz." They discuss what month of the year it might be. Bear Claw says, "Winter's a long time going, huh? Stays a long time this high." He is using "winter" as a double entendre, referring to both the season of the year and Johnson's state of loneliness. Bear Claw, as he is ready to leave, says that Johnson has done well to keep so much of his hair when so many Indians are after it. Then he wishes him well.

The vocalist returns with this song: "The way that you wander is the way that you choose. The day that you tarry is the day that you loose. Sunshine or flowers, a man will always wander where the fair winds blow."

The first person Jeremiah met was Paints His Shirt Red, and the last person he meets is the same. Johnson, sitting on his horse, is perched on a mountain ledge, while the Indian is down below in the valley. Each extends his hand in a sign of peace and as a truce between them. The Indian accepts Johnson as a divine figure, positioned in an ascension scene on the mountain, and Johnson accepts the fact that his vengeance is satisfied and his life as a mountain man has begun again. The narrator, who has been absent since the beginning of the film, now returns and confirms what the scene seems to portray, saying, "And some folks say he's up there still." Then, the vocalist sings, "Jeremiah Johnson made his way into the mountains. He was bettin' on forgettin' all the troubles that he knew." But as the viewer has discovered, Johnson was formed into the man he was by the very troubles that he knew.

The parallel structure of the first four and last four scenes, the last four an inversion of the first four--Johnson with Paints His Shirt Red, Bear Claw, homestead of the crazy woman/Qualen, and Del Grue-- confirms the mythic and cyclical nature of the story. Johnson is no ordinary mountain man. He is a type of son, like Jesus in John's Gospel, who is taught how to survive by a father-figure, Bear Claw, like God, who himself lives in the snowy mountains of the gods. He learns how to die and how to rise. Even his name is significant, since only in Matthew's Gospel do some people consider Jesus to be a reappearance of the prophet Jeremiah, known for his suffering. The last sight of Johnson is a fitting sign with which to end the film. The viewer sees him still alive and alone and still climbing. At the end of John's Gospel, a divine Jesus, who has been in charge of his life throughout the story, repeatedly appears to his followers and convinces them that he has been raised to life and is with them.

"Jeremiah Johnson," because of its lack of dialogue and its use of signs, can help students understand how the author of John's Gospel uses signs to communicate truths concerning Jesus of Nazareth. Chapters 2 through 12 of the gospel are organized around seven major signs, sometimes called the book of signs. The seven--the number itself being a sign of fullness or completion--are: water into wine during the wedding at Cana, the curing of the son of the royal official from Capernaum in Cana, the healing of a paralytic on the Sabbath, the feeding of a large crowd with five barley loaves and two fish (the sum of which is seven), Jesus walking on the sea, the curing of the man born blind, and the raising of Lazarus.

Other than the seven major signs in John's Gospel, there are many minor signs. What follows is not meant to be an exhaustive list but to give the reader a taste of what students can discover in the gospel after watching "Jeremiah Johnson" and learning how to recognize and interpret signs. The "Word" is a sign of God-become-flesh or Jesus, as is the name given to Jesus by John the Baptist: "Lamb of God." "The mother of Jesus," who is never named in John's Gospel, makes only two appearances in the gospel. Thus, she is both a sign and a link between the two scenes in which she appears: the wedding at Cana and at the foot of the cross. There are only "six," an incomplete number, jars of water which become wine at the Cana wedding, and the reader must look for the seventh, to demonstrate that Jesus completes or fulfills his work as redeemer.

Throughout the fourth gospel, the Johannine Jesus refers to himself as "I AM," a sign of the name Yahweh uses to identify God's self when Moses asked the Holy One for God's name. By saying that he is the bread of life, the living bread, the light of the world, the gate, the good shepherd, the resurrection and the life, the way and the truth and the life, and the true vine, the Johannine Jesus not only claims to be God-become-flesh, but to encompass in himself all the qualities of God: source of food, creator, leader, savior.

Some of the signs in John's Gospel are also double entendres. They have more than one meaning. In his dialogue with Nicodemus, Jesus speaks about being born again, which can be understood to mean crawling back into the womb of one's mother, as Nicodemus thought, or as being baptized and beginning a new way of life, as Jesus taught.

Blindness is a sign of both being physically blind, as was the man born blind, and spiritual blindness, as were those who refused to believe that Jesus was the Son of God. In fact, in John's Gospel, the physically blind man sees what the spiritually blind cannot see.

In the bread of life discourse, the Johannine Jesus uses two signs which are also double entendres: bread and wine. Bread can refer to physical bread, such as a loaf, or it can mean Jesus' body. Likewise, wine can be a reference to the fruit of the vine, or it can be a sign of Jesus' blood. When Jesus instructs his followers to eat his body and to drink his blood, they can infer that he is referring to bread and wine or cannibalism.

Probably the most polyvalent sign which serves as a double entendre in John's Gospel is water. In the dialogue with Nicodemus, water refers to baptism. In the story of the woman at the well, it refers to eternal life. During the Festival of Booths, Jesus uses water to refer to the Spirit. Water, used to wash the disciples' feet, becomes a sign of service. And the water, a sign of baptism, and blood, a sign of eucharist, flowing from the side of Jesus after his death, indicate that he has given birth to the church, like God once created Eve from a rib taken from Adam's side.

In a number of references throughout the gospel, Jesus refers to his crucifixion as his "hour," indicating not only the time of his suffering and death, but also the moment of his being "lifted up," itself a reference to his hanging on the cross and his resurrection or return to God. Closely associated with "hour" and "lifted up" is "glory," a sign of Jesus' divinity shown through his death and resurrection. The character of Jesus in John's Gospel is much like the character of Jeremiah in "Jeremiah Johnson," insofar as at the end of both stories they are discovered to be dead and alive: Jesus is raised from the dead; Jeremiah Johnson lives in the mountains eternally.

Exercises and Questions for Discussion

1. Make a list of five signs in "Jeremiah Johnson." For each sign indicate of what it is a sign or what it represents or means.

2. Make a list of three double-entendres in "Jeremiah Johnson." For each list as many meanings as possible.

3. After reading the Gospel According to John in one sitting, make a list of five signs found in it. For each sign indicate of what it is a sign or what it represents or means.

4. Make a list of five double-entendres in John's Gospel. For each list as many meanings as possible.

5. Outline the plot of the film by scene. For each scene indicate its importance to the whole story and what purpose it serves. What scene(s) serve(s) as the pivot point for the film?

6. Outline the plot of John's Gospel by scene. For each scene indicate its importance to the whole story and what purpose it serves. When you look at the outline of the scenes, what do you discover?

7. What do you think is the major truth which the movie attempts to communicate? Is this truth one that endures? Explain.

8. What do you think is the major truth which John's Gospel attempts to communicate? Is this truth one that endures? Explain.

9. Make list of five ways that "Jeremiah Johnson" helped you to better understand John's Gospel.

Teaching John's Gospel

Powder

The Gospel According to John, written near the end of the first century common era, is unlike the synoptic gospels (Mark, Matthew, Luke) in that it does not tell a similar story about Jesus of Nazareth. In fact, the final editor of the gospel is more interested in telling the reader that Jesus is the eternal Word of God become flesh. He who lived in the world above came to the world below to show people how to get to the world above. He became incarnate, taught people a new way of life, and called them to believe that he was the Son of God. After suffering and dying on the cross, he was raised to new life by the Father, whose work he had accomplished. Then, he gives his disciples the gift of the Holy Spirit, the new mode of his presence with them.

In order to help students understand the function of incarnation and the basic story-line of John's Gospel, the film "Powder" (Hollywood Pictures, 1995), may be shown. It is a story about the incarnation of an albino man, his life of compassion for others who harass him because of his strange appearance, his death, and his return to the world above from which he came. The film provides students with a contemporary medium for understanding the character of Jesus in John's Gospel.

The film begins in a thunderstorm with an ambulance arriving at a hospital and a pregnant woman being hauled out of it on a gurney. The time is the present. One nurse looks at the sky as thunder claps. A man holds the hand of the pregnant woman. The viewer feels like he or she is working on a jig-saw puzzle with pieces of the story strewn all over the screen. The film risks losing the viewer of which much is demanded throughout the entirety of the film.

In the next scene, the doctor walks down the hall to a man named Greg, sitting in a waiting room, and tells him that Anna, the woman on the gurney, didn't live. He says that the trauma was too much. The doctor also tells him that the baby did live, but that he is an albino with pale skin and light-sensitive eyes, and that he has experienced everything the mother experienced. Of course, at this point in the film the viewer does not know what that experience was.

Greg goes with the doctor to the incubator where the child is crying and screaming. His head is covered to protect his eyes from the bright lights. His father looks at him while monitors measure his brain waves, which are observed by doctors and the viewer as unusual. Greg says that he is not his son and leaves. The camera focuses on the baby's hand, which is waving near a window in the incubator, and on the paper recording the baby's brain waves, which is covered with black ink. By reading the sign, the viewer concludes that this is no ordinary baby.

Fifteen or more years have passed, and the viewer is taken to the baby's grandparents' farmhouse, where the grandfather has just died. The sheriff, Doug Barnum (Lance Henriksen), his deputy, Harley Duncan (Brandon Smith), and the director of the local boy's home, Jessie Caldwell (Mary Steenburgen), have arrived to investigate the presence of the boy who lives in the cellar below the farmhouse. Barnum tells Caldwell that the neighbors say that he's retarded, deformed, different--a phantom, since they have never seen him, kept as a "family secret."

Jessie goes into the dark cellar to see the boy and observes that the walls are lined with bookshelves crammed with books. As her eyes begin to focus, she notices someone in the darkness, tells him he has no reason to fear, and asks his name. He says that his name is Powder, and tells her about the death of his grandfather. He extends a very white hand toward Caldwell, as the viewer sees a teenager who is totally bald, having no hair anywhere on his body, and displaying a totally white complexion. He tells her that his real name is Jeremy Reed. After discussing why he waited several days to call the sheriff concerning his grandfather's death, Powder tells Caldwell that he was afraid that people would come and take him away.

The viewer concludes that Powder, Jeremy Reed (Sean Patrick Flanery), is the baby-become-teenager seen at the beginning of the film. The viewer must determine that after his father rejected him, his grand-parents accepted him and took him to live in their cellar, where he has been for fifteen to sixteen years.

Meanwhile, Caldwell examines some of the things that Powder has in his cellar sanctuary, such as a toy with a ball that triggers pictures to pop up. He tells her that he works on the farm until the sun gets too bright and sunglasses are no help. She tells him that contact lenses may help. She asks about school, which he says he has never attended, but he has read all the books in the room. He demonstrates that he has a photographic memory by quoting the first few lines from a page of a book which Caldwell randomly pulls off the shelf and opens. Powder knows all the hundreds of books in his library by memory.

Caldwell takes Powder to the "Center," a boarding home for boys who have been abused or abandoned by their parents, where she serves as the director. On their way out of the farmhouse, Powder carries a single suitcase, stopping as Caldwell tells him not to be afraid. He, reading her mind, tells her that she is afraid for him. She drives him away while the sheriff, his deputy, and the neighbors stand around gawking at what they have just seen.

The sheriff calls attention to all the lightning rods on the top of the farmhouse. They are lined up along the top of the roof about a foot apart. Harley tells the sheriff that the coroner said that Powder's grandfather died naturally from a heart attack but that he had received some electric shock. The camera focuses again on the lightening rods to emphasize to the viewer that they form an important piece of the puzzle still to be figured out.

Caldwell and Powder drive through the city of Wheaton and into the country where the home for boys is located while he plays with the electric window switch in the car. On the lawn a group of teenage boys is playing football. They stop and stare at Powder, who, once he enters the building, sits in the hall outside Caldwell's office, while some of the guys stare through a window at him.

In the center's cafeteria, Powder sits at one table eating alone. Some of the boys taunt him. One teenager, named John Box (Bradford Tatum), leads a group over to his table with their trays. All sit and are quiet. Box asks Powder why he looks the way he does. Then, he asks if Powder has cancer or some other disease. Powder just keeps eating. Then, Box suggests that to be properly initiated into the center that Powder must wear a spoon on his nose as another boy, Mitch, demonstrates. If Powder refuses to put it on his nose, Box tells him that he will put it up his ass.

Powder takes the spoon in his hand and rubbing it with his thumb magnetizes it and makes it stand upright in the center of the table. Then, all the eating utensils from around the room are drawn toward it, building a tower of spoons and forks. The room is filled with silence as all the boys sit in astonishment. But there is more to come. One spoon emerges from its place near the serving line, jumps out of the box, leaps up onto the table, and knocks down the tower of other eating utensils. Now, the viewer concludes that Powder has some extraordinary abilities, but he or she still does not know the source.

The story now focuses on Doug Barnum, the sheriff. Upon entering the driveway to his home, he encounters his son, Stephen, who, acknowledging him, walks by him, gets into his car, and drives away. The sheriff goes upstairs, and the viewer sees his wife in bed in a coma. The nurse who cares for her tells Doug that Stephen stayed three hours with his mother and left her a gift, a silver box. The nurse asks about the incidents at the Reed farm and the sheriff talks to his wife, who makes no response. The viewer concludes that the sheriff's wife has been in a coma for a long time and that there is some estrangement between him and his son.

Back in the Center, a doctor examining Powder tells Caldwell that he is a healthy man, except for his lack of body hair. Caldwell tells the doctor that contact lenses are on the way for Powder. Then, after the doctor leaves, Caldwell tells Powder about attending Wheaton High School. She asks him if he would like to go. He says that he would after he gets his contact lenses.

Powder gets off the bus at Wheaton High School while other students gathered near the front door of the school become quiet and stare at him. In the science classroom, the topic is energy and how energy is always relaying, always transforming, even the electric impulses in a person's brain. The teacher, Donald Ripley (Jeff Goldblum), pulls a Jacob's ladder into the center of the classroom to demonstrate how electricity travels. Powder, sitting in the back of the room, is enthralled by the demonstration and the metal objects--paper clip and pen--near him begin to move and spin around. An arc of electricity jumps from the Jacob's ladder to Powder's chest. He is first pushed back against the class-room wall. Then, the arc makes a return connection to the Jacob's ladder and Powder is elevated from the floor by the electric surge. Both Ripley and his students stand against the opposite wall in amazement. Finally, Ripley grabs a stool and smashes the Jacob's letter, stopping the electric charge. Powder falls to the floor with his clothes smoldering. When Ripley touches him to see if he is dead, the hairs on Ripley's arm stand up.

Powder is taken to the hospital, where Ripley tells the sheriff about the experience. The doctor says that there isn't a scratch on Powder. Ripley says there is a hole burned in his shirt and that he attracted the electricity from thirty feet away. Ripley concludes that there is no hair on Powder's body because he is electrolysis, the process used to remove unwanted hair from a body.

Before they can talk to him, Powder escapes from the hospital and begins to walk down a road. After a dog begins to bark at him and he responds by petting it, a girl who was in his science class comes to the fence where he is standing and talks to him. He tells her, "My grandfather used to say that I had an electric personality." She says that he put on "quite a light show." There is a human bonding that is taking place between them. She looks into his eyes to determine the color, but he tells her that he has contacts, which he removes, so that she can see that he has no color in his eyes. Meanwhile, the camera focuses on people in the neighborhood standing in the windows of their homes and staring at Powder.

He asks the girl, "Have you ever listened to people from the inside? You can hear their thoughts and all their memories, places that they don't even know they think from." She learns that Powder can do that. Then, after he asks about the way to the interstate highway, she gives him directions. As he leaves her, she tells him to stay away from electrical outlets.

Powder crosses a railroad trellis where the sheriff and his deputy are waiting for him. Harley, the deputy, tells him that he is being made mad to which Powder tells him that he is afraid of him. Waving the deputy aside, the sheriff tells Powder that he will take him back to the boys' home. While they get into the sheriff's patrol car, he asks Powder about not liking hospitals. Powder tells him that the worse day he can remember was in a hospital. The sheriff asks, "What day was that?" Powder answers, "The day I was born." The viewer now knows that Powder, the baby waving his hand from the incubator at the beginning of the film, was conscious of his father abandoning him. More pieces of the puzzle are coming together.

Back at the Center, Caldwell asks Powder if he had ever been tested to determine his IQ. He tells her that he hasn't, but that he has always been a fast learner. A representative from the state board of education and a group of other professionals, including Donald Ripley, the science teacher, are gathered around a table in a conference room into which Powder is brought and questioned about how he knows so much, especially in light of the fact that he has never listened to the radio or watched TV.

Ripley figures out why he hasn't watched TV and gives a demonstration to the group by turning on the TV set in the room. On it there is no picture. Powder's electromagnetic field interferes with the reception. Then, Ripley tells Powder that he is a genius, that his IQ score is off the charts and so high that there is no classification. Dr. Aaron Stepler from the state board of education tells Powder that he has the most advanced intellect of human kind and asks him if he understands. Powder responds that if Stepler thought he was so advanced, why would he ask Powder if he understood.

Caldwell tells Powder that the people gathered around the table can help him. He says that he just wants to go home. She informs him that the farm is in probate, and he quotes the textbook definition of probate to her from memory. She clarifies what she meant by telling him that the bank owns his grandparents' farm.

Powder reads Stepler's mind, telling him that he thinks that Powder has cheated. The lights in the room blink and go out. The hands on Ripley's wristwatch count off hours in seconds. Powder leaves the room, saying that he is not like other people. As he walks down the hall lined with lockers, the combination locks are drawn outward toward him.

The next scene begins with the boys from the Center along with the sheriff and his deputy on a bus heading to the wilderness for a camping trip. As all are gathered around the camp fire, Powder sits on a log all alone in the darkness. The sheriff sees him and goes to speak to him, telling him that Caldwell told the sheriff that Powder didn't want to go on the camping trip. Powder responds that he doesn't want to be anywhere that's not home. As thunder rumbles in the distance, Powder says, "When thunderstorms come, I can feel it inside. When lightning comes down, I can feel it wanting to come to me. Grandma said it was God. She said the white fire was God." Then, turning to the sheriff, Powder asks him if he believes in God.

Then Powder says that it was God who took his mother. A flashback scene of a pregnant woman getting struck by lightning is remembered by Powder. The viewer now understands the beginning of the film. The pregnant woman on the gurney was Powder's mother, who had been hit by lightning, which made him an electromagnetically charged albino full of extraordinary human powers. The sheriff asks him if his grandfather told him that God took his mother. Powder says, "I remember it."

The next scene shows Powder walking through the woods alone. He is quietly exploring and enjoying the beauty of the wilderness. He observes a salamander in the dried leaves on the ground, puts his hands over the leaves, and watches as many salamanders come to him. The salamanders stop as Powder recognizes two boys from the Center in the woods behind him. John and Mitch emerge from the trees. John has a rifle with a scope on it which he points at Powder while Mitch urges John to stop. John Box, whom the viewer concludes is a tough guy, lowers the rifle as all hear a gun shot in the woods and head to where the sound came from.

Harley Duncan has killed a doe, which he tells the boys around him is a "clean kill," even though the deer is still twitching on the ground. Harley, knowing that he should not have been hunting with the boys and fears that Powder will squeal on him, tells Powder that he didn't see anything. Powder is clearly moved with compassion for the doe which is still twitching from the rifle shot in her neck. He touches the doe over the wound with one hand and grabs Harley's arm with his other hand, forming a conduit for the emotion of fear from the deer to the deputy. All the boys gather around and watch as Harley feels the death of the doe and falls back in amazement. John, brandishing the rifle and pointing it at Powder, tells him to let the deputy go. Another boy knocks down the barrel of the gun as it goes off and the deputy pulls away from Powder. No one is hurt, but the boys are quiet as all observe Powder staying with the deer as she dies. He breaks down in tears.

Back in Caldwell's office, she and the sheriff question Powder about what he did to the deputy. Powder says, "I opened him up and I let him see." He explains that Harley couldn't see what he was doing, so Powder helped him. The sheriff leaves, but Caldwell remains with Powder, who says that he wants to go home. He states, "I saw that I don't like what you do--any of you." As he talks a baseball falls off Caldwell's desk and onto the floor. "You pretend to be my friend, the way you pretend everything." A glass over a picture hanging on the wall shatters and blows outward. "A friend doesn't take you away from your own home and say it's for your own good." The face on the clock on the wall shatters and blows outward and the flourescent light on the ceiling goes out. "How long do you really think I'll let you keep me here?" The glass in the Caldwell's office door explodes into the room as Powder's anger reaches a crescendo. Caldwell stands in astonishment as he opens her windowless office door and leaves.

In the sheriff's home, a doctor explains to him that there is no reason why his wife is still alive, but he wants to take her back to the county hospital. The sheriff says that she keeps holding on and he doesn't know why. The viewer concludes that there is some unfinished business here between the comatose woman, Doug, and their son, Stephen.

In a classroom in the Center, Powder is sitting at a table alone again when Ripley comes to see him. He explains that he has been filled with ideas ever since he touched Powder in the classroom. He asks him about reading Einstein, who believed in life after death because energy relays and transforms but never stops. He says, "If we ever got to the point where we could use all our brain, we'd be pure energy and we wouldn't even need bodies." Then, he says, "You are closer to that energy level as any one body has ever been." Powder says, "So what?"

Ripley launches into the reality of misery and tragedy of being human. He says that humans are stumbling around in a very dark age, trying not to kill each other. He tells Powder that he is different, that he has a mind that people want to evolve to in thousands of years. He says, "You are a man of the future." He tells Powder that he wants to be his friend. Even after Powder tells him that he doesn't need a friend, Ripley extends his hand to Powder, who takes it and makes the hair on Ripley's head stand up straight.

Powder tells Ripley about his grandparents who were afraid to touch him. Ripley touches his face with his hand and then touches Powder's head. Powder lowers his face onto his crossed arms on the table and cries. Ripley has made human contact with a child of lightning. Powder, who knows everything, is gradually becoming more and more of a human being.

The next scene is set at Harley Duncan's home. The sheriff arrives and notices that both of Harley's gun racks are empty. When he asks Harley about that, Harley tells him that he no longer uses them, he no longer participates in shooting competition, and that he has gotten rid of them.

While they walk outside, Harley tells the sheriff what happened in the woods with the doe, recounting step by step what the viewer had seen. Then, Harley says that he could feel the doe dying and that he can't look down the barrel of a gun and kill anymore. He tells the sheriff that Jeremy Reed took what was in the doe and put it into him. The viewer recognizes that Powder has converted the deputy from an animal hunter to an animal-rights activist.

After he leaves Harley, the sheriff visits Powder in his room in the Center and invites him to go home with him. Powder accepts the invitation. As they pull up in the driveway, the sheriff tells Powder that he is not sure if he can help. In the room where Doug's wife lays in the coma, the nurse protests his presence in the house, but the sheriff closes the door on the three of them. Powder touches her head and she frowns. Then, he begins telling her husband what she is saying as he takes her hand in his. Powder says,

> She knows you're here. She can't go until she knows you're going to get through this--both of you--you and Stephen. She wants you to remember the snow when Stephen was younger and all of you were playing and she lost her wedding ring. You looked and looked for it. She cried that both of you loved her so much. She wants you to open the silver box on the table.

The sheriff opens the box and there's her wedding ring. He cries. Powder tells him that Stephen found it at the old house in a garden he was tilling. The viewer realizes that was the gift he had brought to his mother earlier in the film. Powder continues, "She believes in miracles now and you should, too. She thinks I'm an angel come back to take her home and to bring you and Stephen together again, to remind you that you are still in each other's hearts."

Powder continues telling Doug what his wife is saying about their son, Stephen: "He loves you more than any man in the whole world. She won't go until you know that you still have a son. She'd like to feel the ring on her finger." Doug puts the ring on her finger as Powder touches Doug's hand, which is touching his wife's hand. She cries, opens her eyes for a moment, and the sheriff says, "Good-bye."

Meanwhile, Stephen arrives in the driveway and greets Doug, who meets him halfway between the driveway and the house. They embrace and cry. Powder watches their reconciliation from the porch off the upstairs room where Doug's wife and Stephen's mother has died. The viewer realizes that Powder has just healed a family.

The scene changes to a carnival which is attended by Powder, who is stared at by others as he walks through the booths. He makes his way to a picnic table where the girl from his science class--the one he had stopped to talk with when he had decided to run away--is waiting for him. He tells her that some people are wondering if he killed the sheriff's wife.

She asks him, "What are people like on the inside?" He says, "On the inside of most people there's a feeling of being separated from everything. And they're not. They're part of absolutely everyone and everything." After she remarks about being a part of a tree and fishermen in Italy and a man on death row and how come no one recognizes it, Powder touches her forehead and says, "That's because you have this spot you can't see past." He explains that people think they are disconnected from everything. She asks, "So that's what they'd see if they could--that they're connected?" He says, "And how beautiful they really are, and there's no need to hide or lie, and that it's possible without any lies, with no sarcasm, no deception, no exaggeration, or any of the things people use to confuse the truth." She says that she doesn't know a single person who can do that.

Powder asks her to hold out her hand and to put up her fingers. He touches her hand with his and she feels his heartbeat and her own. Then, they begin narrating each other's feelings to the other, delving deeper into each other's self until what she says triggers a hurt in him and he withdraws his hand from hers. She tells him that he has the most beautiful face she has ever seen and kisses him. Just as Powder is again experiencing what it is like to be human, her father sees what is going on, runs over the table, and interrupts them. Just as he grabs Powder, telling him never to touch his daughter again, Caldwell sees what is going on, runs over, and defends Powder. For the first time in the film she calls him "Powder," as up to this point she has always called him "Jeremy."

Back at the Center, he packs his suitcase and prepares to leave. The viewer concludes that he is going back to his grandparents' farmhouse. But as he goes around the outside of the gym, he hears the sounds of a basketball bouncing on the floor and the squeak of sneakers on the hardwood floor. Putting down his suitcase, he walks into the hall separating the gym from the locker room, where, watching one boy take off his shirt, he admires the boy's tanned skin. The viewer concludes that Powder is yearning to be like everyone else.

John Box, the leader of the group in the cafeteria, the boy with the rifle in the wilderness, and the tough man he thinks he is, walks over to Powder and taunts him for being a faggot and no man while grabbing Powder's hat. Reading John's mind, Powder tells him about his father who had beaten him badly and abused him as a child. That only infuriates John, who, while a thunder clap is heard in the distance, grabs Powder and takes him outside. The other four boys who had been playing basketball help him.

Outside, John tears off Powder's coat and shirt to reveal a very white chest. Then, he pulls down his pants as all the boys stare at his lack of pubic hair and the whiteness of his buttocks and legs. Telling him that he needs color, John pushes Powder into a mud puddle and then instructs the others to lift him out of it. More thunder is heard and lightning is seen. Any metal anyone is wearing is drawn toward Powder's magnetic field: A jean's snap pulls its wearer towards him, an earring pulls its wearer towards him, and a necklace with a cross on it pulls its wearer towards him. There is a flash of lightning, which strikes in the center of the group of boys, and all are thrown backward and scattered over the lawn. Rain begins to fall. All the boys get up including Powder, who gets dressed, and goes to John, who is still lying on the now soggy and muddy ground.

One boy listens to John's heart, but there is no beat. Powder puts his hands on John's bare chest and shocks him with electrical volts several times until his heart begins beating again. John coughs and comes back to consciousness. As he looks at Powder, he knows that he has saved his life. One of the boys tells Powder that he knows how to get him away from the Center.

Powder is next seen riding in a hay truck. He arrives at his grandparents' home. When the front door won't open because it is locked, he opens it with his mind, walks in, and goes to his cellar room. Caldwell arrives and finds him sitting on a chair in the empty room. All his books are gone.

She tells him,

> From the first moment I saw you down here in the dark, I had this feeling that you would change everything I knew. This is not the right place for someone as beautiful as you. But if you come with me, I promise you I'll find a place that is.

Just as they are embracing, Ripley arrives and finds them. Then, the sheriff and his deputy arrive. Caldwell tells the sheriff to turn his head and to let them leave.

Thunder is heard. Powder looks at the sky. He begins to walk toward an open field, but stops, turns around, and tells the sheriff that his wife didn't go some place; she is everywhere. Ripley, quoting Ein-stein, says, "Our technology has surpassed our humanity. I look at you and I think that some day our humanity might surpass our technology."

Caldwell and Powder exchange smiles, as he turns and runs into the open field. Again, Caldwell calls him "Powder," and she, the teacher, the sheriff, and the deputy run after him. Powder runs with his hands extended and open as if he were running toward someone. Thunder is heard and a bolt of lightning strikes his chest. He keeps running, now connected by a wave of light to the cloud in the sky. One final burst of light and he's gone. The four, who have run after him, fall to the ground dazed and amazed, much like those who witnessed the transfiguration in the synoptic gospels. Each has a smile on his or her face. The viewer knows that they know that Powder has gone home.

"Powder" updates ancient mythology by using Einstein's theory of energy and natural lightning. God lives in the sky but communicates and incarnates through flashes of lightning. Powder is a type of god. His incarnation through lightning striking his mother can be compared to the Word from above becoming flesh in John's Gospel. Furthermore, using a Johannine image, Powder, like Jesus, becomes a light in the world or bread from heaven.

But Powder needs to experience what it means to be human. He is a god, renounced by his father and abandoned by his mother through death, needing humanization, which is accomplished through Jessie Caldwell, Donald Ripley, and the one female classmate who loves him.

Like Jesus, the eternal Word of God who becomes flesh in space and time, Powder emerges from hiding in the cellar of the home of his grandparents to begin his mission. Like Jesus, we know nothing of his earlier years, except that he was born. He works astounding signs with a spoon and electricity. He is able to read people's minds, and he raises the dead to life. Wherever he goes, he is rejected by his own humankind who consider him so different that they refuse to associate with him and prefer to stare at him from a distance.

Powder's omniscience can be traced to the day of his birth. He remembers the time his mother was struck by lightning. He remembers being born. He remembers his father's declaration that he was not his son. And yet Powder is in sync with the rhythm of life. The salamanders come to him freely. The doe, shot by the deputy, trusts him, as he feels her fear. He does not belong to the world of people; he has no place here, and he wants to go home.

Like Jesus in the beginning of John's Gospel, Powder cleanses the temple of Jessie Caldwell's office of her lack of authenticity. As she speaks about real friendship, he makes her aware of the lack of unity between the words she speaks and the deeds she does. By his shattering glass on a picture, the clock, and her office door, she is shattered, converted, and healed. She becomes his friend in word and in deed.

The albino god heals others, like Jesus did. He connects them to the source of life. The deputy and the doe are connected. He and his female classmate are connected as is he and the science teacher. He connects the sheriff and his wife in a coma. And he reconnects John Box to life. Powder is like the Johannine Jesus, who declares himself to be the vine, the source of life, and everyone else to be branches, who receive life from him.

Powder, like the Johannine Jesus, is stripped naked of all his clothes and crucified by John Box. But his crucifixion is also his baptism, as he is pushed into a puddle of water in which he dies and is reborn. Like the water pouring out of Jesus' side on the cross, muddy water streams down the chest, back, and legs of Powder's white body.

And, finally, once his mission on earth is complete, he is glorified in a brilliant flash of light and returns home to the sky from where he came. Now, he is all over, everywhere. He has triumphed. While's he's no longer physically present in a white body, he lives in the hearts of the men and women whose lives he touched. There is no need for an empty tomb. He's been raised in light, and he's in touch with the electricity of the divine.

The boys in the Center can be likened to the crowd in John's Gospel. They do not like Powder, and they fail to believe in him even after they see the wonders he does. One boy, John Box, is like Judas.

He betrays Powder and crucifies him.

The sheriff, Doug Barnum, is like the unique character of Nicodemus in John's Gospel. Nicodemus, who makes three appearances in the Johannine narrative, first comes to Jesus at night, then advises the council to be fair in its dealings with him, and, finally, helps to bury Jesus after his death. Barnum comes to accept Powder only gradually. Then, like the royal official whose son lay ill in Capernaum, he invites him to his home to awaken his wife from the coma she has been trapped in for years.

Barnum is also like Peter, the leader of the early Christian movement. Barnum needs to be reconciled with his son, Stephen, like Peter needed to be rehabilitated by three-times proclaiming that he loved Jesus in order to undo his three-fold denial.

Harley Duncan, the deputy, can be compared to the man born blind. He is out of touch with the rhythm of life and bent on killing. His eyes are opened and his sight restored once Powder enables him to feel the fear and the death of the doe he shot. Duncan is also like the woman of Samaria, who meets Jesus at the well, insofar as he goes and tells others about what Powder has done to him. He is changed, because he has felt death and life.

Jessie Caldwell, the social worker who runs the Center for boys, is like the unnamed disciple Jesus loved in John's Gospel. Powder loves her even when she is not authentic. Once she is cleansed of her inauthenticity, she, like the unnamed disciple at the foot of the cross, is found to be loyal to Powder to the end.

John Box, who appears at first as Judas because he persecutes and betrays Jesus, is also like Lazarus. Once Box is hit by a lightning strike, Powder does not leave him dead on the ground d. He fills him with the energy of life. And Box regains consciousness.

Donald Ripley, the science teacher, represents the best in humankind, what people can be. He is a type of Johannine John the Baptist, decreasing so that Powder can increase. He both understands and testifies for Powder, like John the Baptist did for Jesus. He sees the potential of what humankind can become in Powder.

The female classmate Powder meets twice is like one of those faithful women disciples who believes in Jesus. She is attracted to Powder's beauty and discovers that he awakens in her a beauty she had not ever experienced. If Powder can be said to bond with any human being, this female classmate is she. She humanizes him more than anyone else, because he feels more what being human is like through her than through anyone else.

The film ends where it began--with a flash of lightning. While the opening scene is of a pregnant woman on a gurney, a flashback later in the film tells the viewer that she had been struck by lightning. At the end of the film, Powder is struck by lightning that takes him home. The Johannine Jesus, the Word of God become flesh, is raised from the dead and returns to the God from whom he came. Both Powder and Jesus have set loose an energy or Spirit which cannot be contained.

Exercises and Questions for Discussion

1. Outline the plot of "Powder" by scene. For each scene indicate its importance to the whole story and what purpose it serves. What scenes serve as the pivot point for the film?

2. After reading the Gospel According to John in one sitting, outline its plot by scene. For each scene indicate its importance to the whole story and what purpose it serves. What scenes serve as the pivot point for the gospel?

3. Make a list of five characters in "Powder" who help you understand five characters in John's Gospel. For each indicate what insight into his or her character you have gained.

4. Make a list of five scenes in "Powder" which help you understand five scenes in John's Gospel. For each indicate what insight into the scene you have gained.

5. Identify three signs used in "Powder" and indicate to what each sign points. For each sign find a comparable sign in John's Gospel and indicate to what each sign points.

6. What do you think is the major truth which the movie attempts to communicate? Is this truth one that endures? Explain.

7. What do you think is the major truth which John's Gospel attempts to communicate? Is this truth one that endures? Explain.

8. What do you think is Powder's major problem that must be solved before the movie can end? Who helps to solve it? How is it solved? Explain.

9. In John's Gospel what do you think is Jesus' major problem that must be solved before the gospel can end? Who helps to solve it? How is it solved? Explain.

Teaching John's Gospel

The Shawshank Redemption

John's Gospel, written near the end of the first century common era, is unlike the synoptic gospels (Mark, Matthew, Luke) in that it does not tell a similar story about Jesus of Nazareth. In fact, the final author of the gospel shows an interest in theological themes which are voiced by Jesus, the eternal Word of God become flesh. Every lengthy story in John's Gospel features Jesus delivering a monologue and explaining how followers at the end of the first century understood not only Jesus and what he taught, but how they had adapted his teaching for a changing world. Jesus became incarnate, taught people a new way of life, and called them to believe that he was the Son of God. After suffering and dying on the cross, he was raised to new life by the Father, whose work he had accomplished. In order to help students understand some of the theological themes, especially that of being born again of water and Spirit, in John's Gospel, "The Shawshank Redemption" (Castle Rock Entertainment, 1994) may be shown.

"The Shawshank Redemption" is a story about a man falsely accused of killing his wife and her golf-pro lover. He is tried in court and found guilty and sent to Shawshank Prison, located in the state of Maine, to serve two life sentences. There, after a struggle to be accepted, he becomes a leader of inmates. After serving nineteen years of his sentence, he escapes from the prison in an elaborate and well-planned scenario, but only after he has transformed the inside of the prison walls by awakening in hardened criminals a humanity most of the world thought they had lost. Furthermore, he imparts to his special friend a hope, a dream of freedom, which materializes on a beach in Mexico.

Andy Dufresne (Tim Robbins) enters Shawshank Prison in 1947 with another group of prisoners on a bus, which pulls into the prison yard and is greeted by inmates lining both sides of the chain-linked fence. As they examine the new inmates, those who have made Shawshank their home place bets on who will and who will not survive the rigors of prison life. The narrator of the film, Ellis Boyd "Red" Redding (Morgan Freeman), says that he didn't think much of Andy when he first saw him.

After a brief orientation by Warden Norton (Bob Gunton), Dufresne is initiated into prison life. He is stripped naked, like a new-born child, and sprayed with water from a fire hose, after which a white powder is thrown onto his wet skin to delouse him. Then, he is given new prison clothes, shoes, and a Bible and is marched naked to his cell. Thus begins his new life as a prisoner in Shawshank.

Dufresne is born again in 1966 when he escapes from Shawshank. After digging a tunnel through a wall in his cell and covering the hole with posters of Rita Heyworth, Marilyn Monroe, and Raquel Welch, successively, to mark the passing of nineteen years, with a rope he ties to his leg a plastic bag containing the warden's clothes and shoes he has stolen, a ledger book, and chess pieces he has carved, and crawls through the dirt birth canal to the water-works area of the prison. There, as thunder strikes and lightning flashes, with a rock he beats on the large sewer pipe until it splits open and, like a woman's water breaking, gushes up its contents.

Red narrates the escape, saying that Andy crawled to freedom through 500 yards of a sewer pipe. The sewer pipe is a birth canal through which Dufresne wiggles his way to new life while being covered with the grime of birth. Once Dufresne emerges from the pipe, he falls into a river and, of course, it is raining. He runs a short distance, strips off his shirt, looks up to the sky, stretches out his arms in a cruciform manner, and laughs. Red says that all the search party found was Dufresne's old prison clothes, a bar of soap, and a worn-out rock hammer. He adds that he remembers thinking that it would take a man 600 years to dig out of Shawshank, but Dufresne did it in less than twenty.

The author of John's Gospel portrays a man named Nicodemus coming to Jesus during the night and entering into dialogue with Jesus concerning how a man can be born again. At first Nicodemus thinks that Jesus is referring to crawling back into his mother's womb and repeating the birth process. But Jesus is referring to being born from above, from the Spirit. Those who believe in Jesus are born of water and Spirit and begin to share eternal life now. Like Dufresne, initiated into prison life with water and initiated into freedom with water, the person who believes in Jesus is baptized into the new life of the freedom of the Spirit according to the Johannine Jesus.

Later in John's Gospel, the author portrays Jesus as returning to the born-again theme by referring to a woman experiencing labor immediately before the birth of her child. The woman feels pain, states the Johannine Jesus, which she no longer remembers once her child is born. The joy of having brought a new human person into the world overshadows the previous labor pains. Likewise, the suffering Dufresne endured in Shawshank, especially the weeks and months he spent in solitary confinement in the hole, are forgotten as he joyously escapes to Mexico and finds a new life there near the Pacific Ocean.

Another Johannine theme that can be found in "The Shawshank Redemption" is that of incarnation. The author of John's Gospel understands Jesus to be the eternal Word of God who became incarnate, that is, took on human flesh. During his nineteen years in prison, Dufresne becomes the incarnation of hope for his friend, Red, who described him as being a quiet man, but one who had a walk and a talk that wasn't normal around Shawshank. Red says that Dufresne strolled like a man in a park who had no cares or worries. Red sums up his impression of Andy by saying that he had an invisible coat that shielded him from Shawshank. In other words, Dufresne was not like the rest of the inmates.

Dufresne also offers hope to Brian Hadley (Clancy Brown), captain of the prison guard who beat an inmate to death with his night stick, by explaining how he could avoid paying taxes on money left to him by his deceased brother. Dufresne offers hope to the other inmates after he becomes the librarian by expanding the prison library and instituting a program for prisoners to study and earn a high school diploma. Dufresne offers hope to the guards by preparing their tax returns for them. Dufresne offers hope to Tommy Williams, who is serving two years for stealing, by teaching him the alphabet, how to read, and enabling him to get his high school diploma.

But it is for Red that Dufresne is the most incarnation of hope. After spending time in the hole for playing a recording of a section from "The Marriage of Figaro" over the public announcement system from the warden's office, Dufresne rejoins his friends in the prison cafeteria. He tells them that while he was in the hole, the music was in his head and in his heart and that can't be taken away from anyone. Then, Dufresne tells them that each one has something inside that the guards can't touch: Hope. Red responds, "Hope is a dangerous thing. Hope can drive a man insane."

After Dufresne spends two months in the hole for telling the warden that he was "obtuse" and unwilling to deal with Andy's discovery that Tommy Williams knew who had killed Dufresne's wife and lover, Red finds him in the exercise yard. Dufresne talks to Red about going to a place in Mexico on the Pacific Ocean that "has no memory," where he wants to open a hotel and buy a worthless old boat and fix it up and use it to take his guests fishing. Red says that he doesn't think that he could make it on the outside since he has been in Shawshank most of his life. He says that he is an institutional man now. Dufresne tells him that he underestimates himself. Dufresne says, "It comes down to a simple choice: Get busy living or get busy dying." Before they separate, Dufresne gives Red directions to a rock fence enclosing a hay field, an oak tree, and a black rock with something buried under it in Buxton, a small town in Maine, and makes him promise to go there if he ever gets paroled.

After he escapes from Shawshank and makes his way toward Mexico, Dufresne continues to be hope for Red, who narrates how he got a blank postcard in the mail with a postmark of Fort Hancock, Texas, which is on the Texas-Mexico border. After looking at an atlas to see exactly where the city was located, Red remembers how Dufresne crawled through a dirty sewer pipe to come out clean on the other side.

A breakthrough for Red begins to take shape. The incarnate hope that Dufresne was for him slowly begins to appear in Red's own flesh. He narrates how he has to remind himself that some birds aren't meant to be caged. He says that when they fly away, one knows it was a sin to lock them up. But the place one lives in is more drab and empty. Red says that he misses his friend, Dufresne.

After his third parole hearing in the film, Red gets paroled. The opportunity for him to become an incarnation of hope is now offered. He is contrasted to another character in the film, Brooks Hadlin (James Whitmore), who, after he was paroled, could not deal with the world outside Shawshank Prison and committed suicide. Red leaves the prison by walking through the same gate as Hadlin did, dressed in the same color of suit, and wearing the same type of hat. Like Hadlin, he rides the bus to town, lives in the same room in the half-way house, and has the same job bagging groceries.

Also like Hadlin, Red doubts his ability to become hope. He's not sure that he can make it outside of Shawshank. He thinks of ways to break his parole so he could get sent back. He declares that it is terrible to live in fear and remembers that Brooks Hadlin knew fear well. He desires to be where things make sense, where he doesn't have to be afraid. Red says, "Only one thing stops me: a promise I made to Andy."

The promise Red made to Andy was to go to the town of Buxton and locate the hay field with the rock fence and oak nearby. Red fulfills his promise. Under the oak tree there is a black rock, and under that there is a tin box with an envelope in a plastic bag. The envelope contains both money and a letter:

> Dear Red, If you're reading this, you've gotten out. And if you've come this far, you're willing to come a little further. You remember the name of the town, don't you? I could use a good man to get my project on wheels. I'll keep an eye out for you and the chessboard ready. Remember, Red, hope is a good thing, maybe the best of things. And no good thing ever dies. I'll be hoping that this letter finds you and finds you well. Your friend, Andy.

Red, moved visibly by the letter, quickly returns to the town where he works. In his room in the half-way house, he repeats Dufresne's word to himself about getting busy living or getting busy dying. Before he leaves the room, near the words carved by one of its previous occupants--"Brooks [Hadlin] was here"--Red carves "so was Red." Unlike Hadlin, he will not commit suicide, but proceeds to buy a bus ticket to Fort Hancock, Texas, get on a bus, and break his parole. As he makes his way to Mexico, now a man of enfleshed hope, Red says that he is excited and that it is the excitement only a free man can feel at the start of a long journey whose conclusion is uncertain. He says, "I hope I can make it across the border. I hope to see my friend and shake his hand. I hope the Pacific is as blue as it has been in my dreams. I hope."

As Red walks along the beach, he spies Dufresne, who is sanding the hull of an old boat. They smile at each other. Hope has met hope in the flesh of two free men, one who was innocent, Andy, and one who was guilty and repented of his crime, Red.

The setting for the film can help students understand the dualism of John's dark-light theme. Johannine dualism is not limited to the dark-light theme, but understanding it may be the vehicle for students to grasp some of the other dualisms, such as matter and spirit, body and soul, death and life, hate and love, evil and good, etc. Shawshank is a maximum security prison, a place of darkness. It's buildings are constructed of gray stone walls surrounded by high gray fences and gray guard towers. Inside, only more gray walls and gray cells and bars await. Prisoners are initiated into prison life in a darkened room. They are given gray shirts and pants to wear. The cafeteria where they eat is painted gray. The library walls are gray. The laundry room, where Dufresne works, is not only painted gray, but the equipment is covered with dull-gray aluminum.

Outside the prison there is light. While most of the movie is set within Shawshank, the viewer sees the colors in the grocery store where Hadlin works, the colors in the park where he feeds the birds, the colors of the room in which he lives, and the colors of the cars passing on the street he is attempting to cross. The viewer also sees the colors of the rock wall, the oak, and the hay field once Red decides to fulfill his promise to Dufresne. What may be the most striking color of all is the blue of the Pacific Ocean, which is seen as Dufresne makes his way to Mexico and which is seen again as Red makes his way to Dufresne.

In terms of characterization, there is no doubt that Andy Dufresne is a type of Jesus of Nazareth character. He is falsely accused of killing his wife and her golf-pro lover and given two life sentences to be served back-to-back in prison. The standard phrase used by all Shawshank inmates when asked by each other why they are there is, "Everybody here is innocent." That's only true of Dufresne, who, as it is proven later in the film, is innocent indeed. Thus, like Jesus of Nazareth, who, according to John's Gospel is sent on a mission from heaven to the world, a place in which he doesn't belong, Dufresne is sent from the world outside to the world inside the prison, where he doesn't belong.

At first, Dufresne is not accepted by some of the cruel members of the prison community. In the gang shower room, he is propositioned by a homosexual named Bogs Diamond (Mark Ralston), a type of Satan, who has his own three or four followers. Later, in the laundry, where Dufresne works, he is attacked by Bogs and two of his disciples in a storage room. Bogs attempts to rape him, but can't. Red narrates that Andy kept getting attacked for two more years. In another scene, Dufresne is attacked by Bogs and three others in the projection room of the prison theater while the inmates are watching a Rita Heyworth film. He is beaten up within an inch of his life and spends one month in the infirmary while Bogs gets a week in the hole. Bogs is removed from the scene once Hadley beats him up with his night stick. Red narrates that the gay prisoners never touched Andy again, and that Bogs, who never walked again, was sent to a minimum security prison where he lived the rest of his life eating and drinking through a straw. In Johannine terms, Dufresne is the light imprisoned in darkness, but the light is breaking out.

Dufresne's first disciple is Red, a Peter-like follower who sees Andy's signs, in Johannine terms, and gradually believes in the hope that Dufresne offers. The viewer meets Red as he appears before the parole board after serving twenty years of a life sentence for murder. He declares that he is the only guilty man in Shawshank. After he states that he has been rehabilitated, learned his lesson, changed, and is no longer a danger to society, "Rejected" is stamped on his parole form.

Ten years later, after Red and Dufresne become friends, Red is summoned to another parole hearing. Now, he has served thirty years of his life sentence. As in the previous hearing, he states that he has been rehabilitated, changed, and is no longer a danger to society. "Rejected" is stamped on his parole form. In the exercise yard of Shawshank, Dufresne presents Red with "a parole-rejected present," a harmonica, an instrument Red said he had once played. At night lock-up, Andy finds a gift from Red--a poster of Marilyn Monroe--on his bed with a note, stating that it is a new girl for his ten-year anniversary. Once the lights are turned out in the prison, Red plays a few notes on the harmonica.

Red's third parole hearing comes after Dufresne's escape from Shawshank. Red has served almost forty years of his life sentence. However, this time the board is made up of new faces, but they ask the same questions. Red declares that he doesn't know what rehabilitation means, but he does feel regret for what he did. He says he was young and stupid and would like to talk to the young man he once was, but he can't. The kid he was is long gone and the old man he is now is all that's left. He challenges the parole board in a confrontational manner. While he walks out of the room, "Approved" is stamped on his parole papers.

Red, the narrator of the action in the film, characterizes himself as a man who can get whatever any inmate wants within reason in Shawshank. He says that he's like a Sears and Roebuck catalogue. Even though he didn't think much of Andy when he first saw him, Red, once he is approached by Dufresne, acquires a rock hammer for his friend who wants to carve chess pieces from rocks.

In 1949, when the roof of the license plate factory needed fixing, Red and Dufresne were two of the twelve men chosen to work on it--an opportunity to labor outside. Red watched Andy perform his first sign which consisted of advising Captain Brian Hadley concerning how to avoid paying inheritance taxes on $35,000 his dead brother left him. In exchange for preparing the paperwork for Hadley, Dufresne requests three beers for each of his "co-workers" on the roof.

Red narrates that on the second to last day of the taring-the-roof job, at ten in the morning, the prisoners sat on the roof drinking icy cold beer. As the camera scans the roof showing the men drinking beer, the viewer counts thirteen--not twelve--prisoners. True, a group of twelve are somewhat huddled together, but sitting alone near the edge of the roof is Dufresne, who refuses a beer when it is offered to him. Clearly, the scene is meant to echo Jesus' multiplication of the loaves and fishes to the astonishment of his twelve apostles, a story which appears in some form in every gospel.

In the next scene, Red and Andy are playing checkers, but Dufresne promises to teach Red how to play chess with the pieces that he is going to carve with his rock hammer as soon as he gets the right type of stones.

Andy's second sign, which takes place immediately after he is assigned as assistant librarian to Brooks, is helping one of the guards set up a trust fund for the education of his children. An unused section of the library is set up as an office, as Dufresne, a former banker, continues to help the guards by preparing their tax returns.

The third sign is Dufresne's proposal to expand the prison library. While the warden is opposed to Andy's writing letters to the state legislature of Maine seeking funds to buy books for the library, he does permit Dufresne to write one letter a week. At first there are no answers to Andy's letters. Then, one day Andy receives a $200 check for his library project and several boxes of books and records. He says that it only took six years.

Dufresne's fourth sign consists of taking one of the records, placing it on a player in the warden's office while he is gone, locking a guard in the warden's bathroom, and turning on the public address system so that all the inmates can hear the music. As all of them stand quietly at attention, listening to a part of the Italian opera "The Marriage of Figaro," and looking at the speaker blasting the music in the exercise yard, Red narrates that it was a religious experience. He says,

> I'd like to think they were singing about something so beautiful it can't be expressed in words and makes your heart ache because of it. I tell you those voices soared higher and farther than anybody in a gray place dares to dream. It was like some beautiful bird flapped into our drab blue cage and made these walls dissolve away. And for the briefest of moments every last man at Shawshank felt free.

Andy's fifth sign is connected to his third one. After increasing his writing to two letters a week to the state legislature requesting more funds for the prison library, he received a check for $500. Red says that Dufresne established the best prison library in New England in 1959. Dufresne used the library to help each prisoner get a high school diploma.

One prisoner in particular, Tommy Williams (Gil Bellows), becomes Andy's sixth sign for Red, or in Red's words, "Andy's new project." Sent to Shawshank for two years for stealing in 1965, Williams has been in and out of prison since he was thirteen years old. Now, in his mid-twenties, Dufresne tells him that he doesn't seem to be a very good thief and that he should try another profession. Dufresne helps him proceed toward that goal by teaching Williams the alphabet and, then, how to read.

By 1966, Williams is ready to take the exam for his high school diploma. After indicating that Williams had used up all the time allotted for the exam, Andy watches as Tommy, upset by what he thinks is his inability to pass the test, wads up the answer sheet and tosses it in the trash can. Dufresne retrieves it, smoothes it out, and sends it in. Later, during mail call, Williams gets a letter from the board of education and learns that he earned his high school diploma. Meanwhile, a guard tells Andy, who is doing time in the hole for speaking back to the warden, that Williams passed the test.

The seventh sign, paralleling the seven signs of Jesus in John's Gospel, performed by Dufresne is his escape from Shawshank, which, as indicated above, employs the Johannine theme of born again. Unknown to anyone in the prison and unknown to the viewer, for nineteen years Andy had been cutting a tunnel through the wall in his cell to the room where he could slip through a sewer pipe to freedom. Using the rock hammer, Dufresne had discovered that he could cut through the wall because pressure and time had caused its hardness to soften. After working at night, the next morning he would tote out to the exercise yard pockets full of the wall. There, he would deposit the debris and watch as it disappeared in the gravel covering the yard.

Red proves his discipleship by keeping his promise to Andy and going to Buxton, Maine, finding the tin box with money under an oak tree next to the rock fence enclosing a hay field, buying a bus ticket to Fort Hancock, Texas, crossing the border into Mexico, and finding Dufresne working on a boat on the beach of the Pacific Ocean. In Johannine terminology, Andy has not only shown Red the way, but he has become for him the way, the truth, and the life. The scene in the last chapter of John's Gospel portraying Jesus fixing breakfast for his disciples on the beach and rehabilitating Peter by asking him three times if he loved him comes to mind as Red walks toward Andy.

Many of the other inmates also become Andy's disciples, especially those numbered among the twelve who share three beers each once the roof on the license place factory is repaired. Some of these are associated with Dufresne as assistants during tax season. In one meal-eating scene in the cafeteria, several express concern and worry about Andy after his last two-month stint in the hole. In another meal-eating scene in the cafeteria after Andy has escaped, his friends are portrayed gathered around a table in an obvious eucharistic-type memorial. Red narrates, "Those of us who knew him best talk about him often." From the laughter of the inmates around the table, there is no doubt that they have been changed by Andy Dufresne. He has become their hero, the one man who escaped from Shawshank, a maximum security prison.

A unique disciple of Andy's is Tommy Williams, the young man Dufresne helps to get his high school diploma. At first, Williams is tough and hard to get to know, but, after observing Andy's way with the other inmates, he asks him to help him earn his high school diploma. In Johannine terminology, Williams is like the man born blind who has his sight restored by Jesus. Dufresne teaches him to read and helps him get his high school diploma.

Williams demonstrates his faith in Dufresne after he and Red have a discussion in the wood shop and he tells Red about a prison cellmate, Elmo Bladge, he had four years previous who told him about killing a golf pro and a banker's wife. Red recognizes this to be Andy's story and has Williams tell Dufresne, who makes a trip to the warden to tell him Williams' story and petition for a chance to get a new hearing. Norton refuses, but later summons Williams to the exercise yard at night. After offering Williams a cigarette and lightning it for him, Norton asks him if what he told Andy is true and if he would swear to it on a Bible. Williams says he just needs the chance. Norton crushes out his cigarette with his foot, an omen of things immediately coming, disappears into the darkness, and Williams is shot three times and killed. Williams has died for his faith in Dufresne, while Norton has protected his money-laundering operation.

Besides teaching Red and others the meaning of hope, Dufresne also teaches the meaning of sacrifice. He risks being thrown off the roof of the license plate factory by Hadley by daring to talk to him and, then, asks for three beers, a biblical sacred number indicating a theophany, for each of the crew. Until Bogs is removed from the prison, Dufresne is beaten on a regular basis, but he demonstrates that he will remain true to himself. He risks upsetting the warden by proposing the expansion of the prison library. He sacrifices two weeks of his life in the hole in order to give his fellow inmates a few minutes of music. Later, after calling the warden "obtuse," he gets one month in the hole, and, after the warden visits him to inform him of the death of Tommy Williams, he gets another month in solitary confinement. In the darkness of the hole, a type of tomb, he symbolically dies, only to emerge filled with more hope than ever. The more he sacrifices his own life and time, the better the prison environment becomes.

Once Dufresne escapes from Shawshank, his cell is compared to the Johannine empty tomb with only a few grave cloths remaining. Red says that all the guards found was a worn-out rock hammer, some old prison clothes, and a bar of soap. During the darkness before the escape, Red says that it was a long night with thunder claps and lightning flashes.

The next morning at cell check, Dufresne was not in his cell. After roll call, one of the guards discovers the cell to be empty. After the warden is informed of the empty cell, he investigates it himself, questioning the guard about Dufresne's absence. Norton says that if Dufresne were in his cell at lights out, it stands to reason that he'd still be there. In an ironic voice, Warden Norton continues, "Lord, it's a miracle. A man up and vanished ...." Red's faith in Andy is confirmed by one line in the letter Dufresne left Red in the tin box with the money under the oak tree about no good thing ever dying. Dufresne is a good man who has not died, but who has been born again to a new life in Mexico, where Red goes to see him and begins his new life.

Other characters in the film who might help students understand men in biblical stories include Brooks Hadlin, Warden Norton, and the judge who sentences Dufresne to life imprisonment.

Hadlin is a type of John the Baptist. After being librarian for over thirty-five years, Dufresne is sent as his assistant. Brooks has prepared the way for Andy to enlarge the prison library. Shortly after Andy's appointment as Brooks' apprentice, Brooks is paroled, but he is not able to live outside the routine of prison life and commits suicide. Like John the Baptist, beheaded by Herod and removed from the gospel so that he decreases and Jesus can increase, Brooks is removed from the film so that Andy's expansion of the library can take place.

The character of John the Baptist in the gospels is modeled after the character of the prophet Elijah in the Hebrew Bible (Old Testament). Elijah, zealous for authentic worship of the one God, demonstrates his God's power to consume a sacrifice with fire and, then, kills all of the 450 prophets of the god Baal, fleeing to Horeb, God's dwelling place. Before this incident, he had predicted a drought, but God had taken care of his prophet by sending ravens who brought bread and meat to him in both the morning and the evening. In "The Shawshank Redemption" Brooks cared for a raven, a type of crow, fallen from its nest.

Warden Norton represents a composite portrait of the Pharisees/Jews, who are portrayed as Jesus' opponents in the gospels. When he first introduced to prisoners in a darkened room, Norton tells them that his first rule is no blasphemy, namely, that he'll not have the Lord's name taken in vain in his prison. He also tells them that they will learn the other rules as they go along. Then, true to Pharisaic form, he continues, "I believe in two things: discipline and the Bible. Here you'll receive both."

Norton's hypocrisy comes through in a scene depicting a surprise cell inspection. When he and Hadley get to Dufresne's cell, Andy is reading the Bible he received when he was initiated into prison life. After

Hadley disrupts Dufresne's cell, turning the bed upside down and knocking everything off of a bookshelf--finding no contraband--Norton takes Andy's Bible and says that he is pleased to see him reading it. Then, he asks him if he has any favorite passages. Dufresne, demonstrating that he is better at Norton's game than Norton is, quotes Mark 13:35: "Watch ye therefore for ye know not when the master of the house commeth." After indicating that his favorite passage is John 8:12, Andy quotes it to him, saying, "I am the light of the world." What Norton fails to realize, along with the viewer at this point in the film, is that Dufresne is light in the world of Shawshank.

Another sign of Norton's darkness is revealed as he hands back the Bible to Andy saying, "Salvation lies within." The significance of that statement is revealed only after Dufresne escapes from prison after having replaced the ledger he kept for Norton in the safe with his Bible. Once Norton opens the safe and recognizes that the ledger is gone, he opens the Bible. A note on the inside front cover states: "Dear Warden, You were right. Salvation lay within. (signed) Andy Dufresne." After turning the page to the beginning of the Book of Exodus, the narrative of Moses leading the Israelites in their escape from Egyptian slavery, Norton discovers the outline of the rock hammer cut into the pages and realizes that Andy had hidden the hammer, the means of his escape from prison, in his Bible.

Norton's hypocrisy comes through again once Dufresne is summoned to his office to be assigned as Brooks' apprentice. Norton, reigning from behind a huge desk, observes as Andy looks at a sampler hanging on the wall. "His judgment cometh and that quite soon" is embroidered on the sampler. Norton tells Dufresne that his wife made it. The significance of the words on the sampler are revealed later in the film as the viewer discovers that it hides the wall safe in which Norton stores the books which contain his records of money-laundering. The last time that Andy places the Bible instead of the ledger in the safe, Norton closes it, humming "A Mighty Fortress is Our God." The next time he approaches it is after he sees the story of his money-laundering printed on the front page of the *Portland Daily Bugle*, a story sent to the editor of the paper by Dufresne. Then, while hearing the sirens of police cars, he glances at the sampler--"His judgment cometh and that right soon"--and both he and the viewer know that the police are coming to arrest him. After discovering the Bible in the safe, he sits at his desk, opens a drawer containing a handgun and bullets, loads the gun, and kills himself. Now, he reigns in death from behind his desk, a hypocrite who preached the Bible but practiced none of it. Red comments that he would like to think the last thing that went through Norton's head, other the that bullet, was to wonder how Dufresne ever got the best of him.

The viewer knows how that happened. Once Norton instigated what Red called his "inside-out program," putting inmates to work outside prison walls in community service projects, Norton began skimming money off of the top of what the prisoners were paid for the work they did. Also, other contractors, who couldn't compete on bids with Norton's labor force, bribed him to bid higher than they so that they would get the jobs. Dufresne, with his background in banking, was put in charge of keeping Norton's books and preparing direct-mail deposits, laundering his money.

In a scene involving only Red and Andy reshelving books in the library, Dufresne tells Red about the "river of dirty money" running through Shawshank and how he has funneled it into different banks under the name of Randall Stevens, a fictitious person who had a birth certificate, a driver's license, and a Social Security number. He was "a phantom" of Dufresne's imagination. Red tells him that he is good. Andy replies that outside Shawshank he was an honest man, and that he had to come to prison to become a crook.

After taking Norton's ledger and escaping from Shawshank, Dufresne, pretending to be Randall Stevens, goes to Main National Bank and withdraws the money Norton had been depositing there. Andy had the right identification, Social Security number, and his signature matched that on file at the bank. He tells the banker that he is going abroad and receives a cashier's check closing the account. Red continues the story explaining how a Mr. Stevens visited nearly a dozen banks in the Portland area and left town with better than $370,000 of Norton's money. Red says that it was severance pay for Dufresne's nineteen years in prison.

The darkness of Norton's hypocrisy comes through in the scene where he summons Williams and has him murdered, staged as an attempted escape, for telling the truth about Dufresne's innocence. After leaving Williams' dead body on the ground, Norton goes to the hole, where Andy is serving a one-month sentence for calling Norton "obtuse." Norton tells him that Williams was shot while trying to escape. Dufresne states that he is stopping everything and won't run Norton's scams anymore. Norton threatens to put him with the sodomites, to brick up the library, and to burn all the books. Then, he sentences Andy to another month in solitary confinement in the hole to reconsider his position. Before he leaves, he asks Andy if he is being "obtuse."

The judge who sentences Andy Dufresne to serve two life sentences for killing his wife and her lover can be compared to Pilate in

John's Gospel. Pilate, who should be in control of Jesus of Nazareth's trial, is out of control. In typical Johannine fashion, Jesus puts Pilate on trial, questioning him and challenging his power. The judge presiding over Dufresne's trial looks like he is in control once Andy is found guilty by the jury. The two life sentences back-to-back handed out by the judge for the State of Maine further emphasize the judge's control. But by the end of the film, the viewer sees that Andy has been in control throughout his nineteen-year stay in Shawshank. He has become the leader of the inmates, taught them, given them hope, sacrificed himself for them, and been born into a new life, a beach on the Pacific Ocean in Mexico, as close to paradise as one can possibly come in a film.

Exercises and Questions for Discussion

1. In what ways does the film illustrate the born-again theme found in John's Gospel?

2. How does the film's use of hope help you understand the Johannine concept of incarnation?

3. In what ways does the film help you understand Johannine dualism?

4. Compare and contrast seven signs in "The Shawshank Redemption" and seven signs in John's Gospel? What do you discover? To what does each sign in the film and in John's Gospel point?

5. What do you think is the major truth which the movie attempts to communicate? Is this truth one that endures? Explain.

6. How is the character of Andy Dufresne a type of Johannine Jesus character? Explain.

7. How is the character of Ellis Boyd Redding (Red) a type of Johannine Peter character? Explain.

8. In what ways are Tommy Williams and the Johannine man born blind alike?

9. In what ways is Andy Dufresne's empty cell like the empty tomb story in John's Gospel? In what ways is it like the empty tomb story in Mark's Gospel?

10. How is the Brooks Hadlin character a type of the Johannine John the Baptist character?

11. How is the Warden Norton character a collective type of Johannine Pharisees/Jews and leaders of the people character?

12. How is the character of the judge, who sentences Andy Dufresne to prison, like the Johannine Pilate character?

Teaching the Acts of the Apostles

The Mission

In scholarly circles, it is generally accepted that the author of the Acts of the Apostles is also the author of Luke's Gospel. Themes, such as the need to witness, the importance of prayer, the guidance of the community by the Holy Spirit, begun in Luke's Gospel are continued in the Acts of the Apostles.

The Acts features two major characters: Peter and Paul. The first half of the book centers on Peter and the establishment and growth of the church within Palestine. Then, once Paul is brought onto the scene and the story of his conversion is told, the Acts focuses on the expansion of the church to the Gentile world and Paul's journey to the ends of the earth (Rome) with the message of the gospel.

Some people think of the Acts of the Apostles as a church history since it narrates the various experiences and speeches of Jesus' first followers. However, it is not a history in terms of a record of past events. It represents the author's idea of how the ideal church should listen to the word of God and practice it. Whatever Jesus is portrayed as doing in Luke's Gospel, such as healing and raising the dead, the apostles, especially Peter and Paul, are portrayed as doing in the Acts of the Apostles. In this second tome of his two-volume work, Luke is interested in the mission of the early Christian community, especially as it was undertaken by its two heroes, Peter and Paul.

Students can gain a good understanding of the Acts of the Apostles by watching the film "The Mission" (Warner Bros., 1986), a story illustrating what happens to the Catholic missions in South America in the eighteenth century when those founded by Spain prohibit slavery and those founded by Portugal permit it and both Spain and Portugal each have Catholic monarchs on their thrones. The missioners are Jesuit priests who have come to convert the natives. The narrator is a former Jesuit, now a Cardinal (Ray McAnally), the pope's representative sent to investigate the problem brewing between Spain and Portugal over slavery and slave-trading and to make a recommendation to the pope as to the solution of the problem. The film is historical insofar as it deals with the real issue of South American slavery in the eighteenth century. The historical events are set in the borderlands of Argentina, Paraguay, and Brazil in 1750. However, the film is not history in the same manner that the Acts of the Apostles is not history and tells its story through the words and deeds of two Jesuits.

The narrator of the "The Mission" is the Cardinal who reads the letter he is sending to the pope about what he has found in his investigation of the missions in South America. He writes that the issue which brought him to South America has been settled, and that the Indians are now free to be enslaved by the Spanish and Portuguese. However, not being pleased with this beginning, he tears up the page upon which is secretary has written this part of the letter and begins again.

> Your Holiness, I write to you in this year of our Lord 1758 from the southern continent of the Americas, from the town of Ascensione in the province of LaPlatta, two-weeks march from the great mission of San Miguel. These missions have provided a refuge for the Indians against the worse depredations of the settlers and have earned much resentment because of it. The noble souls of these Indians incline towards music. Indeed, many a violin played in the academies of Rome itself has been made by their nimble and gifted hands. It was from these missions the Jesuit fathers carried the word of God to the high and undiscovered plateau to those Indians still existing in their natural state and received in return martyrdom.

A scene focuses on a waterfall cascading two-hundred feet over the edge of the plain. Floating on the water is a man nailed to a rough-hewn cross. The time is 1750. The river is flowing through a dense rain forest in South America. The Cardinal writes,

> The death of this priest was to form the first link in the chain of which I now find myself a part. As Your Holiness undoubtedly knows, little in this world unfolds as we predict. Indeed, how could the Indians have supposed that the death of that unsung priest would bring among them a man whose life was to become inextricably intertwined with their own.

As the Cardinal's words fade away, a local Jesuit leader, Father

Gabriel (Jeremy Irons), comes to the waterfall, climbs the rocks to the Altiplano, explores the forest, sits on a rock, and plays a small flute he carries with him. Gradually, the Gurani Indians emerge from the rain forest, accept Father Gabriel, and invite him to follow them. The natives love music, as the Cardinal states, "With an orchestra the Jesuits could have subdued the whole continent." Then, he continues, "So it was that the Indians of the Gurani were brought finally to account for the ever-lasting mercy of God and to the short-lived mercy of man."

The peacefulness of the rain forest gives way to Captain Rodrigo Mendoza (Robert De Niro), a slave-trader, who has a brother named Philippe. Mendoza is selling the natives he captured to Allanzo, a slave buyer for the Portuguese. Father Gabriel, who sees Mendoza hunting Indians in the forest, tells him that the Jesuits are building a mission and that they are going to make Christians out of the natives. The mission Father Gabriel is building is named San Carlos.

After Mendoza delivers a group of slaves to Ascensione, the camera focuses on the woman, Carlotta, Mendoza loves who does not love him as much as she loves his brother, Philippe. After a carnival scene of a parade, Rodrigo goes to his lady's home to find her in bed with Philippe. He turns around and walks away, but Philippe follows. They engage in a sword fight, and Rodrigo kills his brother, Philippe.

Six months pass. Back in mission Ascensione Rodrigo sits in a cell in the Jesuit headquarters doing penance for having killed his brother. Upon the urging by the Jesuit superior, Father Gabriel visits Mendoza. He acknowledges that Mendoza is a mercenary, a slave-trader, and that he killed his brother. Mendoza, who has been sitting in the corner of his cell, stands up, grabs Father Gabriel, and pushes him against the wall, asking him if he is laughing at him. Father Gabriel responds that he is laughing at what he sees is laughable: a man running away, a man hiding from the world, a coward. Father Gabriel continues by telling him that he still has a life and that there is a way out of his depression. Mendoza insists that there is no redemption for him. Father Gabriel tells him that he has the freedom to chose his penance, but Mendoza answers that here is no penance hard enough for him. Father Gabriel dares him to accept his challenge.

For his penance Mendoza chooses to carry his armor and his weapons, including the sword he used to kill his brother, through the rain forest and up the waterfall to the Altiplano. When he reaches the top, one of the natives Mendoza had tried to capture arrives and cuts the cords binding the bundle of metal to Rodrigo, who repents with tears and is converted from his former way of life as a slave-trader to a missioner.

Rodrigo helps to build the mission church above the falls. The Indians paint his chest as a sign that they accept him who once hunted them like animals. Rodrigo joins in a pig hunt, but discovers that he can't kill the wild boar to the disappointment of a little boy. The former slave-trader can be found playing with children on a boat or swimming in the river. He prepares a meal for the Jesuits. During the meal, he thanks Father Gabriel for permitting him to be there. Father Gabriel tells Mendoza that he should thank the Guarani. Mendoza asks him how he can do that. Handing him a copy of the Bible, Father Gabriel tells him to read it.

While reading the Bible, especially the words about love and about putting away childish things in the letter to the Ephesians, Mendoza decides to join the Jesuits. His petition is accepted, and Father Gabriel invests Mendoza with the Jesuit habit and welcomes him into the Jesuit community.

The Cardinal arrives in Ascensione. While his cortege is arriving and unpacking his belongings, he continues to write his letter to the pope, saying,

> This seeking to create a paradise on earth--how easily it offends. Your Holiness is offended because it made a strike from that paradise which is to Rome hereafter. Their majesties of Spain and Portugal are offended because the paradise of the poor is seldom pleasing to those who rule over them. And the settlers here are offended for the same reason. So it was this burden I carried to South America to satisfy the Portuguese wish to enlarge their empire, to satisfy the Spanish desire that this would do them no harm, to satisfy your Holiness that these monarchs of Spain and Portugal would threaten no more the power of the Church, and to ensure for you all that the Jesuits here could no longer deny you these satisfactions.

From dialogue, the viewer learns that the Cardinal was a Jesuit at one time. Then the cardinal says, "So I had arrived in South America, my head replete with the matters of Europe. But I soon began to understand for the first time what a strange world I had been sent to judge."

While presiding over a church tribunal, we learn more about their majesties of Portugal and Spain who want to expand their empires. As they do so, Portugal advocates slavery, while Spain does not. The Cardinal listens to the beautiful sound of the singing of the Indians, as he tries to sort out the mess of the territorial expansion of two Catholic monarchs, one who favors slavery and one who does not, and wonders whether or not the Jesuit missions are under the protection of the Church.

The Cardinal continues his letter to the pope, writing, "Your

Holiness, a surgeon to save the body must often hack off a limb. But in truth nothing had prepared me for the beauty and the power for the limb I had come here to sever."

Meanwhile, Mendoza, who embarrasses Don Kabessa, the Portuguese slave trader, during the tribunal, is ordered to apologize to the Cardinal, who is informed by Father Gabriel concerning Rodrigo's former way of life. But Father Gabriel also tells the Cardinal that he, the Cardinal, and Spain have slaves even though Spain officially does not advocate slavery. The Cardinal leans toward not offering protection for Indian slaves. He says that the issue is the existence of the Jesuits in the area. Before he makes up his mind, Father Gabriel convinces him to visit the missions and see the work that the Jesuits have been doing.

They visit San Miguel mission and observe the successful plantation and wood-working shop run by the natives. During a five-hour candlelight prayer service, during which the Cardinal tries to reach a decision, Father Gabriel invites the Cardinal to San Carlos mission above the falls. The Cardinal, now dressed as a Jesuit, does not climb the falls, like everyone else must do. Upon his flotilla's arrival, he experiences a grand welcome and hears the Indians singing Latin songs and watches a civilized wrestling match. He is visibly moved by what he sees.

He writes,

> Though I knew that everywhere in Europe states were tearing at the authority of the Church, and though I knew well that to preserve itself there the Church must show its authority over the Jesuits here, I still couldn't help wondering whether these Indians would not have preferred that the sea and wind had not brought any of us to them.

However, the Cardinal is not swayed by what he sees. During a meeting with the Jesuits and the Indians of San Carlos mission, the Cardinal, speaking for the Church, tells the Indians that they must leave the mission. Translating for the Indian chief, Father Gabriel tells the Cardinal that they don't want to leave the mission. It is their home. The Cardinal says that they must learn to submit to the will of God. Father Gabriel tells him that the chief says that it was the will of God that they came out of the jungle and built the mission. The chief wants to know if God has changed his mind. The Cardinal says that he cannot hope to understand God's reason. Father Gabriel tells the Cardinal that the chief wants to know how he knows God's will. The Cardinal answers that he does not personally speak for God, but for the Church, which is God's instrument on earth. The Cardinal adds that he has spoken to the king of Portugal, but he will not listen. Father Gabriel tells the Cardinal that the chief says that he is also a king, and he won't listen. The chief also says that he and his people were wrong to have trusted the Jesuits, but now they are going to fight.

The Cardinal tells the Jesuits that if the natives fight, it is absolutely imperative that no one of them should even seem to have encouraged them to do so. Then, he instructs the Jesuits to return with him to Ascensione. To anyone who disobeys he threatens excommunication.

Later in the evening, while the Cardinal and Father Gabriel are standing near the river, the Cardinal asks him why the natives can't return to the jungle and not fight. Father Gabriel tells him that the mission is their home. Then Father Gabriel asks the Cardinal if he knew his decision was going to be to let Portugal have control of the area. After the Cardinal says yes, Father Gabriel asks him why he came to the mission. The Cardinal says that he came to persuade Father Gabriel not to resist the transfer of the mission territories. He tells him that if the Jesuits resist the Portuguese, then he fears that the Jesuit order will be expelled from Portugal. If that happens, he tells Father Gabriel, then the Jesuits could be expelled from Spain, France, Italy, etc. He tells Father Gabriel that for the Jesuits to survive the missions must be sacrificed.

While walking back to the mission buildings, they pass some children who speak to them. The Cardinal asks Father Gabriel about what they were saying. Father Gabriel answers that they don't want to go back to the forest because the devil lives there. The Cardinal asks Father Gabriel about what he said. Father Gabriel responds that the he told them that he would stay with them.

The Indian boy, who had cut the heavy bag of mental from Mendoza's shoulders after he had climbed the falls, retrieves Mendoza's sword from the mud, cleans it, and gives it to him. He takes it, practices with it, and tells Father Gabriel that he is renouncing his vow of obedience. He intends to fight the Portuguese, who are preparing to take control of the land in the Altiplano. Mendoza says that the natives want to live. Father Gabriel tells him that if he dies with blood on his hands, that he betrays everything they have done. Father Gabriel reminds him that he promised his life to God, who is love.

The Cardinal returns to Ascensione. After a scene depicting the transfer of territory to Portugal, the Portuguese army goes to mission San Miguel and wreaks havoc, while mission San Carlos prepares for battle under the direction of Mendoza. Led by some of the Indians, Mendoza manages to steal some of the supplies from the Portuguese while they sleep below the falls. However, one man awakens to catch them in the act and Mendoza kills him.

The Portuguese begin the climb to the Altiplano. They invade the area by marching through the forest and paddling up the river. Meanwhile Father Gabriel and Mendoza meet. Mendoza asks Father Gabriel for his blessing, but Father Gabriel refuses. But Father Gabriel does embrace Rodrigo and gives him the crucifix of the Jesuit who had been crucified and sent down the falls nailed to a cross, shown cascading over the falls at the beginning of the film. Here, the viewer is given a preview of the fate awaiting Mendoza.

Under Mendoza's leadership, some of the Indians attack the Portuguese as they begin to enter the mission, while Father Gabriel leads other Indians in Benediction. The Catholic Portuguese recognize the service, but that does not stop them from setting fire to the mission and attacking the Indians. Father Gabriel continues to pray, leading a procession with the Eucharist in a monstrance and blessing the Indians with it. In the meantime, another Jesuit with several Indians lead some of the Portuguese in a pursuit down the river and over the falls, sacrificing themselves in their attempt to save the mission.

When Mendoza's powder-keg trap for the Portuguese doesn't work, he is killed while watching Father Gabriel continue to lead the procession with the Eucharist, get shot, and die. The mission is destroyed.

In Ascensione, the Cardinal, after hearing about what took place above the falls, asks Don Kabessa if the slaughter was necessary. Kabessa answers that he did what he had to do, given the legitimate purpose sanctioned by the Cardinal. Another Portuguese representative tells the Cardinal that he had no alternative. He says that he must work in the world, and the world is that way. But the Cardinal states that people make the world the way it is, and he, especially, has made this world in South America this way.

Meanwhile, above the falls in San Carlos mission, nine naked children, who have survived, quietly creep into a boat moored on the river and paddle away. The children offer hope that the deaths of the Indians and the Jesuits hasn't been in vain and that a new beginning might take place.

The film returns to the cardinal, who is completing his letter to the pope, reading, "So, your holiness, now your priests are dead and I am left alive, but in truth it is I who am dead and they who live. For as always, your holiness, the spirit of the dead will survive in the memory of the living."

There is no doubt that the film raises the question about the conversion of Rodrigo Mendoza. Was he really changed from a man of the sword to a man of love? At first it looks like that might be the case, but, when love was about to lose, he returns to the sword and falls by it. Of course, the viewer must also question Father Gabriel's submission to a Church advocating slavery. Did he really demonstrate the power of love by peacefully leading some of the Indians in a procession to their slaughter?

Otherwise, the film tells a story similar to that of the Acts of the Apostles. The crucified priest floating down the river and over the waterfall can serve to remind students of the power of Jesus' crucifixion which fuels the Acts of the Apostles. Like the priest, Jesus died on a cross in Luke's Gospel, the first volume of the author's two-volume work (volume two is the Acts). Also, like Jesus who came to show people a better way of life, the Jesuits had come to missionize the Indians according to that very way of life.

Father Gabriel is like Peter in the Acts. He has been sent to spread the good news of the resurrection of Jesus. Peter goes to the Jews, those who were responsible for rejecting Jesus as their messiah and whose elders had been part of the plot to put him to death, like Father Gabriel goes to the very Indians who had crucified the Jesuit priest and sent him over the waterfall.

After spending time with the Indians, Father Gabriel earns their trust and is able to teach them, primarily through music. Likewise, in the Acts of the Apostles, not only Peter, but other apostles, make their way throughout Palestine, perform miracles, preach about the resurrection, and observe how the Holy Spirit converts more and more Jewish believers to what ultimately became known as Christianity. According to tradition, Peter was crucified upside down, because he declared that he was not worthy to die the same way that Jesus did. In "The Mission," Father Gabriel dies carrying the sign of Jesus' death and resurrection, the ultimate love, the Eucharist, the sacrifice of his life for the life of others.

In "The Mission," there is irony in Father Gabriel, who has dedicated his life to working among the Indians. Repeatedly, he attempts to convince the papal representative that the mission territories should not be handed over to the Portuguese. In the end, however, he refuses to fight. Some people would judge him as a failure because he did not support the very cause to which he had dedicated his life.

There is little doubt that Captain Rodrigo Mendoza can serve as a model for understanding the fiery Saul of Tarsus, who is renamed Paul in the Acts. Mendoza is converted from his occupation as a slave-trader and as a killer of his brother, Philippe. But he recognizes his sin, repents, is forgiven by the Indians, and, with Father Gabriel's help, is accepted as a member of San Carlos mission and a member of the Jesuits. In the Acts,

Saul (Paul) has permission from the Jewish high priest to seek out and arrest anyone following the new way of Jesus. He has authority to bring those Christians to Jerusalem in chains. But while he is out Christian-hunting one day, light flashes before him and in a vision he hears Jesus speak to him, as he is blinded by the light.

He is told to go to Damascus and Ananias, who had had a vision concerning Saul (Paul), visits him and lays his hands upon him. He is healed of his blindness and baptized into the very movement he had attempted to wipe out. After Peter launches the mission to the Gentiles, Paul takes over and spreads the good news to the ends of the earth--Rome. Unlike Rodrigo, Paul does not revert to his previous way of life. He is found at the end of the Acts of Apostles under house arrest in Rome awaiting trial. Tradition tells us that he was found guilty of subverting the Roman government and beheaded. From this point of view, he is like Rodrigo, who is guilty of not adhering to his vow of obedience and surrendering the mission to the Portuguese, and who is killed by them. Also, not to be missed is Rodrigo's use of the sword both to kill his brother and to kill the Portugese. Paul is often depicted in popular statuary and iconography holding a sword.

Rodrigo is a man filled with ironic contradictions throughout the film. After he carries his bundle of weapons up the waterfall, it is an Indian who cuts the bundle off of his back. The very people he was capturing and enslaving set him free. With the ceremony of chest-painting, he is accepted by the Indians as a member of their tribe or com-munity. The people he once care nothing about and sold into slavery now accept him as one of their own. Then, Rodrigo, the killer, like Moses, who had had no remorse and was interested in only his personal gain, made vows of poverty, chastity, and obedience.

The persecution that the followers of Jesus' way experience in the Acts can be compared to the persecution the Indians experience from the Portuguese government when it takes over the Spanish missions. The signing of the compromise between the officials representing Portugal and Spain indicates that the Spanish missions will not be protected; in fact, they will be destroyed. According to the Acts of the Apostles, under the Roman government many Christians suffered persecution in various ways, even imprisonment and martyrdom.

The Cardinal sent by the pope to investigate the problems brewing in South America, has no counterpart in the Acts of the Apostles, but his character is worth exploring for its irony. There is little doubt that he is a good man, but he is stuck between the politics of Spain and Portugal. The choice he has to make is between the lesser of two evils:

to allow Portugal the control of the Indian territory and the missions within it which will result in the annihilation of the missions or to deny Portugal control with the result of the "persecution" of the papacy by the Portuguese. He says that to banish the missions would be like severing a beautiful limb from a body, but he ends up severing nevertheless.

The Cardinal also represents the irony of the Church in Rome. The pope had sent the Jesuits to South America. In the end, through the Cardinal's decision, the Church ends up destroying the very missions it had established. Once the Church got embroiled in Spain's and Portugal's politics, destruction was sure to follow.

As the Acts of the Apostles closes, readers are left with the same hope of which the cardinal spoke about in "The Mission." The viewer watches the children from the destroyed mission get into a boat and paddle away. They had been raised in the mission, and they will carry its spirit with them. When the Cardinal writes to the pope, he tells him that the dead Jesuit priests live in the memory of the living. For almost two thousand years, the spirit of Jesus Christ and all those who have followed him continues to survive in the memory of living believers all around the world.

Exercises and Questions for Discussion

1. Identify at least five ways that Father Gabriel in "The Mission" is like Peter in the Acts of the Apostles.

2. Identify at least five ways that Captain Rodrigo Mendoza in "The Mission" is like Paul in the Acts of the Apostles.

3. What parallels, if any, can you find in the Acts of the Apostles for the papal representative, the Cardinal, sent to South America to investigate the activities of Spain and Portugal?

4. Outline the plot of the film by scene. For each scene indicate its importance to the whole story and what purpose it serves.

5. What do you think is the major truth which the movie attempts to communicate? Is this truth one that endures? Explain.

6. In what ways do you think "The Mission" shows a clash between faith and greed? What parallels can you find in the Acts of the Apostles?

7. In what ways do you think "The Mission" shows a clash between wills and cultures? What parallels can you find in the Acts of the Apostles?

8. What do you think is the major truth which the Acts of the Apostles attempts to communicate? Is this truth one that endures? Explain.

9. Make a list of five ways that "The Mission" helped you to better understand the Acts of the Apostles.

Teaching Pauline Theology

Regarding Henry

Paul of Tarsus, the Pharisee Christian-hunter who turned traitor, is the author of most of the letters of the Christian Bible (New Testament). Scholars do not debate the fact that Paul wrote the letters to the Romans, 1 and 2 Corinthians, Galatians, Philippians, 1 Thessalonians, and Philemon between 50 C.E. and 68 C.E., when he was beheaded in Rome. While there is debate about genuine Pauline authorship of Ephesians and Colossians, there is no doubt that they continue Pauline theology. Because of their late date, 1 and 2 Timothy and Titus, sometimes called the pastorals, cannot have been written by Paul, and 2 Thessalonians, somewhat of a summary of 1 Thessalonians, is not from Paul's hand. Hebrews, which at one time carried the superscription as a letter of Paul, is not a Pauline composition. It is also not a letter but a sermon.

The difficulty faced by the teacher when presenting Pauline thought is what to use. The approach I recommend is to present genuine Pauline theology by using "Regarding Henry" (Paramount Pictures, 1991) and then show how Paul's basic understanding of Jesus and his message was expanded by the next generation writing under Paul's name. First, however, it is important to help students understand what a radical conversion Paul underwent when he left his old life as a Christian-hunter behind and began to follow and preach the Way of Jesus Christ.

"Regarding Henry," staring Harrison Ford as Henry Turner, a fast-paced, ruthless lawyer, opens with Turner presenting his closing arguments as the attorney for the defense, North Shore Hospital, in a malpractice suit presented by a Mr. Matthews, a diabetic, who faces living the rest of his life in a wheel chair because, allegedly, a nurse did not hear him tell her that he was a diabetic. Matthews alleges that he did tell her, but the jury finds in favor of the defense.

Back in the elegant law firm offices, Charlie Cameron (Donald Moffat) toasts Turner for his victory. Turner is busy giving directions to his secretary for several actions in rapid succession as he is walking down the hall and smoking like a chimney.

In his elegant and spacious apartment, he disciplines his daughter, Rachel (Mikki Allen), as he and his wife, Sarah (Annette Bening), prepare to leave for a Christmas party and entrust Rachel to the care of the maid, Rosella (Aida Linares).

After the party, Sarah tells Henry that he should apologize to Rachel, but he tells her to call the caterers the next day and tell them that they now have sixty people for the party they are hosting. After walking into Rachel's room and awakening her, Henry tells her about winning his case and quotes her a Latin phrase as the basis for his win ("He who is silent is understood to concert"). She tells him about someone's daughter not getting into the school in which she has been accepted. After several other words of conversation, he leaves her room and goes to his bedroom and looks for cigarettes. When he can't find any, he tells Sarah that he is going out to get some.

After entering the convenience shop and not noticing that he is interrupting a robbery in progress, a young man with a gun points it to-ward Henry and asks him for his wallet. The man shoots him in the shoulder, while Henry says, "Will you just wait a minute?" Then, the man shoots him again in the head and runs out of the store. Henry staggers to the door and falls down.

Police arrive to inform Sarah that Henry has been shot. She goes to the hospital to wait while he's in surgery. She is joined by friends from the law firm and tells Rachel that she doesn't know what will happen next.

In the next scene Sarah speaks to an unconscious Henry, con-nected to all types of machines, lying in a hospital bed. After she leaves, he wakes up when a nurse changes one of his IV bags. A few days later, he is no longer attached to machines, but still in bed and drooling when Sarah comes to see him.

She learns from Henry's doctor that the gunshot caused no major damage to his brain. But the bullet that went into his shoulder hit an artery and caused cardiac arrest. That triggered a lack of oxygen to the brain and there may be some damage. The doctor tells her that he will have a long and tough rehabilitation process that will last longer than three months, that he will be beginning to learn how to speak and how to walk again, and that his memory may be affected. The doctor also tells her that he may not be able to ever regain his speech or physical coordina-tion. But during a meal together, Sarah tells Rachel that he is doing fine and their conversation turns to the topic of getting a puppy for her.

Henry is transferred from the hospital to a rehabilitation center. The chief of staff joins Sarah as she is visiting Henry and asks him if he remembers his daughter or his wife. His facial expressions indicate that he does not.

Back in their apartment, Sarah and Rachel lay on the bed while Rachel asks about their economic status now that Henry is no longer working. Sarah gets angry about a rumor that Rachel tells her a friend of hers told her at school.

In the rahab center, Henry is tested for basic skills, such as colors and shapes. Bradley (Bill Nunni) has been assigned as his physical therapist. After getting Henry out of bed and putting him in a wheel chair, he takes him to an exercise room where he works Henry's leg muscles.

Meanwhile, Sarah gets a job selling real estate. She tells her friend that Henry can't walk, talk, or remember and that she has spoken to their accountant and discovered that they have nothing put away except a few stocks and the value of the apartment. She says that things have to change, but her friend advises that she continue her lifestyle in order to look good with the other wives of the members of the law firm.

After a speech therapist works with Henry to try to get him to say the word "ball" with no success, Bradley takes him to the cafeteria to serve him breakfast. He seasons his eggs with lots of hot sauce and tells Henry that until he starts asking for what he wants, Bradley will continue to serve the eggs with the seasoning. Henry utters his first word in months: Ritz, which Bradley interprets as Henry wanting crackers.

Sarah attends a dinner with Charlie Cameron (Donald Moffat), the head of the law firm, and Bruce (Bruce Altmani), Henry's best friend. After Bruce leaves, Cameron offers Sarah financial help, but she declines and says that she is doing fine.

In rehabilitation Henry continues to improve. Bradley demonstrates how to use a walker and gets Henry to stand up and shuffle his feet. Later, Henry uses the walker to get down a hallway alone. In a series of scenes, he exercises, walks with a cane, walks with a limp without a cane, and walks normally.

The day arrives for Henry to go home. Sarah and Rachel prepare to go get him, but they are not sure how his arrival home will work out. In the rehabilitation center, Henry is painting a picture of a box of Ritz crackers when Bradley arrives and asks him why he isn't packed and ready to go. Henry says, "I'm not going. I've changed my mind. I'm going to stay. I live here." Bradley insists that Henry must go home. Henry says, "I don't know them." After getting angry, he adds, "I just can't remember. I don't know those people."

After Sarah and Rachel arrive to take Henry home, they talk about his coming home. "You've got a life back at home with friends and family and all you could ever want," says Sarah. "All you have to say is you want to come home." Henry replies, "I don't want to."

While Sarah speaks to the chief of staff about Henry's reluctance to want to go home, Bradley talks to Rachel and suggests that she talk to Henry. When she enters his room, he is attempting to tie his shoe. She demonstrates how to do it as he touches her hand and asks her how she learned to tie shoes. She says, "You taught me." At that, he says that he remembers the gray carpeting in their home, goes to the chief of staff's office, and tells Sarah and the chief of staff that he wants to go home. Henry says goodbye to Bradley, who gives him a Walkman, as Henry, Sarah, and Rachel get into a taxi.

The taxi pulls up to the front door of the building in which their apartment is located. The doorman, Eddie, greets the Turners and welcomes Henry home. Henry, totally out of character, hugs Eddie. When he walks into their apartment, Henry says "Wow!" and he sees the elegance of their living space. He comments, "Nice table," in reference to a round dining room table which he had previously ordered to be returned. Henry remembers the smell of the house.

In their bedroom, Sarah shows Henry his side of the bed, getting in cautiously and tossing away several of the pillows he used to require. Sarah turns out the lamp on his nightstand and lays her head on his chest. He tells her that he remembers her hair.

During breakfast the next morning, Henry, Sarah, and Rachel are served breakfast by Rosella. Rachel spills her orange juice all over the table, and Henry says that it is OK because he does it all time. Then, he proceeds to spill his in imitation of her. In the past, he would have yelled at her for her clumsiness.

Henry opens his clothes closets and is astounded by all the suits he has to wear. As he is examining what he owns, Sarah tells him that she is taking Rachel to school. Rosella is left to watch Henry, who, not knowing what to do next, asks her, "What do I do when I'm home?" She tells him, "You're always working." She emphasizes that he works hard all the time.

Exploring the apartment, like a kid in a toy store, Henry finds money and puts it in his pocket. He opens drawer after drawer and takes out items and examines them. A box of letters written on blue paper in blue envelopes catches his attention momentarily, but he does not read any of them.

While Henry continues his exploration of the apartment, Rosella answers the door bell and receives a young man delivering groceries. When she goes to another room to get money for a tip, Henry walks out of the apartment. On the way out of the building, he tells Eddie that he is going for a walk. He is almost hit by a car as he crosses a street.

Of course when Sarah returns, she can't find Henry. He, however, has stopped to purchase a hot dog, explores the streets of the city, answers a public telephone that is ringing, sees part of an X-rated film in a theater, and spies a puppy in the window of a pet shop. He buys the puppy and brings it home, appearing at the front door of the apartment just as Sarah is getting ready to go out and look for him. Rachel is ecstatic as Henry presents the puppy to her.

Rachel's relationship with Henry continues to develop. She takes him to the library, where she has to explain the rules, the proper behavior in such a place. While she is reading and working on a report, he sits across the table from her flipping paper wads at her. Repeatedly, she tells him to stop, but he keeps doing it. She tells him to read the book he has in front of him. Finally, he tells her that he can't read. Back in their apartment, Rachel teaches Henry how to read. As he begins to remember how to read, Henry celebrates by hugging everyone--Sarah, Rachel, and Rosella. They are astonished by his behavior.

One day Bruce, who had been Henry's best friend in the law firm, comes to visit him. Bruce talks about people at their office, but Henry doesn't have any idea about whom he is speaking. Henry asks Bruce, "Were we really good friends?" Bruce replies, "Partners." Then Henry opens the gift Bruce has brought him, a gold picture frame.

At a dinner party made up of members of the law firm and their wives, Henry is toasted by the head of law firm. Then Henry stands up and says, "I don't remember any of you. I don't remember very much of anything. It's all mixed up." Later, Rachel shows Henry some photographs of Henry's past. In the midst of it, she touches his head where he had been shot and he touches her foot, where she has a scar from a bike accident.

Finally, Henry is ready to go back to work. Bruce escorts him to his office and introduces him to his secretary, Jessica. Henry goes to his desk and sits down, after he explores some of the spacious office. Jessica brings in a tray of coffee and proceeds to pour a cup for Henry and tells him to "say when" as she adds cream to it. He never says "when" and she almost makes the cup overflow.

In a series of two scenes, Henry is at home reading with the puppy playing near his chair. Sarah asks him if he would like to have a

Malamar--a type of ice cream bar--his favorite food, but he doesn't remember it was his favorite food. In an office at the firm, Henry is present for a discussion of the strategy being employed for a case, but he seems lost.

Then, during a lunch with several members of the law firm, Henry talks about the last case he won, the one involving the Matthewes, the scene with which the movie began. He reveals that he has found a file of another patient who said that she heard Mr. Matthews tell the nurse that he was diabetic, so the hospital was responsible. Bruce tells Henry to put the file away. Henry comments, "So, what we did was wrong."

Rachel and Henry try to make cookies. Rachel asks him about being scared when he was in the hospital. Then, she tells him that she is going away to school. He asks her if she is scared. After she says that she is, she asks him if he wants her to go. He says "No." He promises to talk to Sarah about Rachel going away to school. When he does, Sarah tells him that it is a great opportunity for Rachel and for them. Getting frustrated with all the change she's been experiencing in him, she tells Henry, "There's got to be a few things we agreed on that I can count on." She also tells him that she has seen a house that would be perfect for them and that she has someone who is interested in buying their apartment.

Together Henry and Sarah take Rachel to the expensive finishing school. As Rachel gets ready to take leave of them, Henry tells her a story about his first day in boarding school and his fear. That gives Rachel some self-confidence, but, as she walks away, he begins to cry. His missing Rachel intensifies later when Sarah finds him on the balcony of their apartment. He tells her how much he misses Rachel. But in the midst of that he begins to remember the names of some stars and points those out to Sarah, who reminds him that they haven't made love since he has returned home. Henry says that he is "really nervous." Taking it slowly, they engage in passionate kissing and make love. Afterward, while lying in bed together, Henry asks Sarah to tell him how they met, and she does.

After Sarah takes Henry to the house she wants to buy and he says that he likes it, they walk down the street together holding hands, something Henry would never have done before. Sarah reminds him that he didn't like showing affection in public. He demonstrates his change in attitude by standing on a park bench, drawing her to himself on the bench, and kissing. Meanwhile, two wives of members of the law firm see them and talk to them.

Back in the law firm, Henry's office has been changed from the spacious window-filled one to a windowless closet. When he asks Jessica to get him files of some of his previous cases, she tells him that she can't, that she's been forbidden to do so by the head of the law firm.

While attending a house warming party for one of the members of the law firm, Henry is found mingling with one of the waiters instead of with some of the partners of the firm. A group of the partners and wives talk about Henry and Sarah, who overhear the negative conversation and leave the party. Henry is hurt by their conversation and won't get out of bed. Sarah tells him, "They don't know you anymore."

In order to help Henry get out of his depression, Sarah invites Bradley over. He and Henry share a beer together. The turning point of the film now beings as Henry tells Bradley, "I thought I could go back to my life, but I don't like who I was. I don't fit in." Bradley tells Henry about wrecking his knees playing football and how he thought his life was over. "It was a test. I had to find a life," he says. Then, he narrates how he decided to become a therapist. Finally, he tells Henry, "Don't listen to nobody trying to tell you who you are. It might take a while, but you'll figure yourself out."

Henry, who has now decided to be his new self, calls Rachel after receiving a letter from her telling him that she is "miserable" in school, but he can't get through to her. Meanwhile, Rosella delivers a just-arrived gift package to Henry, saying, "I'm going to miss you, Mr. Henry. I like you much better now."

The gift is from Bruce and is intended as a house-warming present. A message is written on blue paper in a blue envelope, the likes of which Henry remembers seeing in a box in a drawer one day when he was exploring the apartment. He finds the other blue envelopes and papers and reads them, discovering them to be love notes written to Sarah by Bruce.

Just as Sarah arrives home to tell Henry that they have closed on their new house, he shows her the letters from Bruce. She reveals that she slept with Bruce before Henry was shot, adding that Henry was different then. Henry walks away and goes to the law firm to get a set of files. Bruce meets him, but he walks away with the files.

He goes past a sign, "The Ritz-Carlton Hotel," and remembers that the first word he had said in rehab and the painting he had done of the box of Ritz crackers did not refer to the crackers at all but to the hotel. He gets a room and lays on the bed. But his moment of quiet is interrupted by the doorbell. On the other side of the door is Linda (Rebecca Miller), a member of the law firm. She tells him that she followed him to the hotel. Then she tells him that Bruce really cared for him after he was shot and took over his legal cases. Next, she proceeds to tell him about the affair they used to have and how they would meet every Tuesday and Thursday at the Ritz. Linda reminds Henry that he was going to leave Sarah for her. Startled at this revelation that he has cheated on Sarah like she cheated on him, he walks out of the hotel and strolls along a lake, finally stopping to sit on a park bench.

Taking the subway to the Matthewses' home, he tells Mrs. Matthews that he is sorry for what happened to them in court. He hands her the file with the testimony from the patient who heard Mr. Matthews tell the nurse that he was a diabetic. As he walks away, he says, "I'm sorry. I changed."

Returning to the law firm, Henry interrupts a meeting between Charlie Cameron, head of the law firm, and several Japanese men and tells him that he can't be a lawyer any more. He tells his secretary, Jessica, goodbye and adds, "I had enough. So I said 'when,'" a reference to her instruction to him about telling her how much milk to add to his coffee. He also says goodbye to Linda.

Henry returns home to Sarah. They apologize to each other. Then, Henry tells her, "I don't like my clothes. I don't like eggs or steak. I hate being a lawyer. I want us to be a family for as long as we can. I did like those Malamars."

While Rachel is listening to a lecture on competition, Henry and Sarah arrive to take her home. They have brought Buddy, the puppy, along. Henry, interrupting the lecturer, tells her, "I missed her first eleven years, and I don't want to miss anymore." Rachel joins Henry and Sarah as they leave the building and walk across the lawn of the campus together. Not only Henry is a changed man, but because he has changed, his relationship with Sarah, Rachel, and the law firm has changed too.

While it took a gun shot wound and rehabilitation to change Henry, it took a revelation from God to change Paul. He narrates the experience of his own conversion in his Letter to the Galatians, explaining how he violently persecuted the church and tried to destroy it before he was converted by God's grace and began to preach Jesus Christ among the Gentiles. Using the metaphor of a flash of light, Luke portrays Paul's conversion in the Acts of the Apostles three times, once in narrative and twice in a speech from Paul's own lips. Another version of Paul's conversion can be found in 1 Timothy.

The resemblance does not stop there. Paul was a Pharisee, one who knew the Torah, the law, well. Henry Turner is a member of a law firm and he not only knows the law well, he also knows how to manipulate it in order to win his court cases. After Paul is converted, he comes to understand that the law, while it served the purpose God once intended, has been surpassed by the teaching of Jesus Christ. Paul says that those who follow Jesus have been freed from the law, which kills, but given life in the Spirit. Likewise, once Henry is changed by his experiences of being shot and undergoing rehabilitation, he sees what the law did to Mr. Matthews. He repents. He apologizes. And he puts in motion the steps which are necessary to have the malpractice suit tried again. By handing the file containing the testimony of a patient who heard Mr. Matthews tell the nurse that he was a diabetic, Henry declares Mr. Matthews righteous. Paul, using a metaphor from the law courts of his time, applies the concept of righteousness to God, saying that God declares the sinner righteous through faith. Henry did for Mr. Matthews what the law could not do. Through Christ, says Paul, God has done for people what the Law could not do.

Henry's statements about not liking his clothes, eggs, or being a lawyer and his desire to have a family signal that he has left behind the old man he was and had to rediscover and he has become a new person. Paul refers to this as putting on Christ. Through baptism, one dies to a former way of life and rises to a new life in Christ. Baptism signifies that one is dead to sin, freed from sin. Henry, through his near-death baptism dies to his former hard, uncaring, unsympathetic, non-understanding self and is rehabilitated into a new man who, by touching the lives of Sarah, Rachel, and Bradley, makes a difference.

In this capacity, Henry is a reconciler. He brings together Sarah, Rachel, and himself. He reconciles his past with Mr. Matthews and he attempts to fix other relationships that have gone awry. Paul writes of God reconciling the world through Jesus Christ. Whatever may have separated God from people does so no more. Whatever separated Henry from people has been removed. God, according to Paul, poured grace on the world. Henry poured love and brought together a family.

The most powerful scene of reconciliation occurs after Henry has discovered that Sarah has slept with Bruce and that he had an affair with Linda. Not only has he recognized his wife's sin, but he has also come face to face with his own weakness. Out of his weakness he finds the power to return to Sarah and apologize to her. Paul writes about finding his strength in his weakness. He says that when he was weak, then he was strong. God works through human weakness and not through human power. No one has the right to condemn another person, because all of us are equally sinners in need of redemption.

Henry's desire for Sarah, Rachel, and himself to be a family for as long as they can indicates his desire for unity. Paul speaks of the unity of those who follow Jesus as members of Christ's body. The body of

Christ, animated by the Spirit, is one. Each member possesses special gifts given to him or her for the good of the whole. By serving the needs of each other, the members of the body of Christ serve Christ, whose body they are.

Henry's previous way of life, one marked by his uncaring and uncharitable attitude toward people, is reversed in his new way of life. He learns the meaning of love through Rachel's patience with him in teaching him how to read, how to bake cookies, and how to spill orange juice on the table. Henry learns the meaning of love through Sarah's kindness toward him in their love-making and acceptance of him as he changes. He learns the meaning of love from Bradley's patience with him in teaching him how to walk and talk. All these people are incarnations of Paul's understanding that love is patient and kind, that it is the greatest of virtues, and that we bear each other's burdens because we love, and we forgive each other's faults because love overflows in us.

Henry, who before his life-threatening experience, trusted no one but himself and his own abilities, learns to trust others. He has to believe that his therapist, Bradley, can help him learn to walk and talk again. He learns to trust Rachel when she teaches him how to read. He trusts Sarah when she leads him to make love. In Pauline terms, Henry learns to walk by faith and not by sight. Paul writes about professing faith in God and Jesus Christ and living according to it. Then, what is seen is no longer one's guide for life. What is believed is one's guide for living.

Before Henry was shot, he relied upon the wisdom of the world in terms of being a lawyer in a prestigious law firm, owning a luxurious apartment, and socializing with all the right people in a city. After he is rehabilitated, he rejects the ways of the world, leaving the law firm, moving to a small house, and spending time with the little people. Paul writes about the wisdom of the world in terms of it being folly. He says that it is unable to figure out or recognize what God has done in Christ. Preaching a crucified savior, who has delivered the world from corruption, makes no sense to a world blinded by its own light. Paul uses the cities of the Roman Empire as the bases for his mission to the ends of the earth.

From all appearances, Henry was fully alive before his accident and nearly dead thereafter. He was a valued member of the law firm. He lived in an enviable apartment. He had a wife and one daughter. Henry had plenty of clothes, ate at the most expensive restaurants, and socialized with the elite. But inside, Henry was dead. The irony of the film is that he only comes alive after he nearly dies. Through his rehabilitation, Henry rises from the dead to a new life. He quits the law firm. He moves into a small house. He creates a family. He doesn't like his clothes, rich foods, or high-society groups. But now he is alive.

Often Paul writes about the new life that baptism begins and that will culminate in resurrection to new life on the other side of final death. Paul doesn't know what that new life is like, but he believes that Jesus Christ experienced it and that everyone who follows his way will experience it, too. That's what Paul calls the gospel or good news. It was good news to Henry, and it is good news for everyone.

Bradley, Henry's therapist, illustrates Paul's understanding of the body of the Christ. Bradley uses his gift as a therapist for the good of Henry. In the dialogue between Henry and Bradley in Henry's home, Henry comes to recognize that the new man he has become is for the good of others, especially his family. Bradley recognized this when he has to give up a previous career because of his bad knees and become a therapist. Both men, like Paul, find their existence for others.

Exercises and Questions for Discussion

1. Outline the plot of the film by scene. For each scene indicate its importance to the whole story and what purpose it serves. What scenes serve as the pivot point for the film?

2. After reading Paul's letters to the Romans, 1 and 2 Corinthians, Galatians, Philippians, 1 Thessalonians, and Philemon, what major ideas do you discover that parallel scenes in the movie?

3. Prepare a definition of each of the following Pauline terms: justification, righteousness, redemption, reconciliation, salvation, reckon, grace, sanctification, atonement, victory, and resurrection. What scene, words, incidents in the film can you use as an example that illustrates the meaning of each Pauline term?

4. For each of the following characters in the film, explain what Pauline thought, concept, theological point he or she best represents: Henry Turner, Sarah Turner, Rachel Turner, Charlie Cameron, Bradley, Rosella, Bruce, Linda.

5. Identify a major point which Paul makes and with which you strongly agree. Explain why you agree with Paul.

6. Identify a major point which Paul makes and with which you strongly disagree. Explain why you disagree with Paul.

7. What do you think is the major truth which the movie attempts to communicate? Is this truth one that endures? Explain.

8. What do you think is the major truth which Paul attempts to communicate through his letters? Is this truth one that endures? Explain.

Teaching Pauline Theology

The Doctor

"Conversion" may be one of the most misunderstood concepts in religion. Usually, it refers to a definitive moment in a person's life when he or she adopts a religion. And while not wanting to down-play the importance of locating a specific experience in one's life that leads to an expression of faith, conversion is more of a life-time process than it is one dramatic moment. The process of conversion involves self, one's relationships, and God.

In the Christian Bible (New Testament), the most prominent convert is Saul of Tarsus, known as Paul. It took a revelation from God to change Paul. He narrates the experience of his own conversion in his Letter to the Galatians, explaining how he violently persecuted the church and tried to destroy it before he was converted by God's grace and began to preach Jesus Christ among the Gentiles. Using the metaphor of a flash of light, Luke portrays Paul's conversion in the Acts of the Apostles three times, once in narrative and twice in a speech from Paul's own lips. Another version of Paul's conversion can be found in 1 Timothy.

However, any one of the narratives giving the details of Paul's conversion experience is a synthesis of the stages of the process he must have gone through. In order to help students understand the process of conversion, "The Doctor" (Touchstone Pictures, 1991), can be shown. The film is about a doctor who thought he knew it all until he became a patient. But his conversion is not a single moment in his life; it is a process which entails the doctor, others, and God. The film highlights part of the process.

Jack McKee (William Hurt) is an extraordinary doctor who specializes in lung and heart surgery. In the operating room, he and a team of doctors and nurses prepare a young man, who has a transected aorta, for surgery. The operating room is a place of laughter, where surgeons tell jokes and listen to Country and Western music. Repairing the young man's aorta is no challenge for Jack, who, when finished, quickly moves into the adjoining operating room to consult with a colleague, doctor and rabbi Eli Bloomfield (Adam Arkin), who talks to his patient, even though the man on the operating table is under anesthetic and unconscious. Jack thinks this is cute, and he is above it.

Next, Jack drives to see his own physician, who tells him that his throat is inflamed and slightly swollen. As Jack prepares to leave, his doctor gives him a prescription for antibiotics. Both are confident that this will take care of Jack's hoarseness.

Back in the hospital, Jack examines a woman upon whom he had performed heart surgery. He prepares to remove the staples from her chest, as she asks him about her husband's lack of attraction for her now that she has this huge scar down the center of her chest. Jokingly and without any sensitivity for her feelings and the gravity of her question, he instructs her to tell her husband that she looks like a *Playboy* centerfold and that she has the staple marks to prove it.

As Jack drives home, a woman in a car motions for him to follow her. The viewer discovers that she is Ann McKee (Christine Lahti), Jack's wife. Each discovers that both have forgotten about the other's meeting. Jack has forgotten about a school meeting. Ann has forgotten about an Art Festival meeting during which Jack will accept a check for the hospital. They agree to meet later in the evening for dinner, as they walk through their kitchen which is in the process of renovation. When they do meet, instead of going out for dinner, they decide to return home and eat.

On the way home, they talk and laugh, while Jack takes a call from a patient's wife who is concerned about her husband, whose lung Jack had removed. He wants to mow the lawn. Jack tells her that if her husband feels up to it, mowing the lawn will be good exercise for him.

But just as he is finished with the call, Jack begins a violent coughing spell. Ann finds blood on his shirt and on her dress and hair. Jokingly, Jack tells her that he is not bleeding to death.

In the next scene, Jack takes his residents on rounds in the hospital. As he does so, the viewer gets a clearer picture of this non-sympathetic doctor. He tells them that there is a danger in feeling too strongly about their patients because they will become too involved. He says that surgery is about judgment, and to judge well they will have to be detached. He adds that a surgeon's job is to cut. He says, "You go in. You fix it. You get out."

Together Jack and the resident physicians step into the room of the young man Jack had operated on at the beginning of the film. Jack tells the residents that the young man, named Robert, had walked through a window. As he is leaving, Jack, jokingly, tells Robert that the next time he wants to give himself some real punishment, he should try golf because there's no greater torture. Clearly, Jack has no sympathy for Robert, who has one arm in a cast, one leg in a cast, and a repaired aorta.

Jack sees Leslie Abbott (Wendy Crewson), a throat specialist. She examines his throat and neck and records her work on video tape. When the exam is completed, Doctor Abbott tells Jack that he has a growth, a tumor, on his vocal cords, and she wants to do a biopsy the next day. Jack is shocked into reality. The doctor is going to become a patient.

But he goes home and tells Ann, his wife, that he is fine. When Nicky, his son, is called by Ann to come and talk to his father, he can't believe that his father is home this early in the day and picks up the telephone. Ann knows that something is wrong. So, finding Jack playing a pinball machine, while an electric train runs around a track in their game room in the middle of the night, Ann discovers that Jack is drunk. She asks him to tell her what's wrong. After he explains about the tumor, she says that they can beat it, but, angrily, he answers that they don't have it. "It's not a team game," he tells her. Taking out his frustration on the pinball machine, he beats it with his fist as Ann leaves. Jack has rejected her offer of support.

Later, as he slips into bed, he tells Ann that he has a biopsy the next day and that it is a laryngeal tumor. Ann is dismayed. They hold each other as Jack explains that he has a growth.

The next day, as they wait for Jack's appointment for the biopsy, he makes it clear to the nurse that he's been an attending physician on the staff of the hospital for eleven years and that he doesn't like having to wait nor to fill out all the paperwork. He sends Ann home. Then, he confronts an orderly who arrives with a wheel chair to take him to his room. Jack refuses to sit in the chair and walks to his room. There, he complains to the nurse about not having a private room. She tells him that they have no private rooms. His is visibly displeased that he is not getting special treatment.

The other man in the room, Ralph Brown, introduces himself to Jack, and each tells the other about why he is in the hospital. Ralph is a policeman who has a bowel problem. Murray (Mandy Patinkin), one of Jack's partners, visits him in the room before he is placed on a gurney and wheeled to the operating room. For the first time, Jack experiences the hospital as a patient instead of as a doctor. He discovers a point of view that he has never had, as he sees people and lights from a prone position on the gurney. In the operating room he's given an anesthetic which almost immediately sends him into a state of unconsciousness.

He wakes up in his recovery room with an orderly peering over him. After rolling him to his side, the orderly gives him a barium enema, which is meant for Ralph Brown, his roommate, who is standing in the doorway as the orderly tells Jack what he is going to do. Jack, who can't speak, tries to make the orderly understand that he is not Brown, but the man won't listen to him. Brown leaves.

Later, Ann is found at Jack's bedside as Abbott comes in. She tells them that the tumor is malignant. Both Jack and Ann are clearly shocked by this news. Jack repeats her words. Abbott recommends radiation therapy, but Jack declares that he wants it removed. Abbot replies that if she has to cut, she risks losing Jack's voice. Then, she asks Jack if he knows a good radiation therapist. Jokingly, Jack declares that Clark Kent is terrific. Abbott, not finding any humor in the situation, recommends Doctor Reed to Jack, who asks her about the treatment and tells her that he has open heart surgery scheduled for the next day. She tells him that he has cancer. Ann declares that the next day will be fine.

As Jack is preparing to leave the hospital, he tells Ann that he can get himself dressed, as he sends her to get the car. He is pushed down the hall in a wheel chair by an orderly, who stops when Doctor Bloomfield approaches and offers Jack support by walking down the hall with him. Jack rejects his offer.

Ann drives them home. While in the car, Jack jokes about wanting a cigarette. At home, their kitchen is still in the being re-done stage. But the next day Jack fixes Nicky's bike in their garage and tells him about the growth in his throat. He explains that the kind of tumor he has responds well to radiation before Nicky leaves.

Alone and in the hospital elevator, Jack goes to the Radiation Therapy section, two floors below ground. After getting an MRI, he confronts the nurse with more forms that must be completed and shows that he is upset. Doctor Reed, who is in charge of the radiation department, explains to Jack that he will have to come for a treatment every day for six weeks. He challenges Jack's civility. Jack responds by saying that upstairs they are hostile.

Next, the doctor tells Jack that his chest is clear, but that he will need to get fitted for radiation treatment. If, when the rest of the test results come back, his lymph nodes show signs of cancer, Reed says that he will discuss a different treatment with Abbott and Jack. Reed, like the other doctors, isn't interested in the patient but in the cure.

In a series of scenes, Jack is prepared for treatment on an x-ray table. First, orderlies strap his feet and his wrists, then tape his head to the table. One marks his throat with a pen to designate where the radiation will be aimed. Jack is clearly terrified of these procedures, as they put plastic wrap over his face in order to make a protective plaster mask for his face and head.

Jack arrives at his office, where Murray talks to him about taking some time off while he is undergoing treatment for his cancer. He rejects the care shown by his partner and leaves.

In the next scene, Jack gets his first radiation treatment. An orderly puts a tattoo on his throat to permanently mark the spot where the radiation is aimed. Jack asks for a lead apron to protect his chest, but the orderly tells him that he doesn't need it. The beam of radiation is focused on his larynx. The orderly doesn't care about Jack's concern about radiation.

Returning home, Jack feels sick as he gets out of his car. He finds Ann fixing Nicky's skinned knee and asks if anyone needs a doctor. Then he jokes with Nicky about his tattoo. Jack has not yet accepted the severity of his condition.

Back for another treatment, he gets upset with the nurse when Reed can't be present for the treatment. The nurse apologizes but also makes clear that she doesn't make the rules. Jack responds that in the hospital saying "I'm sorry" should be dropped from conversation.

A woman, June Ellis (Elizabeth Perkins), sitting in the waiting room, tells Jack that there's no point shouting at Laurie, the nurse, because she's just doing her job. Ellis suggests that Jack go shout at a doctor. Jack says, "I am a doctor." Ellis replies, "Not when you're sitting here." Then Jack comments on Ellis' calmness.

Now, June begins to teach Jack, the doctor, about being a patient. She explains that she has a grade-four brain tumor, which took her doctors three months to find. She says that she didn't take it so well. Then, she explains that her doctors really didn't find the tumor until she had been in several car accidents, fell over, and blacked out. She asks Jack if he wouldn't call that negligence. Jack, who is not too eager to learn about being a patient, declines comment. But June does not back down. She accuses Jack of being a member of the club of doctors. June has named the reality: Jack is a doctor and belongs to the "club" of doctors. She's reminding him that now he is also a patient.

Jack asks her if she got tests to find the tumor. June says she had a couple of CAT scans. But before that her doctors had given her aspirin and sent her home. Then, she went through stress management and traffic school. Jack tells her that his father had a patient with the same diagnosis as hers and that that man has grandchildren.

An orderly arrives to get June for her treatment. Jack says that he will see her later, but his tone indicates that he has no intention of doing so.

Jack finds Murray Keplin, one of his partners in the practice, and asks him to get his MRI file and find out the results of the lymph-node tests, as no one else will let him see it. He wants to know if it shows any spread of his cancer to his lymph nodes. Murray obliges and discovers that the tests show no spread of the cancer. They hug and jump for joy in celebration of the good news.

Jack goes home, looking for Ann and Nicky. When he doesn't find them, he prepares a barbecued dinner for them. As Ann arrives, he tells her about his good news, but also discovers that she has already eaten dinner and that Nicky is sleeping over at his friend's house. Ann is upset with Jack because he failed to remember that she works late on Fridays and that he didn't call her to tell her about the tumor or the barbecued dinner.

Ann, with her coat on, asks him if he is cold. Jack responds, "Yeah, you are cold." In anger, Ann tells him that he needs to inform her how he wants her to be because she never knows. She asks him to tell her if they are happy or not happy, close or not close. Husband and wife are drifting further apart.

In the next scene, Jack is back in the hospital waiting room with June. Becoming sensitive to another human being, he asks her if she is angry with him. She responds that he lied to her, explaining, "My tumor-- I see it giving me certain freedoms I never allowed myself." Jack breaks in and accuses her of being incredibly hostile, but June quickly retorts that she is honest and that she expects people around her to be the same.

Obviously now showing some concern, Jack asks her what he lied about. June says that she is dying, and that Jack shouldn't waste her time. Leaning forward, a further indication that he now genuinely cares about June, Jack says that her doctors should have found her tumor, that she was right, that somebody screwed up, and that she should have had an MRI. He explains how insurance companies tell doctors what tests they can and cannot do and that the $1,000 cost of the MRI, which would have found her tumor, kept her doctors from prescribing it. June then asks Jack about his father's patient, the one he had told her recovered. Being truthful, Jack answers that there was no patient, and June accepts his honesty. She tells him not to lie to her again. Jack agrees. A break-through has been made.

Jack McKee continues to grow in sensitivity to and basic human respect for people. While making rounds with a group of residents in the hospital, he asks about the first patient to be seen. One doctor responds by saying that the first is the terminal in room 1217. Clearly upset by the resident's answer, Jack questions referring to a person as terminal. The resident replies that the patient in room 1217 is dying. Jack asks for the patient's name. Another resident steps forward and answers that he is a Mr. Winter. Jack states that Mr. Winter is either alive or dead. Then, looking at the first resident, Jack threatens him, saying that if he refers to another patient as terminal, that he will be describing his career that way.

A brief scene follows of Jack and Ann in bed. While he is asleep, she rolls over and touches his throat and brow with her hand. While there is no doubt that she loves him and wants to support him, she does not know how to communicate with him. He has treated her in the same way that he used to treat his patients and other people: He has kept her at a distance.

However, while his relationship with Ann continues to deteriorate, his friendship with June Ellis continues to grow. In the waiting room outside the radiation therapy department, June announces to the other patients that Barbara died. Everyone knows who Barbara was except Jack. So, June explains to him that she was the older woman with the knitting.

In a long monologue, indicating that Barbara's death has caused her to think about her own imminent death, June tells Jack that Barbara had been knitting a big shawl for her grand-daughter for months, and that she had finally finished it. She tells him that she has never been to London or Italy, never had a baby, never learned to use chopsticks, and had a front row ticket to see the American Indian Dance Theater but couldn't go because of her health.

In an attempt to comfort her, Jack states that the theater will be back, but June responds that it will six months before it returns. She begins to laugh, knowing that she may not be alive in six months. Then, both of them focus on a man who has only small tufts of hair randomly scattered on his head, obviously the result of radiation treatment. He is crying because Barbara has died. Jack is visibly touched by the bond that exists among the patients in the waiting room. It is a bond which he has previously rejected but gradually heading toward.

In Jack's office, he has just finished examining a Mr. Mavis, who is awaiting a heart for transplant surgery, asking if Mr. Mavis has any questions. Mavis says that for him it seems strange that there's somebody alive, walking around, and that something terrible will happen and he or she will die, and he will have that person's heart.   Demonstrating compassion and leaning toward Mavis, Jack says that it may take a while before there is a heart to harvest.

Then, Jack begins a heart-to-heart conversation with Mavis, telling him that it is a good idea for him to set his affairs in order. Looking directly at him, Mavis says that his affairs are in order. Mavis adds that he has confidence in Jack. As Jack extends his hand toward Mavis, the patient not only shakes his hand but hugs Jack, who is startled by the feelings his patient has for him, but he is bonding with his patient and losing some of his arrogance.

In a fast scene, Dr. Reed, the radiation specialist, tells Jack that he wants Jack to have another MRI. The results of the therapy are not what he had hoped for. The tumor has not been reduced.

In the waiting room outside the radiation therapy center, June, sensing that something is wrong, takes Jack's hand. She leads him outside to the roof of the hospital. Then, she explains that she went there after her doctors diagnosed her tumor. She says that she thought she would throw herself over the edge. After a pause, she points out where a bird was perched that kept looking at her in a strange way. She says that she felt stupid and just laughed out loud. Then, she tells Jack that she thinks the bird was an angel. She gives Jack permission to scream, but he declines. She gives him permission to jump, and he declines that, too. Then, she tells him to fight his cancer.

As they are descending in the elevator, Jack asks June if the Indian dancers are still on tour, and she replies that they are. Pulling out of his coat pocket his cellular telephone, Jack begins to dial a number. June interrupts him, saying that she can't go. Jack tells her that he will pay for it, but June says money isn't the issue. Jacks asks her if she is still his intrepid friend. Then, he says that they are going. She hesitates, but agrees. On the telephone, Jack orders two airplane tickets to Nevada, a car, and other things.

In the next scene, Jack is driving his car out of the garage with June in the passenger seat. She asks him if he can just get up and go. Using a line she had said to him, Jack answers, "I see my tumor giving me certain freedoms I never allowed myself." Jack, the doctor, has become a patient.

The scene changes to the Nevada desert. Jack is still driving and June is seated next to him. She begins the conversation by telling him about a dream she had the previous night about flying over his house with a full head of hair. Jack begins to sing, "When this old world starts getting me down and people are just too much for me to face ...." June interrupts him, telling him that she loves the song. Together they sing, "I climb way up to the top of the stairs, and all my cares just drift right into space." June stops singing, but Jack continues, "On the roof is peaceful as can be, and there the world below can't bother me."

June asks Jack if they can stop. Jack says that he doesn't want to miss the concert with the Indians. June explains that her concern is not the concert. She says, "It's the time. It's rushing past me. I don't want to rush past this. I don't want to rush past anything anymore. I can't. I just can't Jack." Jack, better understanding June's needs, says that he will do anything she wants.

The viewer sees them sitting on the ground beside the car and watching the sun set in the desert. Jack realizes that his idea of taking June to the concert was just another way his old self appeared. He tells her that he is sorry for bringing her there. Recalling his advice to his residents, he explains how he has fallen back into his old pattern of fixing things.

Interrupting his self-condemnation, June tells Jack what is truly special for her. Taking off of her head the scarf she's worn throughout the film, she reveals that she has no hair. Jack, visibly touched by her unveiling, a sign of her total self-revelation to him, asks her if she prays and if prayer is what holds her together. She answers that she prays, meditates, eats chocolate, and goes dancing.

Jack is now ready to learn about freedom, which June demonstrates by dancing in the desert as the sun sets. Forming a silhouette with the sun behind them, they dance together, Jack holding her tenderly and lovingly. Then, they dance separately, as she shows him how to be free. He turns and turns in freedom. Rejoining, they finish their dance together and are seen holding hands as the sun slips below the horizon.

In the next scene, June is asleep in the car, while Jack is at a pay telephone in the Nevada desert calling his wife, Ann. He tells her where he is, noting that he went a little crazy. She asks him about what is going on. He tells her that he doesn't think the radiation is working. Ann wants to go and get Jack, but he tells her that he is "with a fellow patient." He explains that June is his friend and that she has a brain tumor. He tells her that he missed a plane and will be home in the next morning. All Ann can say, as she hangs up the telephone, is goodnight.

The next morning, Jack drives June to her apartment and lets her out of the car before heading home. He meets Ann, on her way to work, at an intersection near their home. Ann tells him that she is late. Jack asks her if they can meet. As he drives away, Ann tells him that he is breaking her heart.

Jack's transformation from an uncaring doctor to a loving patient is almost complete. While walking through the parking garage with several of his partners, who are discussing their patients, Jack walks behind them, visibly detached. They spy a man attempting to get into his car who is suing their partnership for malpractice. Jack talks to the man, who, in his attempt to communicate with Jack, reveals that he has a speech impediment. Showing compassion to him, Jack patiently comes to understand that the man has locked his keys in his car. Telling the man to go on, Jack takes his cellular phone from his pocket and tells the man that he'll call someone to help and leave the keys at the front desk for the man.

Jack is examined again by Doctor Leslie Abbott, who had diagnosed his tumor. She reveals that Doctor Reed, the radiation therapist, did not tell Jack the whole truth. Not only has the therapy not reduced the size of the tumor, but the tumor has grown bigger. Jack reveals that he is disappointed and asks her about the prognosis on his vocal cords. Quickly, Abbott calls her secretary to see what possibilities she has for surgery and reveals that she has an afternoon slot open. While she is making arrangements with her secretary, Jack interrupts her, saying that he doesn't want her cutting him in the afternoon because she will be tired, ragged, and hungry, after having been on her feet for hours.

Doctor Abbott, being the type of doctor that Jack used to be, asserts that she is the doctor and that he is her patient. She tells him that the afternoon is when she is available and he needs to have the tumor removed before it does any more damage. Jack is astounded by the insensitivity of her response to him.

In a scene in the operating room, 1920s big band music is playing in the background as Jack and his team of doctors and nurses prepare for surgery. Approaching the patient, Jack pauses for a long time. The other doctors and nurses ask him how he is. Breathing very heavily, he tells them that he can't do the surgery and backs away from the operating table.

Jack goes to June's apartment and knocks on the door, awakening her. She opens the door and he tells her that he "lost it today." Then, reflecting on where he is, he says that he should go home. June invites him in. Jack is visibly shaken and apologizes for awakening June. June reminds him of his wife. Jack says that he has kept her so far away for so long that he doesn't know how to let her get close to him. Then, after a pause, he says, "I have to have the operation, June." Turning away from the door to leave, he says, "I'm sorry." After Jack is gone, June is seen sitting at her desk and writing a letter.

Jack has made up his mind that Doctor Leslie Abbott is not

sensitive enough to his needs. So, the next day he goes to see her without an appointment. Ignoring the nurse at the desk, who calls Abbott to tell her that Jack is coming to see her, he walks down the hall as she emerges from her office, asking her if she has a minute to speak to him. Not concerned about him, she tells him that he can see for himself that she has a waiting room full of patients. Jack responds that she will have one fewer because he is leaving. Angered by all this, Abbott says, "Look, doctor, I know how you must be feeling." Jack interrupts her saying, "That's the problem. You don't have the first idea what I'm feeling."

Jack, who indicates that he has been changed, tells her that she needs to brush up her act. He reminds her that one day she will be sick, that every doctor becomes a patient, and that it will hit her as hard as it has hit him. She responds that she finds him very offensive. Jack tells her that he will just wait for his file. She states that she will get it for him. Coming from the file room, she throws it at him. He says, "Air mail. Thank you."

Now, Jack finds Doctor and Rabbi Eli Bloomfield, the man whom he has joked about and teased for his talking to patients who are under anesthetic and clearly unconscious. Jack finds Eli in the locker room. After acknowledging each other's presence, Jack asks to speak to him. Handing his file to Eli, Jack tells him that he needs a partial laryngectomy and asks him to do it. Jack says, "I don't know a doctor I trust more." Eli, without a moment's hesitation, says that he will do the surgery the next day. Eli's unselfishness comes through to Jack as he explains that he is not working, so he will do it the next day.

After thanking Eli, Jack apologizes to him for his previous behavior, saying that he has insulted Eli in the past and now he is ashamed of his behavior. Eli, accepting his apology and employing Jack's type of humor, declares, "I've always wanted to slit your throat, and now I'm going to get a chance to do that." Together they laugh.

Now that Jack and Eli are reconciled, Jack goes to his partner, Murray, and tells him about the surgery he is having and that he has asked Eli, whom he trusts, to do it. Then, Jack tells Murray that even if he can talk after the surgery that he won't testify on Murray's behalf in the lawsuit because he's discovered that the man had a history which Murray didn't check before Murray performed surgery on him. Murray, visibly shaken, reminds Jack that for fourteen years they have been partners and covered for each other. Using a line that Jack objected to when the nurse in the waiting room used it, he tells Murray that he is sorry. Murray tells him that his neck is on the line, too. Jack, taking Murray's response as a pun about the surgery he's having, agrees. As Murray continues to plead,

Jack leaves the room.

Finding Ann in a waiting room while he's walking down a hall in the hospital, she reveals to him that his secretary has told her about his surgery. He gives her the details of the operation. Then, she asks him if he went to see June the previous night. When he says that he did, she tells him that she doesn't resent her because she must be very special to Jack. What she resents, she says, is that Jack has a friend to go to. She tells him that he used to be her friend, but she finds that she can't go to him. Jack's beeper goes off, and he looks to see who's calling him. Ann says that she has to go. She adds that she has come to realize that she is lonely. Then, she walks away as his beeper sounds again. Jack and Ann are not yet reconciled.

Finding a telephone, Jack answers the page, which summons him to June's room in the hospital. She's in a coma. Sitting in a chair beside her bed and holding her hand, he begins to speak to her, imitating Eli. He tells her that he will have his surgery the next day and that he was hoping she would be there to help him through it. He tells her that he is terrified by the surgery, and that he is telling her the truth. Jack has now faced himself, his fears, and his need for support.

At this point, Jack has become a patient and a compassionate doctor. By facing his own fear and understanding the fear that his patients have had--a fear to which he never was sympathetic before, he is becoming a sympathetic doctor. He continues to talk to June, saying that he knows little about her except that she can dance. He says, "I hope you always fly over my house with your lovely long hair."

Later in the evening, Jack gets into bed with Ann, who has left on the lamp on her night stand. Jack tells her that June died. Ann says nothing, but rolls over toward Jack and holds him.

The next morning in the operating room, Eli tells Jack that he'll explain everything that he's doing to him, even though Jack will be under total anesthetic. Eli also tells him that he has a treat for Jack. One of Jack's favorite Country and Western songs blasts through the intercom and the nurse, who has assisted Jack many times in the operating room, sings for him. He reaches out and holds her hand, while she is amazed at his behavior.

In the next scene we see Eli walking down a hall in the hospital toward Ann. The surgery is over. Eli gives Ann his report, saying that he got the tumor, but he was not able to save all the vocal cords. He tells her that he is not able to make any guarantee about Jack's voice. He will have to wait and see.

Jack arrives home with Ann and Nicky. As they pass through the kitchen, still in the process of renovation, Ann gives him a whistle which he can use to get their attention, since he is not supposed to try to speak. Jack, looking at Nicky, blows the whistle in an attempt to tell him that he loves him.

After falling asleep in a chair in an upstairs room, Jack is awakened by the sound of Ann arguing with the kitchen remodelers. Walking down the steps, he blows the whistle, grabs Ann by the arm, and takes her outside on the patio to talk. He has a small white board around his neck. With a magic marker he writes, "Yell at me." Ann refuses. On the other side of the board he writes, "Kitchen my idea." Ann tries to go inside, but Jack pushes her away until she agrees to yell at him inside the house.

Inside, Jack blows his whistle. Ann says, "Look, Jack, I don't know what you want from me." He writes, "I need you." She says, "No you don't. You don't need me." But he points to the words on the board. She says, "No. I don't believe you. I was there. I was there for you, Jack, and you didn't need me." He writes, "Sorry." She says, "Yeah, me too, me too." Jack blows his whistle again. Ann says, "Stop it. Stop blowing that thing. Stop it." Holding up the board with "I need you" on it, Jack blows the whistle even more as Ann walks away. Jack stops and writes, "Start again." Ann says, "Start again. Jesus!" But Jack keeps blowing the whistle. Ann yells, "Stop it!"

Holding up the board, Jack points to "I need you." Then, taking the whistle from his neck, he hands it to her. She cries. He smiles. Ann says she regrets giving him the whistle. Jack mumbles, "I love you." Then, imitating the dance June taught him in the desert, he stands in the middle of the kitchen and dances in freedom. Ann laughs. They hug and kiss. At last, Jack has reconciled himself with his wife.

Weeks later, Jack is healed and able to talk. In a hospital room he sees Mr. Mavis, the man who needs the heart transplant. While Mavis is sitting on his bed surrounded by members of his family, Jack tells him that the heart is being harvested and that it will be flown in from New York. In Spanish, Mavis explains what Jack said to his wife, who does not understand English. Seeing a questioning look on her face, Jack asks Mavis about it. He says that his wife wants to know if the things people say, like kind-hearted and good-hearted, come from the heart. Jack says, "Tell her I think they do." Never would Jack had said something like that before.

Later, in the operating room, Jack, imitating Eli's practice, speaks to Mavis, who is unconscious as Jack attaches the new heart in Mavis' chest cavity. Watching the heart to see if it begins beating, Jack tells the heart to start beating. Leaving toward Mavis, he tells him that his wife will be delighted. Then, touching him on the forehead, he tells him that the new heart is beautiful.

Jack picks up a letter from a nurse as he passes by her station on his way to meet his residents. Handing hospital gowns to all of them, he instructs them to strip naked and put on the hospital gowns as quickly as they can. Once all appear as patients, Jack begins a monologue of instruction to them which indicates how much of a transformation he has undergone.

Jack tells the residents that they have spent a lot of time learning the Latin names for diseases their patients might have, but now it's time for them to learn something simpler about their patients. He states,

> Patients have their own names: Sarah, Alick, Jack. They feel frightened, embarrassed, and vulnerable, and they feel sick. Most of all, they want to get better. They put their lives in our hands. I could try to explain what that means until I'm blue in the face, but you know something: It wouldn't mean a thing. It sure as hell never did to me. So, for the next seventy-two hours you'll each be allocated a particular disease. You'll sleep in hospital beds, eat hospital food, be given all the appropriate tests, tests you will one day prescribe.

Jack opens the double doors into the ward and a whole troop of nurses walk in with equipment for administering tests. Jack tells the residents that they are no longer doctors; now they are hospital patients. He says that he will see them on his rounds.

As he walks out of the ward, he pulls the letter he picked up earlier from his pocket, opens it, and begins to read it. The viewer realizes that this letter is the one June wrote after Jack had visited her. Her voice is heard reading the letter as Jack reads it quietly to himself.

She explains that she was worried about him after he left her apartment because he didn't know about how to let Ann get close. She tells him that she has composed the following story for him which she hopes he reads before his operation.

Jack goes to the roof of the hospital, the place June had taken him once before. She continues to read the letter:

> There was a farmer who had a lot of fields and he kept all of the birds and creatures away from his crops with traps and fences. He was very successful, but he was very lonely. So, one day he stood in the middle of his fields to welcome the animals. He stayed there from dawn to dusk with his arms outstretched, calling to them, but not a single animal came. Not a single creature appeared. They were terrified, you see, of

the farmer's new scarecrow. Dear Jack, just let down your arms and we'll all come to you.

Jack laughs as he gazes toward the Golden Gate bridge. He knows that he has already let down his arms and seen how many people have come to him, including Ann. He's been converted, changed, from being an extraordinary doctor to being an extraordinary person and an ordinary patient.

Saul of Tarsus, the strict Pharisee who converted to Christianity after an experience which made him see the error of his ways, is the author of most of the letters of the Christian Bible (New Testament). Scholars do not debate the fact that Paul wrote the letters to the Romans, 1 and 2 Corinthians, Galatians, Philippians, 1 Thessalonians, and Philemon between 50 C.E. and 68 C.E., when he was beheaded in Rome. While there is debate about genuine Pauline authorship of Ephesians and Colossians, there is no doubt that they continue Pauline theology. Because of their late date, 1 and 2 Timothy and Titus, sometimes called the pastorals, cannot have been written by Paul, and 2 Thessalonians, somewhat of a summary of 1 Thessalonians, is not from Paul's hand. Hebrews, which at one time carried the superscription as a letter of Paul, is not only not a Pauline composition, it is also not a letter but a sermon.

The resemblance between Jack McKee and Paul does not stop with their conversions. As a Pharisee, Paul knew the Torah, the law. As a physician, Jack is not only a member of a practice, but he is known for his specialty in heart and lungs. After Paul is converted, he comes to understand that the law, while it served the purpose God once intended, has been surpassed by the teaching of Jesus Christ. Paul says that those who follow Jesus have been freed from the law, which kills, but given life in the Spirit. Likewise, once Jack is changed by his experiences of cancer and being a patient, he sees, especially with the help of June Ellis, that he's out of contact with himself and his patients. But he changes. He becomes both doctor and patient to those whom he serves. And he puts in motion the steps which are necessary to insure that his residents are not as out of touch with their patients as he once was.

Jack's bold move to dismiss his doctor, Leslie Abbott, and go to the man whom he has made the butt of his jokes, Eli Bloomfield, signals that he has left behind the old man he was and has discovered that he has become a new person. His new-person status is confirmed as he prepares his residents to be patients for three days. Paul refers to this as putting on Christ, much like the residents put on patients' clothes. Through baptism, one dies to a former way of life and rises to a new life in Christ. Baptism signifies that one is dead to sin, freed from sin. Jack, through his cancer surgery, dies--put under anesthesia--to his former hard, uncaring, unsympathetic, non-understanding self and is rehabilitated into a new man who, by touching the lives of Mr. Mavis, Ann, Nicky, his residents, and his partners in their practice, makes a difference.

In this capacity, Jack is a reconciler, especially with his wife, Ann. He brings them together, just as he had kept them apart. He reconciles his past with Murray, Eli, and Ann, attempting to fix relationships that have gone awry. Paul writes of God reconciling the world through Jesus Christ. Whatever may have separated God from people does so no more. Whatever separated Jack from people has been removed. God, according to Paul, poured grace on the world. Jack, with June's help, poured love and brought together lots of people.

The most powerful scene of reconciliation occurs after Jack has returned home and is recuperating from his surgery. He will not let Ann walk away from him as he had walked away from her. In a sense, the whistle she gave him becomes the vehicle for bringing them together. He has come face to face with his own weakness, embraced it, and been altered by it. Out of his weakness he finds Ann and urges her to do the same. Paul writes about finding his strength in his weakness. He says that when he was weak, then he was strong. God works through human weakness and not through human power. June is the shining example of this. No one has the right to condemn another person, because all of us are equally sinners in need of redemption.

Jack's advice to his residents about going in, fixing the problem, and getting out is transformed. His warning to them about being involved with their patients turns one hundred eighty degrees. Once he experiences the distance between doctor and patient, such as that between Abbott and himself, Jack desires unity. June teaches him that compassion fosters unity. Paul speaks of the unity of those who follow Jesus as members of Christ's body. The body of Christ, animated by the Spirit, is one. It is a unity the cancer patients show Jack when June announces the death of Barbara. Each member possesses special gifts given to him or her for the good of the whole. By serving the needs of each other, the members of the body of Christ serve Christ, whose body they are. Jack, a healer, only understands the power of his gift when he becomes the patient who needs to be healed.

Jack's previous way of life, one marked by his uncaring and uncharitable attitude toward people, his arrogance and his pride, is reversed in his new way of life. He learns the meaning of love and truth through June's patience with him in teaching him how really to live, how to be honest, and how to dance. Jack learns the meaning of love through

Mr. Mavis, who is not afraid to embrace him and tell him how much he trusts him. He learns the meaning of love through Eli, who forgives him for the way Jack has treated him in the past and willingly gives up his day off to perform the surgery on Jack. All these people are incarnations of Paul's understanding that love is patient and kind, that it is the greatest of virtues, that we bear each other's burdens because we love, and we forgive each other's faults because love overflows in us.

Jack, who before his voice-threatening cancer trusted no one but himself and his own abilities, learns to trust others. He has to believe that his doctors, Abbott and Reed, can help him. He learns to trust Eli, and later imitates him, when it becomes clear that he must have surgery. He trusts June when she teaches him the freedom of dance. In Pauline terms, Jack learns to walk by faith and not by sight. Paul writes about professing faith in God and Jesus Christ and living according to it. Then, what is seen is no longer one's guide for life. What is believed is one's guide for living. Jack demonstrates that he has embraced a new way of living.

Before Jack was diagnosed with cancer, he relied upon his expertise in medicine. After he is healed, he rejects his own wisdom and begins to see how smart his patients and partners are. Paul writes about the wisdom of the world in terms of it being folly. He says that it is unable to figure out or recognize what God has done in Christ. Preaching a crucified savior, who has delivered the world from corruption, makes no sense to a world blinded by its own light. At first for Jack learning from his patients was not an option. After he becomes a patient, learning from those he serves becomes his choice.

From all appearances, Jack was fully alive before his cancer. He was a valued member of a medical practice. He lived in a nice home. He had a wife and a son. Jack had it all. But inside, he was dead. He only comes alive after he brushes against cancer and the possibility of losing his voice. Through his experiences leading up to his surgery and flowing from it, Jack rises from the dead to a new life. He leaves Abbott behind. He tells Murray that he can't and won't back him when the lawsuit comes to court. He holds the hand of a nurse. And he begins to practice what he learned as a patient. Now he is alive.

Often Paul writes about the new life that baptism begins and that will culminate in resurrection to new life on the other side of final death. Paul doesn't know what that new life is like, but he believes that Jesus Christ experienced it and that everyone who follows his way will experience it, too. That's what Paul calls the gospel or good news. It was good news to Jack, and it is good news for everyone.

Eli, Jack's partner and surgeon, illustrates Paul's understanding of the body of the Christ. Eli uses his gift as a doctor for the good of his patients. In the dialogue between Jack and Eli in the locker room, Jack tells Eli about the new man he has become. Eli recognizes this when he forgives Jack. Later, Jack imitates Eli's manner of speaking to his unconscious patients while Jack does heart replacement surgery on Mr. Mavis. Both Eli and Jack, like Paul, find that their existence is for others and not for themselves.

Exercises and Questions for Discussion

1. Outline the plot of "The Doctor" by scene. For each scene indicate its importance to the whole story and what purpose it serves. What scenes serve as the pivot point for the film?

2. After reading Paul's letters to the Romans, 1 and 2 Corinthians, Galatians, Philippians, 1 Thessalonians, and Philemon, what major ideas do you discover that parallel scenes in the movie?

3. Prepare a definition of each of the following Pauline terms: justification, righteousness, redemption, reconciliation, salvation, reckon, grace, sanctification, atonement, victory, and resurrection. What scene, words, incidents in the film can you use as an example that illustrates the meaning of each Pauline term?

4. For each of the following characters in the film, explain what Pauline thought, concept, or theological point he or she best represents: Jack McKee, Ann McKee, June Ellis, Eli Bloomfield, Leslie Abbott, Murray, Mr. Mavis, Nicky McKee.

5. Identify a major point which Paul makes and with which you strongly agree. Explain why you agree with Paul.

6. Identify a major point which Paul makes and with which you strongly disagree. Explain why you disagree with Paul.

8. What do you think is the major truth which Paul attempts to communicate through his letters? Is this truth one that endures? Explain.

9. What is the significance of Jack receiving June's letter after his surgery and recovery? Why does he go to the roof of the hospital to read it?

10. We don't discover the city in which the film is set until the end. What is the setting? Why is it significant that the movie-maker chose to wait until the end to tell us the location?

Teaching the Book of Revelation

Pale Rider

"Which is more powerful: the force of good or the force of evil?" That's a question which people have been trying to answer for hundreds of years. It was a question which the author of the Book of Revelation attempted to answer near the end of the first century, as followers of Jesus believed that God's force of good was more powerful, but they experienced the Roman occupation government, the force of evil, as being powerful enough to persecute them mercilessly.

As Christians experienced the chaos of their first-century world and were persecuted by Rome, the anonymous author of the Book of Revelation defiantly declares that the kingdom of the world has become the kingdom of God and of the Messiah, who will reign forever. The kingdom of God is more powerful.

The literary genre called apocalyptic portrays the huge force of evil oppressing the tiny force of good. However, in the end, God's good will trample and imprison all that is evil, and those who remain faithful will live forever.

Apocalyptic literature was written during a time of crisis to offer hope to an oppressed people. The writer sees the world rushing toward a tragic climax, and there is no hope, other than through divine intervention, to save it. The author of apocalyptic literature finds hope in the future, when God will intervene, destroy the wickedness of this world, and establish a new world, a new age of order. Such literature was needed during times of crisis to offer hope to people who felt oppressed and lost. It offers an alternate view of reality in the midst of a crisis that is either real or perceived.

The apocalypticist views the world in dualistic terms. In the world above, the good God lives, and in the world below, people live and are facing a crisis in which it looks like the beast, evil, Satan, or wickedness will be the victor. The apocalyptic author believes that salvation from crisis, or chaos, or war, or despair comes only from beyond human history or beyond linear time, from the world above. When God intervenes, the world above is united to the world below and evil proves that it is no contest for God.

Once evil is destroyed by divine intervention, people living in a crisis will be saved. Apocalyptic is designed to offer hope to those who suffer for whatever reason by providing a vision of a new world which is divinely ordered. By reading the author's narrative of good destroying evil, the reader obtains hope that the worldly crisis in which he or she is involved will soon pass away and all order will be restored. Thus, an apocalyptic work elicits faithfulness from the reader. It tells him or her to stay calm, not to panic, and to remain faithful. God will take care of the rest.

"Pale Rider" (Warner Bros., 1985) can help students understand some of the aspects of the unique genre called apocalyptic. The title of the film comes from the Book of Revelation, the Christian Bible's contribution to the genre. The visionary sees four horses each with a rider. The fourth is "a pale green horse!" Its rider's name was Death (Revelation 6:8). Thus, just from the title of the film, students can conclude that it is about a man riding a pale horse and inflicting death.

The film begins with a scene of high mountains, traditionally the dwelling place of gods. From the mountains, which are partially covered with snow, emerge twelve horsemen riding hard and fast down the valley, through the trees, and across a river. The number twelve signifies both the tribes of Israel and the apostles of Jesus. It represents a group chosen for a particular purpose. As the horsemen get closer to their destination, the camp of the tinpaners, the sound of the galloping hooves deafens the ears of the hearer (viewer).

In the camp of miners, called tinpaners because they pan for gold instead of using other methods, children are playing, men are mining and sluicing, a dog licks the face of a young man, and a woman hangs laundry on a line to dry. The camp is the epitome of domesticity and life, which is about to be attacked.

The horsemen pass through the camp, shooting their guns in the air, knocking over fences, cabins, and tents, knocking over people, trampling everything underfoot, killing a milk cow and a small dog belonging to a girl, and scaring everyone before leaving. As the tinpaners emerge from their hiding places to assess their loses, the girl, Megan Wheeler (Sydney Penny), mourns her dead dog, buries it in the forest, and marks the grave with a stick.

Then Megan prays what the viewer recognizes as Psalm 23: "The Lord is my shepherd. I shall not want." But she interrupts her prayer with commentary, saying, "But I do want." Then, continuing with the psalm and alternating with commentary, she says, "He leadeth me beside still waters. He restoreth my soul." Commentary: "But they killed my dog." Prayer: "Yea, though I walk through the valley of the shadow of death, I shall fear no evil." Commentary: "But I am afraid." Prayer: For thou art with me. Thy rod and thy staff--they comfort me." Commentary: "But I need a miracle." Prayer: "Thy loving kindness and mercy shall follow me all the days of my life." Commentary: "If you exist." Prayer: "And I shall dwell in the house of the Lord forever." Commentary: "I'd like to get more of this life first. If you don't help us, we're all going to die. Please. Just one miracle." Prayer: "Amen."

Not only does Megan's prayer and commentary disclose that she and the tinpaner's camp in which she lives is in a crisis and needs divine intervention, but she and those with whom she lives are reaching a point of despair. Their world, their camp in Carbon Canyon, representing the force of good, has just been destroyed by the twelve horsemen, representing the force of evil. And it looks like evil may win the day.

Except that out of the snow-covered mountains and over the snow-dusted meadows there rides another man on a speckled gray and white horse. Dressed in a dark gray coat and wearing a black hat, the stranger heads to the town of LaHood, California, named after the man who mines the earth with high-powered water canons: Coy LaHood. The small town consists of one street with three or four stores on either side.

Hull Barret (Michael Moriarity), the weak leader of the Carbon Canon settlement, declares that he is not quitting in the face of the destruction wreaked upon his people. He heads to town, even though his fellow tinpaners ask him if that is a smart move to make "after what happened last time." After arriving in LaHood in his buckboard, Barret goes to the general store to buy supplies needed to fix up the camp. Four men watch him. The proprietor tells him that he's a fool for coming to town to which Barret replies that Coy LaHood doesn't own him.

After gathering all the supplies he needs, Barret walks out of the store to his wagon, while each of the four men grab ax handles from a container in front of the store, surround Barret, and taunt him. The man on the pale horse watches from afar, but the wind blows and he disappears. As the men begin to strike Barret with the wooden handles, some of the business people of the town stare out their windows at the beating taking place in the street. Just as one of the men is about to set fire to

Barret's wagon, the man who had been watching from afar throws a bucket of water on the man with the match, saying, "You shouldn't play with matches."

He is called "Preacher" (Clint Eastwood). He grabs the last ax handle and proceeds to beat every one of Barret's opponents, striking all of them and leaving the street strewn with aching bodies. When he has finished, he comments on the hickory axe handle. Then, as he starts to walk away, Barret, who crawled under the wagon for protection, thanks him.

As Preacher rides out of town, Barret follows him in his wagon, catches up with him, and invites him to use one of his two rooms in his cabin in Carbon Canyon. Preacher accepts. On the way there, Barret meets Ulrich Linquist, who's moving out and leaving the canyon.

In Megan's home, while she reads from the Book of Revelation, her mother, Sarah Wheeler (Carrie Snodgrass), stands at the stove and cooks. Megan reads,

> And power was given to him that sat thereon to take peace from the earth. And that they should kill one another. And there was given unto him a great sword. And when he had opened the third seal, I heard the third beast say, "Come and see."

Sarah interrupts Megan's reading to ask her to get butter and syrup for her.
Megan continues,

> And I beheld and, lo, a black horse. And he that sat on him had a pair of balances in his hand. And I heard a voice in the midst of the four beasts say, "A measure of wheat for a penny and three measures of barley for a penny. And see thou hurt not the oil and the wine." And when he had opened the fourth seal, I heard the voice of the fourth beast say, "Come and see." And I looked. And, behold, a pale horse and his name that sat on him was death. And hell followed with him.

Throughout the reading from the Book of Revelation, the camera has repeatedly focused out of the window of the Wheelers' cabin. Just as Megan reads the words about "a pale horse," the man who had helped Barret in LaHood, Preacher, appears and is framed by the window. Both Megan and Sarah look through the window and stare at him.

The passage read by Megan from the Book of Revelation serves as an outline or a prophecy for the rest of the film. Peace has vanished from Carbon Canyon, and LaHood's men are killing tinpaners and forbidding them to go to town. The rider of the black horse carries a scale which is not balanced. Evil outweighs good. But the rider of the pale horse has appeared, and he will bring death to all who oppose good. Those who confront him will think that they have entered hell.

There is something mysterious about the pale rider who helped Barret defeat LaHood's evil men in town. As Barret makes the now shirtless man feel comfortable in his room, offering him a towel after he washes his face in preparation for dinner, Barret notices a pattern of six scars on the man's back. They are the result of the healing of gunshot wounds. There are six, because six is an incomplete number. In other words, the man may have been shot six times, but he isn't dead!

Meanwhile, Barret tells Megan and Sarah about the man and how he saved his life. They discuss what's happening to their colony in Carbon Canyon. Megan, who is fourteen years old, declares that she is not leaving until LaHood's men are whipped. They continue to talk about the man and wonder if he is a hired gun. Suddenly, the door opens and the man enters the room wearing an episcopal-style collar and black rabat. Barret, Sarah, and Megan are shocked. The man picks up a bottle and pours himself a shot of whiskey. All Barret can say is, "I'll be damned!" As they seat themselves around the table, Megan asks the man to say grace, which he does, and to which all three respond "Amen." The viewer concludes that this is no ordinary minister, who reveals his name to be merely "Preacher."

Now, the camera contrasts Carbon Canyon with LaHood's camp and mining operation. LaHood uses hydro power to blast away dirt, mud, and rocks. Only men work in the camp under the direction of LaHood's son, Josh (Christopher Penn). Their dark clothes match the dreariness of the camp. As the trio, each wearing a bandage or bearing a wound of some kind, reports to Josh about what happened to them in town, he calls a huge and tall man from his tent and instructs him to accompany Josh, who has decided to pay a visit to Carbon Canyon.

In Carbon Canyon, Barret, while taking Preacher on a tour of the camp, explains to him how LaHood uses hydro power for mining and how he has been persecuting the tinpaners. LaHood, who has no lawful right to Carbon Canyon, wants to mine it, but the only way he can lay claim to the land is if the tinpaners leave. Megan appears in the scene and tells Preacher that LaHood's men killed her dog and her grandfather.

Preacher asks about local law enforcement. Barret tells him that LaHood "owns" or controls everyone, and, if there were a lawman, La-Hood would own him, too. Barret explains that he takes care of Megan and Sarah, whose husband abandoned her, since Megan's grandfather died of a heart attack after a previous raid of their camp by LaHood's men.

In a surprise move to Barret, Preacher asks to be put to work, saying, "Spirit ain't worth spit without a little exercise." Barret points to a huge rock in the middle of the stream flowing through Carbon Canyon and indicates that under it there might be gold. After handing a sledge hammer to Preacher, who begins to strike the rock with it, Barret gets another hammer and joins in. Megan and Sarah watch from a cliff above, and others members of the camp watch from their front porches and yards.

Megan points out the arrival of Josh LaHood and the big man with him. Both are on horseback. Josh asks Barret about the new man in their camp. Barret tells him that Preacher is their new preacher. Josh tells Preacher to get out of Carbon Canyon. Preacher replies, "Well, there's a lot of sinners hereabouts. You wouldn't want me to leave before I finish my work, would you?" Such words only inflame Josh, who orders the big man to dismount.

As he walks toward Preacher, the big man rolls up his shirt sleeves, picks up a sledge hammer, emits a loud groan, raises the hammer, and strikes the rock in the middle of the stream, splitting it into two pieces. All watch in amazement. When the big man begins to strike Preacher with the sledge hammer, Preacher blocks his blow with his own hammer, hits the man on the forehead with the hammer and then strikes him in the groin with it. The big man doubles over, moaning in pain. Preacher helps him to his horse, tells him to put ice on his bruises, and watches as Josh and he ride away. Preacher comments, "The Lord certainly does work in mysterious ways." The men of the colony join Preacher and Barret and gather around the rock in the steam. Each wields a sledge hammer toward the rock. They are united in the task ahead. Preacher has bonded them into a force of good ready to face the power of evil.

And the power of evil arrives. Pulled by a black engine belching black smoke, the train arrives in LaHood, and Coy LaHood emerges from it dressed in black pants, black vest, black coat, and black hat. From the color of his wardrobe there is little doubt which force he represents. Greeted by his son, Josh, and several other men, Josh fills in his father about what has happened in their mining camp while LaHood was in Sacramento, about their raid on Carbon Canyon, and about the "stranger" who is now living there.

When they tell LaHood that the stranger is a preacher, he angrily and rhetorically asks, "You let a preacher in Carbon Canyon?" Then he continues by reminding them that before he left for Sacramento that the tinpans had all but given up and their spirit was nearly broken. He states, "And a man without spirit is whipped. But a preacher--he could give them faith." Then, LaHood tells them that with one ounce of faith the tinpans will dig in deeper than ticks on a dog. Indeed, LaHood knows what he is up against when faced with an apocalyptic force of good. Faith inspires a spirit of hopefulness. And with hope the tinpaners will not leave Carbon Canyon--at least not willingly.

LaHood tells his son and the other men to bring the preacher to him. But then, after thinking about it for a moment, he changes his mind, saying, "Don't want to give them a martyr." Again, LaHood knows that the death of one man, standing firm in his conviction, can give hope to many who are faltering.

LaHood tells Josh about his meeting in Sacramento with the politicians, some of whom want to do away with hydraulic mining. LaHood says that they call it "raping the land." LaHood says that they have to move fast, before the politicians can act, that the tinpaners have to go, and, that he has to find a way to deal with their preacher.

In the Wheeler home, Megan asks her mother, Sarah, about her marriage and her parents' reaction when she told them who she was going to marry. Sarah reveals that she is not sure if she wants to marry Hull Barret. Then Megan asks her if preachers get married. Sarah replies that she can see no reason they do not. Their conversation is interrupted by Barret, who, finding a four-ounce gold nugget under the rock in the stream, rushes up to the cabin and shows it to Sarah. Barret wants to celebrate. Megan suggests they go to town. They know what might happen if they do. Preacher appears and says, "We've got as much right to go to town as the next person."

Barret drives the wagon over a snow dusted road to town. In the front seat with him sits Preacher, and in the back are Megan and Sarah. LaHood's main street is covered with snow. Barret parks the wagon and goes to the general store to settle his account there with his gold nugget, while the others wait in the wagon. To Preacher Megan points out Josh, who walks toward the wagon and tells Preacher that his father wants to see him. Preacher gets down from the wagon and goes with Josh to his father's office in which are LaHood and several of his men.

LaHood invites Preacher to come to town and make the town his parish. LaHood tells him that he will build a new church for him. Preach-er responds that he would be tempted by an offer like that. LaHood agrees. Preacher says that then he would want new clothes, and LaHood says that he would have them tailor-made. Then, Preacher says that he would want money, and LaHood tells him he would make him a wealthy man. Preacher concludes, "That's why it wouldn't work. You can't serve God and mammon both--mammon being money."

LaHood, realizing that he has met his match, states that he opened that country and made the town what it is, bringing in jobs and industry. He says that he built an empire with his own two hands and never asked help from anyone. He concludes, "Those squatters, reverend, are standing in the way of progress." All Preacher asks is, "Theirs or yours?"

Now getting angry, LaHood shows Preacher a document from Sacramento giving him the mineral rights to Carbon Canyon. Preacher says that he'd exercised those rights by now if he had them legally. The people there have legal claim, and LaHood can't mine the land until they're gone. Preacher tells LaHood that his document isn't worth the paper it's printed on. Otherwise, LaHood wouldn't be trying to bribe him. LaHood tells Preacher that he has twenty-four hours to pack up and leave or his men will ride into Carbon Canyon. He vows to fight for what he claims is his. Then, he threatens Preacher by saying that he will call in a law officer named Stockburn, and he will take care of this problem.

Preacher asks LaHood if he will buy out the claims in Carbon Canyon. LaHood says he will at one hundred dollars a claim. But Preacher asks for a thousand dollars a claim. LaHood laughs, but Preacher remind him that Stockburn and his deputies will cost him a lot more than that. Then, Preacher asks him how much it is worth for him to have a clear conscience. LaHood agrees to one thousand dollars a claim, but wants the tinpaners out of Carbon Canyon in twenty-four hours.

Barret emerges from the general store, goes to his wagon, and from Sarah and Megan finds out that Preacher was summoned to La-Hood's office. Just as Barret is ready to head toward the office, Preach-er emerges. After returning to Carbon Canyon, Barret and Preacher join the men around a campfire that evening to discuss LaHood's offer to buy each claim for one thousand dollars. One of them asks Preacher what he thinks, but he tells them to sleep on it and decide in the morning. However, he does relay LaHood's threat to call in Stockburn if they refuse to sell their claims.

Preacher explains that Stockburn is no ordinary marshal, that he travels with six deputies, that they uphold whatever law pays them the most, and that killing is a way of life with them. He says that he is telling them this because if they decide against LaHood's offer, they will meet Stockburn and his deputies. One of the men asks, "You know this Stockburn?" Preacher responds, "I've heard of him."

The men continue to discuss LaHood's offer. They evaluate their ability to fight LaHood as well as the pros and cons of starting over somewhere else. Barret emerges as a leader of the tinpaners, urging them to see their problem from a moral point of view. He tells them that if they are in Carbon Canyon only for money, then they are no better than LaHood. Barret reminds them that if any one of them found a thousand dollar gold nugget, he would not quit but, instead, use the money to provide for his family.

In a long speech appealing to each man's personal integrity, Barret reminds the men that they came to Carbon Canyon to raise their families. He tells them that Carbon Canyon is their home and dream. He reminds them that they have sunk roots there and buried members of their families there. He asks them if they are going to take a thousand dollars and leave the graves of their family members unattended. Appealing to their higher sense of morality, he tells the men that they owe their dead more than that and they owe themselves more than that. He asks them, "... If we sell out now, what price do we put on our dignity next time: two thousand dollars? Less? Or just the best offer?"

Just as the men had joined Preacher and Barret earlier and signified their bond together by striking the rock in the stream with sledge hammers, so now, gathered in a circle around the fire, they vote to stay in Carbon Canyon, to reject LaHood's offer, and to fight for their dignity. Once all make their verbal pledge to each other, they leave the campfire and return to their homes.

Preacher takes a walk in the woods, where he finds Megan standing near the place where she buried her dog. After she points out the grave to him, he tells her that it is hallowed ground. Then, Megan tells him that she said a prayer for her dog after the raid. She states, "I prayed for a miracle." Preacher says, "Well, maybe someday you'll get that miracle." Megan informs him, "It was the day you arrived."

However, Megan more than believes that Preacher is the answer to her prayer for deliverance from the power of her evil enemies. As hinted earlier in the film in the dialogue between Megan and her mother, Megan tells him that she thinks she loves him. Preacher tells her that there's nothing wrong with that. He adds that if there were more love in the world, there probably would be a lot less dying.

The general love of humanity which Preacher speaks about is not what Megan has in mind. She states that there can't be anything wrong with making love. Preacher, keeping the conversation on the general level, declares that he thinks it is best to practice loving for a while before she thinks about making love. Megan, who can't be sidetracked, says, "If I practice just loving for a while, will you teach me the other?" Emphatically, Preacher answers, "Megan, most folks abound here kinda associate that with marriage."

Now, Megan appeals to her age, saying, "I'll be fifteen next month. Mama was married when she was fifteen. Will you teach me then?" Preacher answers, "Ninety-nine out of a hundred men would be proud to say yes to that, Megan, but a young girl, young woman, like you --you wouldn't want to spend your future with a man like me." Megan asks, "Why not?" And Preacher replies, "That's just the way it is."

Megan, who begins to get agitated by Preacher's unwillingness to love her in the manner she wants tells him that she doesn't understand, that she doesn't believe him, and that what he is saying isn't true and isn't fair. Preacher cajoles her, urging her to trust. "If you love someone, you gotta try to trust that what they tell you is true," he says. Megan asks, "Even if it means they can't be together?" Preacher, taking the wider vision, tells her, "Someday a young man is going to come along, the right man, and none of this will matter anymore."

Then, attempting to end the conversation, Preacher tells her that her mother is probably worried about where she is. However, that statement only adds fuel to Megan's fire, as she states that she thinks he loves her mother. Preacher says that her mother, like her, is a fine woman. But Megan, who has paid attention to her mother's manners around Preacher, says that she has observed the way he looks at her mother and the way she looks at him. She tells him that he can have her mother and that she never wants to see him again. As Megan runs back home, Preacher calls her name. She stops, turns around, and says, "I hope you die, and I hope you go to hell."

The next morning, Preacher, dressed in his collar, rides through and inspects LaHood's mining operations. When he sees Josh, he instructs him, "Tell you father they (the tinpaners) turned him down." Then, he continues to ride through LaHood's camp.

The train arrives in town as Preacher watches from a distance. After a brief stop, it continues, but Preacher disappears. The station-master, who saw Preacher on the other side of the tracks, sends a tele-graph message delivered by one of LaHood's men.

Back in Carbon Canyon, Barret discovers that Preacher is gone, and he tells Sarah and Megan. Sarah says that he probably went to tell LaHood about the vote the men had taken the night before. Then, Barret and Sarah argue about the way the men voted and Barret's role in urging them to vote to stay. Sarah declares that the men were counting on Preacher for help, but now he's gone. Their conversation is interrupted by a huge explosion upstream. As all rush out of their cabins and tents, they see that the river has been dammed by LaHood's men. Sarah tells Barret that if he would have accepted LaHood's offer, this never would have happened.

In a pivotal scene, Preacher goes to a bank and hands the teller a key to a safe deposit box. He opens the box to reveal two handguns and a holster. After removing the weapons, he drops his collar in the box. Drastic times demand drastic measures, so the viewer concludes. La-Hood's evil violence will have to be met with a comparable good violence if he is to be defeated. In other words, a showdown is about to occur.

In a series of scenes, Barret, who has begun to grow a beard--a sign of a lifestyle change--informs the other men in Carbon Canyon that Preacher is gone. While they are trying to decide what to do next, Stockburn and his six deputies are seen riding over the snow-dusted plain toward LaHood. Then, Spider Conway (Doug McGrath) finds a huge gold nugget in the dry creek bed and wants to celebrate by going to town. Barret finds Sarah and apologizes for anything he may have said or done, asks Sarah to take Megan and leave Carbon Canyon with him and start over, and asks Sarah to give him the truth about their relationship. Sarah tells Barret that there is a possibility of them getting together, so he talks more about leaving and beginning again. Clearly, Barret has joined the rest of the men in the canyon in their state of despair without Preacher.

Meanwhile, Megan, who has asked Barret if she could borrow his horse for a ride, travels to LaHood's mining site. Josh, who is on horseback patrolling the operations, finds her, shows her around, and explains how hydromining works. Megan, looking out over the wrecked landscape, says, "It looks like hell." Josh, dismounting, takes Megan from her horse and carries her toward a group of men in the camp. He forces a kiss on her, then, falling down on her on the ground, tries to rape her, first tearing her dress.

Just at that moment, Megan is rescued. Preacher arrives, fires one shot in the air, and Josh stops. All the men, who had been urging Josh on, stand in fear of Preacher, since they have seen what he did to four of their number previously. However, Josh draws his gun. Preacher draws his faster, fires, and knocks the gun out of Josh's hand. But Josh is not smart. He attempts to pick up the gun from the ground, and Preacher shoots him in the hand. Then, in anger, Preacher shoots the gun several more times as a warning, helps Megan get behind him on his horse, and gallops back to Carbon Canyon.

Conway, who has gone to town to celebrate his good luck, stands in the middle of LaHood's street holding the gold nugget in one hand and a half-empty bottle of whiskey in the other. In his drunken state, he harasses LaHood, who is standing at his office window. Conway's two sons also watch through the window in the general store, where they are gathering supplies.

In LaHood's office is Stockburn (John Russell) and his six deputies. While Conway is in the street shouting, LaHood explains the situation concerning Preacher to Stockburn. Then, LaHood describes Preacher to Stockburn, adding, "His eyes--something strange about them." Stockburn declares, "Sounds like a man I once knew." LaHood: "He recognized your name." But Stockburn says, "Couldn't be. The man I'm thinking about is dead."

Conway, who has fallen over in the street, stands up as Stockburn and his deputies emerge from LaHood's office. All seven of them are dressed in long, dark cream-colored coats with lighter cream-colored hats. They form a single line on the wooden sidewalk in front of La-Hood's office, three on one side of Stockburn and three on the other side, facing Conway. Simultaneously, all of them pull back their coats and put their hands on their guns. Stockburn fires at Conway's feet in order to make him dance. As Conway's sons rush out of the general store at the sound of gunfire, all the deputies begin firing at Conway's feet. He jumps around from one foot to another in order to avoid being hit. Next, Stockburn shoots the bottle out of his hand, then the rock with the gold in it out of the other hand. Then, all seven of them shoot him multiple times, filling his body with bullets from head to toe. Conway falls down in the street, and Stockburn, firing one final bullet right into the middle of his forehead, tells Conway's sons to take back their father to Carbon Canyon and tell Preacher to meet him in town the next morning. Perfect evil violence, in terms of seven--Stockburn and his six deputies--seems to be in control of the town of LaHood.

As Preacher delivers Megan to Carbon Canyon, he's told about the damming of the stream and Conway's death in town. He drops off Megan at her home, where Sarah sees his holster and gun. Barret arrives and spies the holster and gun and leads Preacher to the wagon with the body of Conway in it. Conway's sons deliver Stockburn's message to Preacher. One of the men asks Preacher if he knew Stockburn.

But Preacher, not answering his question, attempts to solidify them as a group again. He tells them that their vote to stay shows courage. He reminds them that they voted to stick together and that's what they should do. Using Spider Conway as an example, he says that he made a mistake by going into town alone. "A man alone is easy prey. Only by standing together are you going to be able to beat the LaHoods of the world. No matter what happens tomorrow, don't you forget that."

Later, while Preacher cleans and prepares his guns for the coming battle between evil and good, Sarah comes to his room. Preacher asks about Megan, whom Sarah says is feeling better. Then, Sarah says that she knew he was a gunfighter. They talk about him going to town the next day to meet Stockburn, and Sarah asks him not to go. Preacher tells her, "It's an old score. Time to settle it." Sarah, who tells him that she wishes she could change his mind, also tells him that when he left (to go get his guns), his leaving reminded her of her husband who had left her. Then, she reveals to him that she has feelings for him, but she states that she needs a man who would never leave her, and she knows that he will leave. He affirms her statement.

Sarah informs Preacher that she is going to marry Barret, but, moving toward him and preparing to kiss him, she says, "This is just so I won't spend the rest of my life wondering." As she moves toward the door, a voice can be heard in the distance, calling, "Preacher. Preacher." She asks about it. Preacher answers, "A voice from the past." He tells her to close the door. She asks, "Who are you? Who are you really?" Preacher answers, "It really doesn't matter, does it?" Sarah says, "No." And the voice is heard again in the distance.

The next morning, Preacher mounts his horse and, just as he is about to begin riding, he discovers Barret, who is already mounted on his horse, waiting for him and holding a buffalo rifle in one hand. After telling Preacher that he wants to go with him, Preacher tells him that his rifle will not be of much use but he can follow. They head toward La-Hood's mining operations, where they toss lit sticks of dynamite at the equipment and the buildings in the camp, blowing up everything. Josh, emerging from one of the cabins with a rifle, prepares to shoot Preacher in the back when the big man, whom Preacher had whipped, comes up from behind him and knocks the rifle from his hand. Tipping his hat toward the big man in appreciation, Preacher rides on out of the camp.

As both he and Barret continue lighting sticks of dynamite and destroying LaHood's operation, one of the lit sticks falls out of Preacher's hand. Quickly, Barret dismounts, picks it up, and tosses it over a cliff. While Barret is performing this good deed, Preacher takes his horse and gallops away, telling Barret that he is a good man and that he should take care of Sarah and Megan As Barret is left standing there, he says good-bye to Preacher.

Meanwhile, in Sarah's and Megan's cabin, Megan awakens and she and her mother discuss how they both love Preacher. Sarah discloses that she said good-bye to him, but Megan didn't get a chance. She runs out of the house.

Preacher arrives in LaHood, rides down the street, goes to the general store, gets a cup of coffee, and tells the proprietor and his wife to leave. LaHood's men, who were standing near the street and watching the Preacher ride in, go to the general store, see him sitting inside drinking his coffee with his back to the window, draw their guns, and go in firing. After they run out of bullets shooting up the place, they discover that he's not there! But, while they are attempting to reload their guns, he re-appears. Two of them run away, but he kills four of them who stay. Then, he walks out into the street, turns around, and reloads his gun.

LaHood and Stockburn, who have been watching all this from LaHood's office window, asks Stockburn about what Preacher is doing. Stockburn answers, "Inviting us to join him." So, Stockburn and his deputies go outside and stand in a row as they did when confronting Conway, but Preacher has disappeared again, leaving only his hat sitting on the ground in the middle of the street. Stockburn tells the deputies to fan out and to find him. The six deputies begin their search through the town, but Preacher kills them one at a time until all six are dead.

Then, he steps out into the middle of the street, picks up his hat, puts it on his head, and faces Stockburn, who is standing in the middle of the street at its other end. As Preacher walks toward Stockburn, he re-cognizes him, saying, "You! You!" Stockburn draws his gun, but Preacher is faster. Preacher fires six bullets into Stockburn's chest. As he begins to fall face down to the ground, the viewer notices that the pattern formed by the bullet holes in Stockburn's back matches the one seen on Preacher's back. Then, just as Stockburn is about to roll over dead, Preacher fires one more bullet into the middle of his forehead, matching the bullet Stockburn had fired into Conway's head. Seven bullets from the good Preacher have defeated evil Stockburn.

But all evil is not yet eliminated. As LaHood continues to watch what Preacher has done to the force he brought into town to stop him, he aims his rifle to shoot Preacher. Barret comes in the back door of La-Hood's office, quickly sizes up the situation, and, aiming and firing his buffalo gun at LaHood, blasts him through the window. Barret, then, goes outside to see Preacher, who rides on his horse out of a stable, stops when he approaches Barret, and says, "Long walk," referring to Barret's walk from LaHood's camp to town. Barret affirms Preacher's statement as he sees the bullet pattern in Stockburn's back and the corpses of the six deputies littering the street. Barret understands. Preacher rides toward the mountains.

Megan arrives in a buckboard and townsfolk come out of hiding to view the carnage. Megan asks Barret where Preacher is, and Barret tells her that he left. But she runs to the end of town and yells, "Preacher, Preacher," the sound of which can be heard echoing through the valley.

"We all love you, Preacher," she says. "I love you." As Preacher rides through the snow-covered meadow, Megan says, "Thank you. Good-bye."

Barret helps Megan get into the wagon, and they head back to Carbon Canyon. They leave a few townsfolk in the street, which is strewn with the seven dead bodies of Stockburn and his six deputies. Meanwhile, Preacher keeps riding into the mountains until he disappears.

There is no doubt that Preacher is a god-figure, who comes from the mountains, the traditional place where gods live, and returns there. He is a Christ-figure, like the lamb who was slain and now lives, who possesses six bullet holes in his back. He once was dead--in fact his name is Death--but the incompleteness of six bullet holes indicates that he isn't totally dead and still lives. He has come back from the dead to complete his work. Thus, while he represents the fourth man on a pale green horse whose name was Death and after whom Hades or hell followed, he is also the Book of Revelation's rider on a white horse who is called Faithful and True and who judges in righteousness and makes war.

Preacher is the savior for whom Megan prayed. He is tempted by LaHood with the offer of religion--the town can be his parish, with the offer of clothes--a position in society, and with the offer of money--wealth. But, like Jesus, Preacher knows that one cannot serve both God and the world. As a man he is tempted with sex, first by Megan and then by Sarah, both of whom profess to love him. He succumbs to none of the temptations, but remains focused on his mission to unite the tinpaners as a community standing against the evil (LaHood's force) in the world.

In fact, Preacher offers himself as a sacrifice to save the tinpaners. His strategy is to defeat the enemy, LaHood's men and Stockburn and his six deputies, one man at a time. When the force of good stands together, then it can beat the LaHoods of the world. When the force of good separates, when there is no community, evil wipes out good one person at a time. Preacher demonstrates that evil has no power when it is not united. First, he eliminates LaHood's men. Then, he picks off the six deputies, one at a time, before confronting Stockburn and killing him with a mortal wound of seven complete bullets. Preacher had been shot only six times and he lived, but the six deputies were killed with one bullet each and Stockburn was killed with seven, one in the middle of the forehead to indicate he was indeed dead.

Preacher, whose eyes fascinate LaHood and are recognized by Stockburn, is the Book of Revelation's rider on a white horse whose eyes are like flames of fire. He has a name no one knows, since throughout the film he is only called Preacher. Once he completes his work of answering Megan's prayer for deliverance, he returns to the world above, signified by the mountains, from which he came. The dualism of the Book of Revelation is clearly mirrored in "Pale Rider."

Megan can be considered a type of zealot, who prays to God for deliverance from the evil force of domination, asking for a miracle. She, a woman, contrasted to all the men, is the only person in the tinpaner's camp who maintains a fighting spirit until Preacher arrives. Repeatedly, she maintains that she will not run away in the face of evil, but she will keep her stand and not leave her home until LaHood's men are defeated.

Some students might also see Megan Wheeler as a type of Mary Magdalen since she tempts the Preacher with sexual favors one time. Moreso, after he rescues her from LaHood's camp and Josh's attempt to rape her, she goes to town looking for him. Like Mary Magdalen looking for the body of Jesus, Megan can't find Preacher, who has returned (died and risen) to the mountains from where he came.

Sarah, Megan's mother, can also be considered a type of Mary Magdalen, since she too tempts Preacher with sex and marriage. She tells him of how much he reminds her of her husband who loved her passionately but abandoned her. She knows that he cannot stay, even though she kisses him. She knows that Hull Barret will make her a better husband.

From another point of view, both Megan and Sarah can be compared to the woman who gives birth to a child destined to rule the nations but sought after by the dragon in the Book of Revelation. Megan prays for the deliverer to come and save the colony, and Preacher is the answer to her prayer. Sarah, who at first doesn't believe in him, comes to understand his ways, declaring him to be a gunfighter and offering him her support. From this point of view, Megan and Sarah are contrasted to the many men in the camp who keep wavering in their allegiance to Preacher as they prepare to confront the dragon, the deceiver of the world, LaHood and his hired gunmen.

Hull Barret is a John the Baptist type of character. He prepares the way for Preacher, after Preacher saves him from a beating with ax handles by LaHood's men in town. He invites Preacher to his cabin, offers him one of the two rooms, and repeatedly rallies the men of Carbon Canyon to follow Preacher's course of action and not sell their claims to LaHood.

Barret, however, also has his moments of doubt, especially when Preacher disappears from the camp for a while. In this regard he is a type of Peter. He follows Preacher, but he is never one hundred percent sure of himself. He joins Preacher with a sledgehammer in breaking up the rock in the center of the stream. He helps Preacher pitch lit sticks of dynamite into LaHood's mining camp to destroy it. He saves Preacher's life by shooting LaHood after the final showdown of Preacher's killing of Stockburn and his six deputies. Preacher's last words to Barret, "Long walk," can be understood to imply that the Christian life is a long and hard journey fraught with doubts and insecurities, as Barret demonstrates throughout the film.

From the Book of Revelation's perspective, Barret can be compared to John, the receiver of God's revelation. Barret receives Preacher into his home before he knows that he is a clergyman. He listens, understands, and learns from Preacher, delivering what he hears to the other men in Carbon Canyon. In the monologue he delivers around the campfire, he gets to the heart of why the tinpaners came to live in Carbon Canyon. After reminding them that their fundamental value is not gold but family, Barret appeals to their human dignity, urging them not to give in to evil but to stand up and face it with the hope of defeating it. In this regard, he is like the Book of Revelation's John who delivers the message of hope to those who were being persecuted by Roman occupation forces near the end of the first century common era.

The Roman occupation forces, called the whore of Babylon in the Book of Revelation, consist of LaHood's men and Stockburn and his deputies. There can be no doubt that LaHood, who first appears getting off a black train belching black smoke and dressed from head to toe in black, is Satan, the first beast, the incarnation of evil. Furthermore, he advocates a method of mining that rapes the land. When his own forces of evil cannot eliminate the tinpaners from Carbon Canyon, he employs the epitome of evil, perfect evil, signified by marshal Stockburn and his sex deputies who follow whatever law pays them the most. Collectively, Stockburn and his deputies represent the second beast. The viewer should not fail to note that the six deputies are incomplete without Stockburn.

Preacher defeats evil by dividing it up and conquering it one man at a time. His force of good, while smaller, is greater than that of evil. It takes only one bullet each for Preacher to kill the six deputies, whereas it took hundreds of bullets for the deputies and Stockburn to kill Conway. Using seven bullets to kill Stockburn, indicates that the Preacher has defeated evil with perfect good.

It is at this point in the film that the viewer discovers himself or herself in a conundrum. When Preacher removes his collar and straps a gun on his hip, he declares that his message of peace and non-violence cannot defeat the power of evil in the world. The only way that evil can be defeated is with its own power--guns and bullets. However, in some ways the Book of Revelation operates off of the same principle. Michael wins the war in heaven against the dragon and his angels. And the rider on a white horse rules the nations with a rod of iron, and with his sharp sword he strikes them down. He conquers and captures the beast and his forces and casts them into the lake of fire.

Students may also notice similarities between all the things made of gold--crowns, lampstands, censer, measuring rod--in the Book of Revelation and the search for gold by miners. Both camps revolve around finding gold, even though Barret makes it clear that the tinpaners value family above gold.

The stream flowing through the middle of the tinpaner's camp in Carbon Canyon is the Book of Revelation's river of life coming from God's temple. The water gives life to trees, animals, men and women and children in the tinpaner's camp until LaHood dams it. LaHood uses water, but he misuses it by destroying the land, raping it of life, and exploiting it for profit. Even with all the water power LaHood has in his camp, there are only men, who don't know how to treat a woman properly and who live in the most dreary of environments. The destruction of LaHood's mining operation by Preacher and Barret is like the fall of Babylon in the Book of Revelation.

The seven bowls of God's wrath, each poured out on the earth in the Book of Revelation, is comparable to Preacher's destruction of Stockburn and his six deputies. Also, they are like the seven kings who make war on the Lamb but, ultimately, are conquered by the Lamb and those called chosen and faithful who follow him. Preacher defeats Stockburn and his six deputies, but Barret kills LaHood.

The Book of Revelation's key of death is paralleled in the film by the key Preacher gives to the bank teller. The key opens his safe deposit box which contains his holster and guns. With them he fulfills the meaning of his name--Death, the rider on a pale horse. Just as Stockburn had sealed Conway with death by firing a bullet into the middle of his forehead, so Preacher seals Stockburn with death by firing his seventh bullet into the middle of his forehead. Indeed, as Sarah had read from the Book of Revelation as Preacher entered the tinpaner's camp, hell followed with him.

Exercises and Questions for Discussion

1. By comparing the title of the film to the Book of Revelation (6:7-8), what can you conclude the film is about even before viewing it? Explain.

2. After reading the entire Book of Revelation in one sitting and watching the movie "Pale Rider," make a list of ten comparisons between the Book of Revelation and the film.

3. Make a list of five comparisons of characters between "Pale Rider" and the Book of Revelation.

4. In "Pale Rider," what is power? Explain. In the Book of Revelation, what is power? Explain.

5. What do you think is the real issue with which "Pale Rider" deals? What do you think is the real issue with which the Book of Revelation deals?

6. How does "Pale Rider" offer hope to people? How does the Book of Revelation offer hope to people.

7. Do you agree with the way the problem is solved in "Pale Rider?" Explain. Do you agree with the way the problem is solved in the Book of Revelation? Explain.

8. Using three examples, compare and contrast the two camps in "Pale Rider." What do you discover?

9. What do you think is the major truth which the movie attempts to communicate? Is this truth one that endures? Explain.

10. What do you think is the major truth which the Book of Revelation attempts to communicate? Is this truth one that endures? Explain.

11. What do you think is the significance of the opening scene of "Pale Rider" in which men on horseback rush toward Carbon Canyon and destroy the tinpaners' camp?

12. Does good always triumph over evil? Give examples to support your answer and explain.

Teaching the Book of Revelation

The Milagro Beanfield War

"Who is running the world?" That's a question which begs for an answer. It was a question which the author of the Book of Revelation attempted to answer near the end of the first century common era as followers of Jesus believed that God was running the world, but the Roman occupation government believed that Caesar was in charge.

That question seems to be asked more intently as groups of people discover themselves to be in a crisis, a chaotic moment in their existence. As Christians are being persecuted by Rome, the anonymous author of the Book of Revelation declares that the kingdom of the world has become the kingdom of God and of the Messiah, who will reign forever. The kingdom of God is now.

The literary genre called apocalyptic is set within a narrative framework in which a human recipient receives a revelation from an out-side-of-this-world being (such as an angel). The revelatory message is attributed to God, who, in the ancient view of the world, lived above the vault of the earth and sent messages down to the earth about the imminent destruction of evil in the world.

Apocalyptic literature was written during a time of crisis or chaos, such as during a period of foreign military occupation; or when a group felt alienated from the rest of society, such as the Jews in their own homeland; or when approaching a millennium, when people were experiencing despair about their world; or during a natural disaster, such as an earthquake or a flood. An apocalyptic writer sees the world as rushing toward a tragic climax, and there is no hope, other than in a divine intervention, to save it. The author of apocalyptic literature finds hope in the future, when God will intervene, destroy the wickedness of the world, and establish a new world, a new age of order. Such literature was needed during times of crisis to offer hope to people who felt oppressed and lost. It offers an alternate view of reality in the midst of a crisis that is either real or perceived.

The human recipient of the revelation receives it in the form of a dream or a vision, the meaning of which is interpreted by an intermediary, usually an angel as in the case of Revelation. The author lives much later than the angel's appearance and writes pseudonymously. That technique lends credibility and postulates authority to the apocalyptic work.

The author of apocalyptic literature does not share our linear notion of time as past, present, and future. In other words, he could not draw a time line and place upon it past, present, and future events. In apocalyptic there is only the present age and the age to come. In the present there is no hope for redemption from evil, but in the age to come there is great hope that God will triumph.

The apocalypticist views the world in dualistic terms. There exists only the world above, where the good God lives with his angels, and the world below, where people live and are facing a crisis in which it looks like the beast, evil, Satan, or wickedness, will be the victor. Sometimes referred to as the horizontal dimension of apocalyptic literature, the apocalyptic author believes that salvation from crisis, or chaos, or war, or despair comes only from beyond human history or beyond linear time. There is also a vertical dimension to this genre, which unites the world above to the world below and offers descriptions of angels and demons going up from earth to heaven or coming down from heaven to earth.

Once evil is destroyed by divine intervention, people living in a crisis will be saved. Apocalyptic is designed to offer hope to those who suffer for whatever reason by providing a vision of a new world which is divinely ordered. By reading the author's narrative of good destroying evil, the reader obtains hope that the worldly crisis in which he or she is involved will soon pass away and all order will be restored. Thus, an apocalyptic work elicits faithfulness from the reader. It tells him or her to stay calm, not to panic, and to remain faithful. God will take care of the rest.

"The Milagro Beanfield War" (Universal, 1988) can help students begin to understand the unique genre that apocalyptic is. The film is set in Milagro, New Mexico, a town at an elevation of 8,400 feet and with a population of 426. Nothing had changed in Milagro, a name meaning "miracle," for 300 years, but something was about to happen.

At sunset, the viewer hears the wind, sees the moon, and watches as the breeze rustles the leaves and blows up a pillar of dirt into a dust devil. Then, a man with a beard, wearing a large sombrero and a blanket appears dancing through town and playing a concertina. He's an angel, who has come to help the people of Milagro deal with the crisis they are about to face.

Next, we are introduced to Amarante Cordova (Carlos Riquelme), an old man, who, after waking up, gets out of bed and thanks God for letting him have another day. He goes outside his small three-room adobe house to draw water from the well and talks to Coyote Angel (Robert Carricart) who is sitting in an old car. Angel tells him, "It's your town that's dying," as the wind is heard and the angel disappears. Meanwhile, Amarante calls his pet pig, who serves the same purpose as a dog--a sign of domestication--but the pig has run off to the home of Joe Mandragon (Chick Vennera) where he pulls down the clothes line.

Next, we meet Ruby Archeleta (Sonya Braga), who owns and operates the local auto repair shop, and Bernie Montoya (Ruben Blades), sheriff in the town, who says, "There is something about this day," as he gets into his patrol car which won't start.

Not too far outside of the town of Milagro, a bulldozer pushes over a tree and a crane hoists into place a huge sign bearing the name "Miracle Valley Recreation Area." It represents the transformation of the area by Ladd Divine (Richard Bradford), a rich land developer. While the sign is put in place, Joe drives up in his old truck and asks Horsethief Shorty (James Gammon), one of Divine's crew members, for a job, but Shorty tells him nothing is available.

A party, celebrating the opening of Miracle Valley, is in full progress at Divine's other development, Dancing Trout Resort. Divine heralds Miracle Valley as the largest leisure-time development in the history of New Mexico.

Meanwhile, Joe goes to the barren bean field once owned by his father and now his. The field is not cultivated because Joe does not have access to water, but water flows through the ditch above his field. The only problem is the water is owned by Divine. As Joe passes the valve which keeps water from flowing into his field, he breaks it with a kick, and the water begins to seep onto his property.

Amarante, who lives nearby, talks to Joe about his father's plans for the bean field. Joe says that his father has been dead for six years, and he's going to sell the property. But Amarante sees the water flowing into the field and Joe standing in it and dipping his hands into it. Joe tells Amarante that he ought to shut off the water, but thinks that he will sleep on it. Back home, Joe kisses his wife, Nancy, greets his children, and reminisces about the relationship he had with his father.

Meanwhile, more trees are bulldozed to make way for development at Miracle Valley and one of Divine's men drives by Joe's bean field and sees the water flowing into it.

Amarante, dressed in a black hat and black pants and a black coat with a sheriff's badge pinned on it, enters the town's bar. The bartender asks him how he is and he replies, "Still living, thanks to God." After a few moments he tells the men in the bar that Joe let water into his father's beanfield. All of the men in the bar get very quiet as Amarante declares, "I'm not saying its good, and I'm not saying its bad."

One man, Martinez, who has only one arm, leaves the bar and goes to the general store where he tells everyone there that Joe is irrigating his father's bean field. Like in the bar, everyone gets extremely quiet. While Joe works in the field, rumors of what he has done circulate throughout Milagro. Even a boy on a bike rides to the site to verify the truth, and Sammy Cantu (Freddy Fender) finds the sheriff at Ruby's garage and tells him what is going on.

Ruby immediately gets into her truck and drives to Joe's field to verify the fact that he is irrigating it. To herself she says, "I knew Joe Mandragon couldn't go through his entire life without attempting at least one great thing." She gets back in her truck and drives away.

After working in his field, Joe returns home to find his three children watching TV. He turns it off and sends them outside while he and Nancy discuss and then argue about his action of irrigating the bean field. He tells her that he is determined to plant the bean field.

However, someone does give a damn, and he is Divine. During a meeting with other officials of the project and of the town, Divine hears about Joe's irrigation of the field, which is a plot of a section of land not owned yet by Divine but an important part of the master plan for the recreation area. Bernie, the sheriff, says that arresting Joe will not solve the problem. Jerry (Ronald G. Joseph), the local Forest Service representative who carries a gun, says that Joe should be arrested. After thinking about it, Divine decides to call the governor and ask him to do something.

Meanwhile, people from the town line up all along the fence around Joe's bean field to watch him sitting on a tractor plowing it. Once he finishes the plowing, he opens the valve and permits the water to flow in between the rows of soil in the field. Angel watches and laughs.

Ruby goes to see Charlie Bloom (John Heard), a lawyer-turned-newspaper owner, who is working in his garden and complaining about Amarante's pig, who has rooted up some of his plants. Ruby asks Bloom about the newspaper due to be published next week and indicates that she wants him to write an article on Joe's bean field in order to draw attention to the Miracle Valley project. Bloom says that he thinks that such an article will upset a lot of people and will cause some to get hurt. After he tells her that he thinks that Joe's is a lost cause, she tells him that she will write the article and pay him to print it.

Back in Milagro, Herbert (Herbie) Platt (Daniel Stern), a young man working on a degree in sociology from New York University, gets off a bus. He has a tape recorder strapped around his neck, a stack of books in one hand, and a bag of clothes in the other. After asking several people for help, he finally finds Mayor Cantu, who knows nothing about Platt's arrival. Platt explains that he is writing a thesis and doing research and staying in Milagro for six months on a grant and that he needs a place to live.

Meanwhile, Joe comes to town to buy beans to plant in his field. The owner of the general store will not advance his credit for the beans, so Joe must use his last paper money to pay for them. While Cantu continues to tell Platt that he doesn't remember him coming, Platt offers to teach in exchange for a place to live. Cantu says, "If we don't know it by now, chances are we're not interested in learning it." Certainly, that summarizes the passive state of affairs in Milagro.

Since he has no place to live, Platt begins walking down the road. Joe stops, picks him up, and offers him a room in exchange for help in his bean field. Joe takes Platt to a cabin whose door falls off the hinges when it is opened. It more closely resembles a storage shed filled with garbage, but Joe tells Platt that he'll get him a cot and a heater.

The governor wants the Miracle Valley project to proceed as planned in order to bring tourists to New Mexico and boost the economy. In his office, he discuses the development with some of his officials, saying that he wants no publicity as the result of arrests being made. He has employed Kyril Montana (Christopher Walken), a professional law man, who is more like a hired gun, to go to Milagro and figure out a way to stop Joe Mandragon from planting his bean field.

Bernie goes to the field and talks to Joe and asks him to think about what he is doing. Joe says that he will stop when he thinks he is doing something wrong. Then, as both he and Bernie look at the field and the beauty of the land beyond it, Joe says, "It's beautiful, isn't it?" Bernie says, "Yes, it is."

As Amarante is walking along the road with a staff in his hand and his pig at his side, Montana passes by, driving a car he has beat up in an attempt to deceive the townsfolk, who figure out who he is immediately. Angel tells Amarante, "I don't think the boy (Joe) knows what he's in for." Amarante replies, "Nobody would do anything if they knew what they were in for." Angel: "Maybe so, but the boogeyman (Montana) just came to town."

Montana goes to the newspaper office to hunt for Bloom, whom he thinks is behind Joe's bean field activities. The office of *La Voz Del Norte* (*The Voice of the North*), *The Newspaper of San Juan County*, is closed. Montana walks away. But then Bloom drives up and enters the office. Ruby arrives, bringing the article she wrote about Joe's bean field. He tells her that he wrote one. They discuss each article. Then, Ruby tells Bloom that she wants him to give the people of Milagro an idea of what is going to happen to their valley if the recreation area is built. She gets him to agree to attend a meeting she is calling to inform the people about the plans that Divine has for his Miracle Valley Recreation Area.

Meanwhile, Platt hears Amarante talking to himself one night. While he is helping Joe plant beans the next day, he asks him about Amarante. Joe tells him that Amarante is the oldest man in Milagro. While Amarante sits on his porch in a chair with his pig at his side, Joe adds, "He was probably talking to a saint or an angel." Platt asks, "What?!"

Divine finds a cross in his driveway which he brings to a meeting with Bernie, Montana, and Shorty. On the cross are the words "El Brazo Onofre," which Bernie explains to Montana refer to Martinez's arm. He tells Montana that Martinez lost his arm it in an accident, but nobody ever found it. So, Bernie tells Montana, that people around there think it has a life of its own.

Montana asks about Bernie's surveillance of Bloom because he doesn't think Joe decided to plant the bean field without Bloom's help. The plan is made for the members of Divine's staff to pick up all the copies of the next issue of Bloom's paper as soon as they are delivered and burn them. That way no one will be further provoked to follow in Joe's footsteps. And so as Ruby attempts to buy a paper in the general store, she finds out that they are all sold already.

While one of Divine's staff is burning the newspapers in a trash barrel, Angel appears, creating a wind which lifts the papers from their stacks in a gentle tornado motion and carries them into town where they are dropped everywhere and people can pick them up and read them. This action by Angel insures a large crowd of people at the meeting, which is held in the Catholic Church.

Before the meeting begins, Ruby lights the candles in the sanctuary. Everyone from Milagro is present. Ruby begins by reminding them of a time when their poverty did not shame them, when their children stayed home and raised their children in Milagro. She tells them that they could become a town of old men and old women. She also reminds them that they are family. She says, "I think of Ladd Divine and the development. And I know if it comes, it means the end for most of us." Then, she tells them that if they want to fight the recreation area, they have to understand it because it is very complicated. She says that she has asked Charlie Bloom to explain it to them.

Two police officers are standing outside the church as Bloom stands up to talk. He had told Ruby that he didn't want to get involved this way. But that, of course, hadn't stopped her. He explains that once wealthy people move in, they will want new schools for their children, new roads, new sewer systems, and cleaner water. He tells them that the wealthy are able to pay for all those things, but at the same time the people of Milagro will also have to pay. Bloom says,

> Your taxes are going to go sky high. And it is doubtful, very, very doubtful that any of you will be holding the new higher-paying jobs unless, of course, you happen to be a golf pro. So, my guess is most of you will be forced to sell out and to move elsewhere.

The meeting breaks out in chaos, which Ruby quiets by saying that she was hoping they could form themselves into a group to protect their town. But more chaos erupts and a fight breaks out. The police officers enter the church and arrest Bloom for disturbing the peace.

Angel, rubbing his sore feet, sits in a chair outside Amarante's home with him and says, "Idiots. Full of sound and fury signifying nothing. What a start for a revolution!" Amarante replies, "Milagro will wake up. You'll see. The people will fight Divine." Angel: "Will they fight their feared enemies?" Just then Platt comes along and witnesses Amarante talking to Angel, whom Platt cannot see. Platt introduces himself to Amarante, tells him that he is a sociologist, and wants to ask him some questions.

First, Platt asks, "What does Milagro mean?" Amarante replies, "Miracle, like the town." Then Platt asks him about the statue he saw on the altar outside of Amarante's house. Amarante tells him it is a statue of St. Jude, the patron saint of desperate causes, who pulled him through six operations. Platt asks how the saint did that. Amarante explains, "You have to put out for him a nice meal .... Then you talk to him and ask for help. People now, I don't know, they have forgotten how to act with saints or talk to angels." Platt: "Angels?" Amarante: "Yes, they're around here. They've been dead a while." Platt: "You actually talk to angels?" Amarante: "Those are the only ones around got time to spare."

Ruby posts bail for Bloom and gets him out of the San Juan

County Jail, but he won't get into her truck so that she can take him to his vehicle, which he left the previous night at the church. As he walks down the road, Ruby catches up to him in her truck and tells him that he was right about the people of the town not being ready for a meeting. She proposes that the best way to accomplish the stopping of the development is to get the people to sign a petition. She begins circulating the petition, but no one in town will sign it. Montana watches her activity.

Amarante, who has become a good friend of Platt, pays him a visit. "I brought you a St. Ignacio," he says. "He helps smart people." Then, Amarante tells him that he could use a couple of other saints, too.

A sequence of scenes follow showing Amarante and Angel sitting at a table playing checkers, Amarante and Platt talking and walking together, the pig eating a sheet of paper in Platt's typewriter, Platt showing Amarante how his Walkman works, and Amarante showing Platt the town cemetery. Meanwhile, bulldozers continue to move earth on the Miracle Valley site while Divine and his wife, Flossie (Melanie Griffith), stop during a horseback ride to view the valley from on top a hill and he explains the development to her. The only problem is that Joe's bean field is in the way.

Montana, Jerry the Forest Service agent, and others plot a way to get Joe's cow to wonder into the National Forest so that they can take the cow and levy a fine of $100 on Joe. After putting down a plywood walkway over the cattle guard, they lure the cow across it with a bucket of food and take her to the Forest Service holding pen.

A truckload of old men go to the bean field to tell Joe about his cow. Joe goes home, gets his rifle, and heads to the Forest Service pen to get his cow. The truckload of men follow him. While Joe is leading the cow out of the pen, Jerry comes out of his office, draws his handgun, and tells Joe to stop. Each of the old men raises a rifle and aims it at Jerry. Bernie arrives to mediate the dispute. After several attempts, he tells Jerry that the cow didn't eat enough Forest Service grass to warrant this behavior. Jerry agrees. All lower their guns, and Joe takes home his cow.

Flossie Divine receives a package in the mail and opens it to discover a box of fish heads. After finishing a day's work in the bean field, Joe and Platt are beaten up by two men who come out of the shadows. Bloom has a friend of his in his bedroom when Ruby arrives to ask him if he's heard about Joe and his cow and she informs him that when the beans are ready to be harvested, there will be a party. Meanwhile, rumors are passed from one person to another throughout the town.

Amarante, kneeling, prays quietly in front of his household shrine, which contains numerous burning candles. Then, he straps on a holster, finds his handgun in a tin box, places it in the holster, and walks out the door. Angel appears, saying, "I see desperate times call for desperate measures." Meanwhile, more land is being moved at the development site.

In the general store, Amarante buys bullets for his gun with food stamps. Then, he goes to the bar, puts bullets in the gun, aims at a bottle on a shelf, shoots the gun, and shatters the bottle. All the eyes of the men in the bar are upon him. Then, he leaves and returns to his home near the bean field. He sits and waits with his pig at his side while Platt works on fence repair.

A new strategy to deal with Joe and his bean field is developed by Divine. He will offer Joe a job building cabins and pay him such a salary that he will have to take the job. That will get him away from the bean field. When Joe returns home, after being offered the job, Ruby is waiting for him. He tells her about the job offer. She asks about him giving up the bean field, and tells him that Divine is trying to buy him. The conversation is stopped by a sudden gunshot through the window.

In imitation of Amarante, all the men of the town appear at the general store and buy bullets for their rifles and handguns. Meanwhile, Montana goes to see the Miracle Valley sign which has been set on fire. Divine arrives, too, sees the sign, and lets out a ferocious scream that echoes through the valley. Horsethief Shorty suggests that maybe Martinez's arm did it. Later in the day, a flaming arrow appears on the Forest Service sign. Jerry, standing nearby, removes it. That evening, while sitting in bed with his wife, Divine tries to figure out what is going on.

Angel dances to Amarante's house. The old man is sound asleep in bed, but Angel, standing outside and peering through the window, awakens him. "That bean field don't look so bad," Angels says. "I've seen worse." Amarante replies, "No thanks to you. I thought you were going to do something." Angel: "I don't do things. I give advice." Amarante: "You have some advice?" Angel: "You're going to need a big sacrifice here."

The next morning one of Divine's men shows up with a bulldozer on the outskirts of Joe's bean field. He lowers the bucket and begins to destroy the plants. Amarante draws his pistol and fires two shots toward him. That makes him stop and get off the bulldozer. Amarante climbs onto the bulldozer, puts it in gear, and it begins to tear down the fence, part of a house, and heads for a cliff. Clearly, Amarante does not know what he is doing. Just as the bulldozer is about to go over the cliff, Amarante jumps off of it. It hurls over the cliff, crashing onto the rocks and breaking up into multiple pieces. Meanwhile, Martinez explains to

Platt how 1,000 butterflies took his arm.

Joe arrives at the bean field and sees the pig eating his beans. He takes his rifle from the truck and shoots at the pig, who begins to chase him. Taking another shot, he hits the pig, stopping him, but he does not kill the pig. Amarante appears shooting at Joe, but Joe can't tell who it is because the sun is behind Amarante. Joe defends himself by firing his rifle and hitting Amarante. Martinez and others arrive and tell Joe that he had better run away while they take Amarante to the clinic.

Joe heads home to tell Nancy what has happened. Ruby is there and hears the whole tale. At the clinic, Amarante lies in bed while Platt and Martinez wait for him to regain consciousness. Ruby goes to Bloom's newspaper office, tells him about Joe, and asks him to represent Joe. Montana shows up and reminds them that both of them know that Joe is a fugitive from justice. Ruby retorts that Joe is a fugitive anyway. Montana threatens them with prosecution if they know where Joe is but don't tell him. This infuriates Bloom, who says, "I'm Joe Mandragon's lawyer and he has certain rights with which I'm sure you are familiar." Then, he tells Montana that if he and his deputies go after Joe and shoot him or manhandle him, he will prosecute them all the way to the Supreme Court. Montana leaves and goes to his motel room to get his rifle.

When Montana arrives in town, Bernie has about thirty men waiting to form a posse on horseback to search for Joe. As they head toward the hills, they begin to sing. Montana tells them to stop. At a rest stop, Montana tells Bernie that his posse couldn't find itself. Bernie replies that it could if it wanted to. Montana tells Bernie that he has decided to go after Joe alone and he is sending back Bernie and the posse. Bernie says, "If I thought you had a chance, I wouldn't go back." As they head back to town, all the men in the posse sing "De Colores."

Back in the clinic Ruby, Platt, and others wait for Amarante to regain consciousness. Platt goes to Amarante's house and prepares food and beer and places them in front of St. Jude's statue in Amarante's household shrine. Platt says, "No tamales. I hope the tacos are OK." Then, he gets on his knees and prays, saying, "I'm sorry if I'm not doing this right. I don't want to insult you or anything. But I'd really appreciate it if you could help my friend, Amarante. He's a good man."

While Angel plays his concertina, Ruby finds Bloom at Joe's bean field, which he has watered. He says, "It would be a shame to let it all die now." Ruby asks him if he hears the music coming from the concertina, but Bloom shakes his head no. "You don't hear anything?" she asks again. "No," he says. At the clinic, the shadow of Angel appears on the wall of Amarante's room.

Out in the mountains, Joe faces a cliff he must climb, while Montana tracks him. At the clinic, Amarante opens his eyes, mumbles a few words in Spanish, and then, looking at the crowd around his bedside, asks, "What are you all doing here? Where's my pistola?" Bernie tells Amarante, "I found one of your bullets in Joe Mandragon's wall." Then he asks if anyone knows anything about burning Divine's sign, the crosses, the dead fish heads, the flaming arrow. Of course, no one knows anything.

Montana spots Joe through his binoculars and heads after him. He fires at Joe, who, running for cover, drops his rifle. Then, Montana talks to him, attempting to get him to come out. But from another direction gunshots are fired at Montana, who, losing his balance, rolls down a hill behind him. Horsethief Shorty appears on horseback and tells Joe that Amarante is going to live. Then, Shorty rides away.

Joe heads home, where Martinez, Ruby, and Bloom are waiting for him. He signs Ruby's petition, then heads to his field to pick beans. A procession of trucks filled with people from the town follows him. More and more people get into the caravan as the church bell signals the start of the harvest. There is hardly enough room for parking when all arrive in trucks at Joe's bean field and distribute baskets to help Joe pick his beans.

But then a procession of police cars arrives with Montana in the lead. Getting out of his car, he arrests Joe, charging him with attempted murder and flight to avoid prosecution. After handcuffing him, he begins to lead him away toward his car. The townsfolk, one by one, get their rifles from their trucks. One police officer on the radio with the governor says, "We're about to have a war."

Bernie arrives and takes charge of the situation, saying that Amarante refuses to press charges. Then, Bernie tells Montana that he is deputizing everyone in the crowd for crowd control duty. Meanwhile, Montana gets a call from the governor over the radio and is ordered to stop everything. Sarcastically, Bernie asks Montana if the name Custer rings a bell. Montana tells his officers to let Joe go. The crowd sings, shooting rifles into the sky, and the police force leaves. The governor, placing a call to Divine, tells him that the Miracle Valley Recreation Area is being put on the back burner.

Once the beans are harvested, the celebration begins in the field. All are engaged in dancing to the music being played by the townsfolk. Ruby tells Bloom that she has signatures on her petition from everyone and how the present moment is wonderful.

Amarante, who has escaped from the clinic, walks down the road toward the party. Angel appears and joins him, saying, "Hey, compadre, where are you going?" Amarante: "I've got to get to the bean field." Angel: "Ah, yes. There's one hell of a party going on. Come on. I know a short cut. My feet are killing me." Amarante says, "Sometimes you do not act like an angel." Angel replies, "I want to tell you something." Amarante says, "I don't want to know anything." And they keep talking and walking down the road together.

There is no doubt that the film is making a statement about the world of land development versus the world of small-town life. But through the use of Coyote Angel, the film places the discussion in an apocalyptic context and, as such, can help students grasp some of the basic characteristics of apocalyptic found in the Book of Revelation. This can best be accomplished by analyzing the characters in the film.

Coyote Angel represents the world above in the apocalyptic genre. He appears after the wind blows. He brings a message that Milagro is dying and, in order for it to be resurrected, a big sacrifice will be needed. Angel assists people in determining what the next step needs to be taken in the course of action to stop the development site and preserve the way of life of Milagro. He is like the angel sent to John in the Book of Revelation to show him what will take place soon. Angel is not beyond getting involved in human affairs, especially if they are not going the way he thinks they should, such as causing the windstorm that carries the newspapers away from the man burning them and into the town so that all find out about the town meeting set to discuss the development area.

Angel is sent to Amarante, a very religious man and one of the few humans who still maintains some contact with the divine through prayer and the practice of religious devotion. Like John in the Book of Revelation, Amarante speaks freely to Angel, criticizes him for not doing anything, and assures him that Milagro will wake up and fight Ladd Divine and stop Miracle Valley Recreation Area from becoming a reality. Amarante accepts Angel's message that a big sacrifice is needed, and he willingly becomes that sacrifice.

Amarante is also a teacher, like John in the Book of Revelation. He explains his devotion to St. Jude to Herbie Platt, the sociologist, the one studying people's behavior. Platt not only absorbs Amarante's teaching, but, when Amarante is in the clinic, he practices it, making an offering to the saint and praying for Amarante's recovery. From Amarante he learns how important it is to take time for God in order to understand God's ways in the world. From Amarante he learns that all of life is dependent upon God, whom Amarante thanks every morning for giving him one more day. Indeed, that's an interesting message for a sociologist to hear, let alone to believe and practice.

Ruby, a woman who represents the traditions of Milagro, symbolically gives birth to the man who saves it. She is like the woman who gives birth to her child and must flee from the dragon in the Book of Revelation. Ruby's objective is to stop the Miracle Valley Recreation Area by prodding Charlie Bloom to support the old way of agricultural life represented by the bean field, which is located right in the middle of the land development area.

Like Coyote Angel, she is a trickster, luring Bloom to the town meeting and putting him on the spot to explain what will happen if the development continues. When part of her plan fails, she intercedes by paying Bloom's bail and getting him out of jail. After Joe shoots Amarante, she pleads with Bloom to represent him. Finally, Bloom comes to birth and decides to save not only Joe, but the town as well.

Ruby also supports Joe's activities of cultivating, irrigating, and planting his father's bean field. Repeatedly, she assures him that he is doing the right thing. She has confidence that he is doing a great thing by defying Ladd Divine and writes an article she wants published in the local paper to prove it. When Joe is offered a job to build cabins for Divine, she reminds him that he is being bought. She asks Bloom to represent him, and she plans the celebration that will take place in the bean field. In many ways, Ruby is the female counterpart to Angel insofar as she, like Amarante, can hear the music he plays on his concertina. Through her actions, she is able to breathe new life into Milagro.

Joe Mandragon represents the force of good. He is like those who faithfully follow the lamb in the Book of Revelation. He is the typical man with a wife and three children who struggles to make both ends meet. As one of the downtrodden of society, he picks his father's small beanfield to represent his stand against the force of evil, Ladd Divine, whose sign is the bulldozer knocking over trees and tearing up the earth. With gentleness Joe plows the bean field, repairs its fence, irrigates it, and places the seeds into the soil with his bare hands. He represents the traditional and agricultural way of life of his Spanish ancestors, especially his father. He is contrasted to Divine, whose yellow bulldozer destroys the earth. It is only when the huge bulldozer is brought to the bean field that the war between good and evil really begins.

The bean field can be compared to Armageddon in the Book of Revelation. It is the place where many previous battles have taken place and been won. Another one is about to begin, and there is little doubt that Joe will win. In fact, Amarante, the holy man, demonstrates how easy it is to defeat evil by stealing the bulldozer and driving it the end of a cliff where it falls to its death. Those who stand fast in faith are saved from the power of evil, says the Book of Revelation, and nothing can hurt them.

The beanfield also represents the town of Milagro. It is a miniature of the town. Meaning "miracle," Milagro is the Book of Revelation's new Jerusalem come down from heaven. It is like the old Jerusalem insofar as it hasn't changed in 300 years, but it is like the new Jerusalem insofar as it is awakened to new life. It is contrasted to the Miracle Valley Recreation Area, which is supposed to be the location of new life for the area but ends up getting put on the back burner. There is no miracle in Miracle Valley; the miracle takes place in a Milagro bean field.

Kyril Montana, the professional police officer/hired gun sent by the governor to put a stop to Joe Mandragon's defiance of progress by planting his bean field, represents the might-makes-right attitude. Montana, the rich and powerful servant of the state who is equipped with plans and weapons and sent to insure the triumph of land development, is contrasted with Mandragon, the poor and weak citizen of Milagro who has no plans, who possesses a rifle that he leaves in the wilderness, and who believes that the old way of life, coaxing the land to yield a harvest, is somehow better than ravaging it by uprooting its trees and plowing under its topsoil. Montana may be legally correct, but Mandragon is morally right. In the Book of Revelation, Montana would be one of the beasts, while Mandragon would be one of the servants of God who has been sealed.

The contrast is so well presented to Horsethief Shorty that he is converted. Shorty, a member of Divine's crew, upholds and defends the land development and participates in all of the schemes pieced together by Divine, the governor, and Montana. But once Shorty realizes the immorality of it all, he changes sides and demonstrates his conversion by defending Joe and shooting at Montana. Then, knowing that he did the right thing, he rides off and is never seen again in the film. He would be counted among those who are sealed in the Book of Revelation.

Ladd Devine--notice the name--represents the harlot Babylon in the Book of Revelation. Devine is defeated, like Babylon (representing the power of Rome) is destroyed. The traditional way of life is preserved in Milagro, and God comes to live with the faithful and good people in the Book of Revelation.

In "The Milagro Beanfield War," water plays a key role. It is the lack of water that has prohibited Joe from planting his bean field. But once he opens the valve, he is refreshed by the sight of water coursing through his field. His resolve is to plant the field and recover his heritage.

Repeatedly, the film focuses on the ditch from which the water flows. The townsfolk of Milagro are drawn to the irrigated field. After Joe runs into the hills, Bloom goes to Joe's field and irrigates it. The water in the bean field is more than water. It is Revelation's river of life bringing healing to all people. In the film, water flowing into a dry bean field heals the people of Milagro of their inability to be a community and forms them into a people who remember, celebrate, and adhere to their traditional way of life. In other words, water precipitates a miracle in Milagro. In the Book of Revelation, water flows from God's throne and calls all people to come and drink and be one with the God who calls them to be a chosen and saved people. Water saves the way of life of the citizens of Milagro with a little help from God's agents: Coyote Angel, Amarante Cordova, Ruby Archeleta, and Herbert Platt. Anything can happen in Milagro.

Exercises and Questions for Discussion

1. Make a list of five comparisons of themes between "The Milagro Beanfield War" and the Book of Revelation.

2. Make a list of five comparisons of characters between "The Milagro Beanfield War" and the Book of Revelation.

3. Outline the plot of the film by scene. For each scene indicate its importance to the whole story and what purpose it serves.

4. Outline the plot of the Book of Revelation by scene. For each scene indicate its importance to the whole story and what purpose it serves.

5. What do you think is the major truth which the movie attempts to communicate? Is this truth one that endures? Explain.

6. What do you think is the major truth which the Book of Revelation attempts to communicate? Is this truth one that endures? Explain.

7. Identify the apocalyptic elements in "The Milagro Beanfield War." For each specify how it is used and what it means.

8. Compare and contrast life in Milagro with life in Miracle Valley Recreation Area. Then, compare and contrast life in the world with life in the new Jerusalem in the Book of Revelation. What do you discover?

9. Why do you think specific locations are so important in "The Milagro Beanfield War" (such as the bean field, development site) and in the Book of Revelation (cities of seven churches, Armageddon, new Jerusalem)? Make a list of the specific places "seen" in the film and those described or mentioned in the Book of Revelation. Identify the significance of each.

10. In "The Milagro Beanfield War," who do you think was responsible for the crosses, the fish heads in a box, burning the Miracle Valley sign, and the flaming arrow shot onto the Forest Service sign? Explain your answer.

11. In "The Milagro Beandfield War," what do you think is the function/role of the old woman who throws small stones at people?

Teaching the Book of Revelation

Waterworld

"When will Jesus return?" is an urgent question which expects an immediate answer. It was a question which was already being asked in the middle of the first century common era, as can be seen by the answers given by the writers of gospels and Paul before them. It was a question which the author of the Book of Revelation attempted to answer near the end of the first century common era.

The question seems to be asked more intently as people discover themselves to be in a crisis, a chaotic moment in their existence, or as they approach a millennium. What was true of the first followers of Jesus remains true 2000 years later. We want an answer to this question: "When will Jesus return?"

The anonymous author of the Book of Revelation declares that the kingdom of the world has become the kingdom of God and of the Messiah, who will reign forever. The apocalyptic work portrays a worship ceremony taking place. Those present sing about God having begun God's reign. Again and again, the author of the book makes it clear that the kingdom of God is now, that salvation and power and kingdom have come.

Later in the book, the author describes the end of the world as a harvest. The Son of Man is told to use the sickle in his hand and to reap because the harvest of the earth is ripe. Once the good is harvested, an angel is told to harvest all that is bad and throw it into the wine press of God's wrath. Thus, the author of Revelation understands the kingdom to be a present reality with the harvest and separation of the good from the bad to take place at a future date, when Jesus will return.

But seventy years had passed and two generations had believed and been laid to rest and there was no sign that Jesus was coming. It was becoming an embarrassing question for those end-of-the-first-century believers.

Apocalyptic literature supplied the means to deal with the embarrassing question. Apocalyptic, a genre of literature, was available from 200 B.C.E. to 200 C.E. That 400-year period was the "golden age" of apocalyptic literature. Apocalyptic permits the "predicting" of the future by using the past. The future is not available to our experience, as are some events beyond the realm of our experience (such as beyond death and resurrection). But by coding historical events in signs, an author can place them as predictions on the lips of a character and, then, proceed to make them unfold in the narrative.

Apocalyptic literature describes the kingdom, which Jesus preached as a present reality, to be a future event, maybe present in some small degree now, but not yet realized in its fullness. The historical Jesus' teaching was apocalypticized by the culture in which he lived. The ancient authors couldn't help being influenced by the apocalyptic milieu in which they lived and wrote. Likewise, their audiences could not but be influenced by the same milieu.

Did the historical Jesus of Nazareth say that he would return? Probably not. As a human being, just to be raised from the dead by God would have been beyond his wildest imaginings! Returning would have been even further from his thoughts. However, that did not stop his first followers from believing that Jesus would return again to finish the rescue of Israel from the hands of its 500-year domination by foreign powers. The mind-set of the first century would have found it inconceivable that the Messiah had not restored the political rule of the Davidic monarch. Popular Jewish understanding was that the Messiah would come as a warrior-king, like David, who represented the epitome of what a warrior-king should be and do.

By the end of the first century common era, the restoration of Israel's Davidic dynasty had not been accomplished. Rome still occupied the land. The people were still ruled by a foreign government. Roman soldiers still patrolled the country. Taxes were paid to an emperor across the Mediterranean Sea. So, the mission of the Messiah, in popular though, had not been accomplished. Therefore, the author of the Book of Revelation thought Jesus of Nazareth must return to finish what he, supposedly, started.

In order to fully understand the genre of literature named apocalyptic, we first identify three English words derived from the Greek word "apocalypsis": apocalypse, apocalyptic, and apocalypticism. "Apocalypsis" means "revelation," or "uncovered," or "a drawn back curtain." Sometimes biblical scholars add "apocalyptic eschatology" to the above-mentioned list of words. "Apocalyptic eschatology" refers to an author's attempt to describe what God will do in the future. However, as already mentioned above, the future is not available to human experience. Therefore, "apocalyptic eschatology" is an educated guess as to what God might do in the future. It is based on what humans have reflected on and believed to be what God has done in the past.

The literary genre called apocalyptic is set within a narrative framework in which a human recipient receives a revelation from an outside-of-this-world being (such as an angel). The revelatory message is attributed to God, who, in the ancient view of the world, lived above the vault of the earth and sent messages down to the earth about the imminent destruction of evil in the world. The best example of apocalyptic in the Christian Bible (New Testament) is the Book of Revelation, also known as "The Apocalypse."

Apocalyptic literature was written during a time of crisis or chaos, such as during a period of foreign military occupation; or when a group felt alienated from the rest of society, such as the Jews in their own homeland; or when approaching a millennium, when people were experiencing despair about their world; or during a natural disaster, such as an earthquake or a flood. An apocalyptic writer sees the world as rushing toward a tragic climax, and there is no hope, other than in a divine intervention, to save it. The author of apocalyptic literature finds hope in the future, when God will intervene, destroy the wickedness of this world, and establish a new world, a new age of order. Such literature was needed during times of crisis to offer hope to people who felt oppressed and lost. It offers an alternate view of reality in the midst of a crisis that is either real or perceived.

The human recipient of the revelation receives it in the form of a dream or a vision, the meaning of which is interpreted by an intermediary, usually an angel as in the case of Revelation. The author lives much later than the angel's appearance and writes pseudonymously. That technique lends credibility and postulates authority to the apocalyptic work.

The author of apocalyptic literature does not share our linear notion of time as past, present, and future. In other words, he could not draw a time line and place upon it past, present, and future events. In apocalyptic there is only the present age and the age to come. In the present there is no hope for redemption from evil, but in the age to come there is great hope that God will triumph.

There can be no past in apocalyptic because the author codes the events of the past in signs, which would have been familiar to his audience when he was writing--otherwise, the reader would not have been able to decode the work. In the time-frame of his narrative, the apocalyptic writer pretends that a certain event has not yet taken place, predicts that it will or quotes another writer as prophesying that it will, and then proceeds to show how it did happen as it was prophesied. Thus, the author is always one hundred percent correct. This makes dating an apocalyptic work rather easy. All that one has to do is to decode the last predicted and fulfilled event in narrative time and discover when it took place in real, historical, or linear time. An apocalypticist will not predict the future in linear time because he cannot humanly know it and, should he attempt to do so and it not happen, his credibility and the authority of his work would be questionable.

The authors of the Christian Bible take a great risk in portraying Jesus as "predicting" his return. However, they only take the risk after establishing his credibility by portraying him "predicting" his future death and resurrection in story-time and showing how it was fulfilled in story-time. In other words, in the Christian Bible (New Testament) the only event "predicted" to happen outside of story-time and not fulfilled within it is Jesus' return, and it is "predicted" only after carefully establishing Jesus' credibility to "predict" his own suffering and death in story-time and demonstrate their fulfillment.

The apocalypticist views the world in dualistic terms. There exists only the world above, where the good God lives with his angels, and the world below, where people live and are facing a crisis in which it looks like evil, Satan, or wickedness will be the victor. Sometimes referred to as the horizontal dimension of apocalyptic literature, the apocalyptic author believes that salvation from crisis, or chaos, or war, or despair comes only from beyond human history or beyond linear time. There is also a vertical dimension to this genre, which unites the world above to the world below and offers descriptions of angels in heaven and demons in hell coming down from heaven to earth or going up from earth to heaven.

Important to the vertical dimension are the signs of the end of time which the recipient of the visions and dreams gets from the intermediary. These are usually cataclysmic, such as earthquakes, volcanic eruptions, floods, wars, famines, etc. Since these are known to destruct the earth in linear time, the writer uses them to describe how all evil will be destroyed in the future. Using the past, the author "foretells" the future --something which is impossible in linear time.

Once evil is destroyed by divine intervention, people living in a crisis will be saved. Apocalyptic is designed to offer hope to those who suffer for whatever reason by providing a vision of a new world which is divinely ordered. By reading the author's narrative of good destroying evil, the reader obtains hope that the worldly crisis in which he or she is involved will soon pass away and all order will be restored. Thus, an apocalyptic work elicits faithfulness from the reader. It tells him or her to stay calm, not to panic, and to remain faithful. God will take care of the rest.

Apocalyptic literature can also be considered a protest. In its coded images it names the enemy, who might be political, military, social, or theological. Since it is non-confrontational, this genre of literature urges the reader to stand firm in non-compliance with political authorities, such as emperors or military personnel. It calls the reader not to give in to acceptable social standards or watered down theological positions. Of course the supreme form of protest which apocalyptic literature advocates is martyrdom. A faithful person gives his or her life as a refusal to accept the world view of oppressors. In essence, the martyr says that true power and authority in the world belong only to God. Apocalyptic aids the martyr by saying that all wrongs will be righted, all evil will be punished, all crisis and chaos will be resolved in the future--in the world beyond death. Of course, that future is based on a faith that there is life after death, that God does raise people from the dead. Such a future has no proof!

Finally, apocalyptic literature which is misunderstood, that is, not read as apocalyptic literature, has a tendency to believe itself. Authors who do not understand how the genre works read it literally. By incorporating it into their work, they postulate that they can predict the future because they understand what they read to do so. Of course, as we saw above, no one can predict the future. No one knows what is on the other side of the present moment, let alone on the other side of death!

Some people are still waiting for Jesus to return today. We live in a world of chaos--people shooting people drive-by style, earthquakes causing billions of dollars of damage and harming millions of people, the planet experiencing global warming and destruction of its species. We live in a world of crisis--blue and white collar jobs are lost to computers, children are abused sexually and emotionally, marriages last for only a few years.

People are on the move, immigrating from one country to another; when they are denied entrance, they threaten mass suicide. The daily paper's headlines reveal the state of chaos: "Mom, two kids found killed in beds," "Explosive fire sends hundreds fleeing," and "FBI agent shoots suspect in bank heists."

Even the popular "Frank and Ernest" cartoon strip by Bob Thaves captures the feeling. In one strip Frank and Ernest pass by a man holding a placard, which states, "The end is near!" Ernie asks, "Do you think that's right, Frank?" Frank replies, "Don't be silly, Ernie. They haven't even started rolling the credits yet!" And in another strip, Frank carries a placard which states, "World ends at midnight!," while Ernie carries another one behind him, stating, "Have a nice day."

One of Dik Browne's "Hagar the Horrible" cartoon strips features one person with "The end is coming" sign. One of Hagar's friends says, "His sign says the world will end soon." Hagar replies, "I hope it's not until after Alf's stag party."

In a "Non Sequitur" cartoon by Wiley, people are ascending a heavenly staircase at the top of which is located a podium and several angels. One of those ascending the stairs carries "The world will end today" sign and turns to the person behind him, saying, "Well, I figured I'd be right eventually."

Leigh Rubin's "Rubes" shows a man on the corner of a street bearing a placard "The End is near" with an arrow pointing to "The End" storefront. On the window are signs, stating, "For all your doomsday prophecy needs!," "Stock up now before it's too late!" and "All sales final!"

Every October even Charlie Brown gets into the apocalyptic picture as he and his friends in a pumpkin patch await the arrival of "The Great Pumpkin" and wonder how come he has delayed his coming for another year.

Various right-wing groups gather in secluded compounds for security and arm themselves with the best munitions in order to fight and win the battle with evil chaos, which is named "the government," "blacks," or "Jews." When, in their paranoia, they fail to win, after having predicted the end of the world, they have but two choices left: They can either repredict, like the Jehovah Witnesses and the Seventh Day Adventists have done, or they can bring about the end, like the Branch Davidians or the Swiss Order of the Solar Temple cult have done.

People seek escape from the crisis and chaos by running after UFOs, Marian apparitions, and weeping statues. They read books, like *After Life* by Carol Neiman and Emily Goldman, which presents new beliefs about life after death; *Embraced by the Light* by Betty J. Eadie, the story of a clinically dead woman, her journey to heaven, and her revival; *The Burning Within* by Ranelle Wallace, another account of a near-death experience; and *The Apocalypse Watch* by Robert Ludlum, a novel about the imminent destruction of the major cities of the world. The classic book not to be missed, of course, is Hal Lindsey's famous *The Late, Great Planet Earth.*

Apocalyptic movies are on the rise. "The Day After" depicts what a nuclear apocalypse would be like. Other films deal with life after death, such as "Ghost," "Ghost Dad," "Field of Dreams," "Defending Your Life," "Always." Still other movies investigate the other side of consciousness, such as "Flatliners" or "Powder." Not to be missed are television shows and movies about angels, heavenly visitors who help people in need.

The "Doomsday Clock's" hands may be set to fourteen minutes before midnight, the hour that signifies nuclear apocalypse, but about six out of ten Americans believe that the world will come to an end or be destroyed within a few years. The books they read and the movies they watch give them a sense of control over the chaos and hope that order will be the final result. People need hope in the midst of their confusion. We want hope that God will save us from evil and restore the world to some type of order.

Hope comes in the form of predictions from various fundamentalist groups concerning the end of the world--another way of answering the question, "When will Jesus return?" Lest we think that we live in a world entirely different from that of about 2000 years ago, many are ready and willing to insist that the end of the world is near. Crisis will end. Chaos will be over. Jesus will come (sometimes called the rapture) on a certain day and at a certain time and all that is good will be preserved, while all that is evil will be destroyed.

A milder form of apocalyptic is found in the Season of Advent for Roman Catholics and some other mainline denominations. Advent is a season of waiting for Jesus to return. It focuses on his birth as his first coming. Now he comes in the seven sacraments. But one day he will return in glory. However, while the four weeks of Advent focus on the return of Jesus, every Mass contains a number of references to waiting in joyful hope for his coming in glory.

Like its "The end is near" companions, Mort Walker's "Beetle Bailey" cartoon strip incorporates both destruction and hope in a series of six panels. While reading the paper in the sergeant's office, Beetle says, "Boy! Things are really bad!" The sergeant responds,

> Son, you don't know what bad is. I've been through the big depression, three wars, floods, epidemics, inflation, vast unemployment, strikes, volcanic eruptions, hurricanes, earthquakes, assassinations, riots, crisis after crisis! Nothing going on now even compares with the past sixty years. Today, most people have jobs, food, homes, and we're at peace!

Beetle says, "Yeah, I guess things are pretty good," and the sergeant says, "Hey! They're not that good!"

"Waterworld" (Universal, 1995), staring Kevin Kostner, can help students begin to understand the unique genre that apocalyptic is. The film presumes that the world has been flooded and only a small child knows the way to one spot of land. A narrator tells the viewer, "The future: The polar ice caps have meted, covering the Earth with water. Those who survived have adapted to a new world." The movie illustrates not only how they have adapted, but it also reveals the search for order, Dryland, out of the chaos of the ocean. The viewer can't help but think of the first story of creation in the Hebrew Bible (Old Testament) Book of Genesis in which God creates the Earth and orders the chaotic seas to retreat to the boundaries God has set.

The hero of the movie is the Mariner (Kevin Costner). He is not like the rest of humankind left to survive on the sea. He is a mutant, possessing gills behind his ears which enable him to breath under water and webbed feet which facilitate his movement down to the depths of the ocean. In apocalyptic language, he is an angel who has arrived to both interpret and guide a small group of survivors to Dryland.

As the film opens, showing the single Mariner standing on his boat sailing the infinite blue ocean below and the bright sun shining above, the viewer can't help but think of Samuel Taylor Coleridge's "The Rime of the Ancient Mariner":

> The sun came up upon the left,
> Out of the sea came he--
> And he shone bright, and on the right
> Went down into the sea.
> ...
> Alone, alone, all, all alone,
> Alone on a wide, wide sea!
> And never a saint took pity on
> My soul in agony.

Unlike the Mariner in Coleridge's poem, the one in "Waterworld" demonstrates that the flooding of the Earth with salt water has meant a limited supply of fresh water. After urinating in a cup, the Mariner pours his waste into a filtering device which purifies it and makes it immediately drinkable as fresh water. One lime tree in a pot reminds the viewer that citrus is still necessary to prevent scurvy.

The Mariner stops his boat, dives into the ocean, and rises with a bag of artifacts from the world that used to exist on the Earth. In other words, he returns to the past before launching forward into the future.

Meanwhile, another man on a skiff appears and steals all of the limes from the Mariner's tree. The Mariner spots the drifter's boat, talks with him, and finds out that there is an atoll about eight days journey East.

Both spot Smokers, who represent the epitome of darkness and evil. Already, the good-versus-evil dualistic theme is put into motion. As the drifter sails away, he shows the Mariner the limes he has stolen. The Mariner raises his sails and heads after the drifter while the Smokers head after the Mariner. Catching up with the drifter, the Mariner rams his boat, breaks his mast, and leaves him for the Smokers, who promptly kill him with a machine gun.

Eight days later--eight being a significant apocalyptic number indicating perfection--the Mariner arrives at the atoll, a circular floating fort defended by metal walls and a double metal gate. He shows the guards at the gate a jar of dirt which prompts them to open the gates and to let him sail into the fort. He notices that members of the atoll are recycling a dead woman; in this new world everything is reused in some form. The Peacekeeper (R. D. Call) tells the Mariner that he has two hours to trade and then he must leave.

The Mariner trades his 3.2 kilos of dirt for 124 chits, a monetary unit, and overhears one man telling another about a child with a map on her back showing the way to Dryland. The child lives in the atoll. Meanwhile, the Mariner proceeds to buy two rounds of water for himself, much like one would buy a whiskey at a bar in an old west movie, talks to the man who points out the child--named Enola (Tina Majorino) with a map on her back, and buys a tomato plant and the empty shelves of what resembles a general store run by Helen (Jeanne Tripplehorn) for half of his chits.

While carrying his purchases back to his boat, a group of citizens of the atoll asks the Mariner for his seed for one of their daughters in order to continue the human race and prohibit inbreeding. When the Mariner attempts to board his boat and leave, he is stopped and discovered to be a mutant with gills. A fight erupts and the Mariner kills a man, but other men capture him with a net.

Peacekeeper arrives to defend the Mariner from the crowd which is ready to kill him. Peacekeeper puts the Mariner in a single bared cage which is suspended above the water while the citizens decide his fate. During the darkness of the night, the Mariner sees a Smoker spy, one of the men he has spoken to earlier, leave the atoll.

While the Mariner awaits his fate, Gregor (Michael Jeter), an old inventor, looks at the map on Enola's back and observes the pictures she draws of animals who live on the land. From their conversation, the viewer concludes that they plan on leaving the atoll by using a device Gregor has invented. It looks like a balloon.

Gregor goes to talk to the Mariner, noticing his webbed feet and asking him about the functionality of his gills. Gregor wants to learn more about the Mariner, who is not interesting in divulging any information other than he is the only one of his kind left. Gregor asks about where the dirt came from and talks about the ancients doing something bad hundreds of years ago to cause the Earth to be covered by water. The Mariner, bargaining with Gregor, says that he will tell him the story if he opens the cell door. Gregor says that he wants to know more about Dryland, telling the Mariner, "Don't let it die with you." Before Gregor can free the Mariner, Peacekeeper arrives and tells him to get away from the prisoner.

The next day a council of citizens of the atoll sentences the Mariner to recycling because, as a mutant, he is a threat to them. Just as Peacekeeper begins to lower him into the recycling pit, a Smokers' alert is sounded as they approach the atoll and begin to attack it. The Smokers ride on self-propelled water sled-motorcycle vehicles each of which carries a machine gun. Other boats accompany them and they carry other types of rapid-fire weapons. As they encircle the atoll, their leader is revealed to be Deacon (Dennis Hopper), evil, the devil, Satan in human disguise.

The first battle of good versus evil takes place. The Smokers' guns blast holes into the sides of the metal fort, while the Mariner attempts to escape from his cage. Using a huge slide, Smokers riding water craft jump over the atoll's walls and one slams into the Mariner's cell, knocking it into the recycling pit. Getting the Smoker's knife, the Mariner tries to pry open the lock as he continues to sink into the yellow liquid of the pit.

Meanwhile, Gregor prepares the balloon for Helen and Enola and his own escape, but it inflates faster than he had expected and he lifts off from the atoll without them. Helen, seeing that her only way out of the atoll is now gone, rushes to the Mariner's cage and makes him agree to take her and Enola with him if she sets him free. Once he is released, he tells Helen to open the gate of the atoll while he lifts the sails and unties his boat.

The viewer learns that the Smokers are after "the girl," Enola, whose name is the same as that of the plane which dropped the bombs on Hiroshima and Nagasaki, Japan, at the end of World War II. When the gate gets stuck half-way open, Enola shows the Mariner how to set the gears to make it open all the way, then she and Helen jump onto the Mariner's boat and escape from the atoll. Just as the Smokers see what is going on and begin to attack the Mariner, he shoots a metal line to their boat with the big gun on it, gradually turning it around so that they end up firing on their own men. Sailing out into the deep blue ocean, the Mariner is no longer alone, but he has Helen and Enola with him while the Smokers comb what's left of the atoll looking for the girl. Deacon, who has been hit in the right eye with bullet, investigates the girl's disappearance and questions some of the citizens who remain on the atoll, but they know nothing, and he orders them to be killed. The first battle is over, and good has won. But evil is not yet defeated.

On the Mariner's boat Helen says to him, "You've been there, haven't you? Dryland. You know where it is." He says, "Yes, I know where it is." Helen: "And we're going?" Mariner: "You and I are. The kid we got to pitch over the side." Helen: "What!" Mariner: "My boat's tore up. I'm taking on water. I'll be lucky to get a half a hydro ration out of that," as he points to the water-purifying machine. Helen: "I won't drink." Mariner: "Twelve days?"

The Mariner explains, "It's better one of you dies now than one of you dies slow." Helen: "Wait. We saved your life. We got you out." Mariner: "No, you got me out so you could get out. We're even." Helen begins to plead with the Mariner to save Enola's life by appealing to her ability to cook and fish. As a last resort, she offers herself to him to save the girl's life. While he is tempted, he tells her, "You got nothing I need." Meanwhile, Enola, who was sent down below, explores the Mariner's collection of artifacts and finds a box of Crayolas. Helen, now desperate, threatens the Mariner with a gun, but he lowers the sail on her and, picking up a boat paddle, strikes her while she is trapped under the canvas. Then, they sail on the wide, blue ocean.

On the Smokers' ship, Deacon gets a huge glass eye, but it won't stay in so he covers the hole with a patch. He is told about a problem in the pit, the tank containing crude oil used for fuel, so he is driven in a rust-covered car without tires, only rims, to the source of the problem. As he goes along, he throws out cigarettes to the crowd, like one distributes candy during a parade. From the old man with a beard who lives on a canoe in the pit, Deacon finds out that only four feet and nine inches of oil, enough for three "refuelers," is left. He decides to spare nothing in order to find the girl.

Back on the Mariner's boat, Enola draws pictures on flat surfaces of the boat using the crayons she had discovered. Angered, the Mariner tells Helen to teach her the rules if they are going to stay. The Mariner, who was going to throw Enola overboard, has changed his mind. Later,

Enola tells the Mariner that he isn't so tough. She asks him about how many people he has killed. He tells her that she talks too much. She responds by saying that she is not afraid of him. Picking her up, he tosses her overboard as Helen screams that she cannot swim and jumps in to save Enola. The Mariner turns the boat and rescues both of them.

But the Smokers' plane spots them in the water. One Smoker, wielding a machine gun, begins firing on the Mariner, Helen, and Enola. Helen fires a line from the boat to the plane, which begins making smaller and smaller circles closer and closer to the boat as he wraps the line around the boat's mast. The Mariner climbs the mast to cut loose the plane which is about to crash into the boat. After he does so, he angrily grabs Helen and cuts off her hair. She tells him she is sorry. He tells her not to touch anything on the boat again. Enola, watching all this take place, says, "She said she was sorry. That means you're supposed to say something back." Next, the Mariner discovers more of Enola's drawings on the mast, and Deacon, hearing from the men in the plane, calculates where he can capture the Mariner.

The Mariner meets a drifter, who talks to himself. They bargain for food. Then, the drifter tries to buy the women from the Mariner in exchange for paper with writing on it in a tube. The Mariner agrees to give Helen to him for one-half an hour. After the drifter and Helen go below, the drifter removes his shirt and approaches Helen, while the Mariner removes the paper from the tube and examines it. The Mariner rushes below deck and declares that the trade is off; he has changed his mind. The drifter is not pleased and begins a fight. In the next scene, he emerges from the lower deck with a stream of blood flowing down his back. He collapses on the deck and dies. The Mariner takes what he wants from the drifter's boat, cuts it loose from his, and shoves the drifter's body overboard.

Because Helen and Enola are hungry, the Mariner dives into the ocean with a gun. A huge fish emerges and is killed. All sit on the deck eating fish steaks which are grilled on a Hibachi. Meanwhile, Enola sings and notices that the Mariner is disturbed. She says, "You don't like my singing, do you?" He asks her, "Have you ever tried to listen to the sound of the world?" They continue to banter.

Later, Helen delivers to the Mariner a picture drawn by Enola and a crayon she has kept. They talk about Enola and the marks on her back. Helen says, "Enola draws what she sees. The folks on the atoll thought she was a freak. I thought she was special." The Mariner says that he will "loan" the crayon to Enola. Helen moves their conversation to the topic of Dryland, asking, "Is Dryland beautiful?" The Mariner replies, "You'll see." Then, looking at the picture Enola drew, the viewer sees that it consists of three stick people--a man, a woman, and a child--holding hands. Enola has imagined the Mariner, Helen, and herself to be a family.

Helen is shocked the next morning to see the Mariner and Enola playing in the ocean. He teaches her how to swim, instructing her to hold on to his neck while they dive below the surface. The friction between them has been washed away to Helen's amazement.

As the Mariner, Helen, and Enola approach a border outpost, a floating tower, they discover that all the men on it are dead, except for Deacon and his assistant. Using an underwater device, the Mariner spots Smokers waiting below the surface and turns the boat away from the outpost. The Smokers begin to chase the Mariner, who clears their net and causes them to crash into each other. However, while raising an extra sail to escape them, Deacon fires one shot from a long-range rifle and wings the Mariner in his side.

As he sits bandaging his wound, the Mariner asks Helen about the meaning of the marks on Enola's back. Helen says that they represent the "way to Dryland." The Mariner says, "Dryland doesn't exist; it's a myth." Helen: "No, you said yourself you knew where it is." Mariner: "You're a fool to believe in something you've never seen before. It doesn't exist. I've sailed farther than most have dreamed, and I've never seen it." Helen asks about the artifacts he has on the boat, the shells, the music box, and other items, saying, "Where did they come from?" He decides that he will take her to Dryland, but it isn't the Dryland she thinks exists.

Helen gets under a glass bell jar, attached to a line from the boat, and the Mariner takes her down to the ocean depths to see what used to be Dryland. Helen sees the shell of former skyscrapers, other buildings, a city, sand, and an old Pepsi can. After they resurface, she says, "I didn't know." The Mariner says, "Nobody does."

Meanwhile, the Smokers have found the Mariner's boat and surrounded it, but they have not found Enola, who was left on it. Deacon grabs both Helen and the Mariner and, after questioning them, throws them down. He threatens to shoot them if they don't tell him where she is. He fires several bullets over their heads and Enola screams, betraying her hiding place. The Smokers grab her while the Mariner and Helen dive under the water to escape the Smokers' gunfire. She tells him that she can't breathe under the water, but he tells her that he will breathe for them. Placing his lips against hers he shares his breath with her, while on the ocean's surface the Smokers torch his boat and take off with Enola. When

Helen and the Mariner resurface, there is very little left of his boat.

On Deacon's ship, where he has Enola held as a prisoner, he asks her to explain the map on her back. He offers her a cigarette, the sign of being a Smoker, and tempts her into talking by offering her a magic marker with which she can draw pictures. She tells him that the tattoo on her back is a map of the way to Dryland. After more questions from Deacon about the tattoo, the conversation turns to talk about the Mariner. "He'll come for me," states Enola. "I know he will."

On their destroyed boat, Helen ask the Mariner if they're going to die. Then, she asks him why he didn't take her when she offered herself to him in exchange for Enola's life. The Mariner tells her that he really didn't want her then, but he does now. The under-the-ocean exchange of air which turned into an extended kiss now becomes full-fledged love-making and bonding.

The Mariner proceeds to search for scrap metal under the ocean to use in fixing his boat. While diving, he discovers a chest full of old *National Geographic* magazines. Comparing their covers to the pictures Enola drew, he begins to realize that Dryland really does exist somewhere. Helen tells him, "We weren't made for the sea." And that is the reason she believes in Dryland.

Just as a hopelessness of ever fixing the boat enough to make it sail again is about to descend upon the Mariner and Helen, Gregor appears in his balloon, and Helen tells him about Enola being captured by the Smokers. The Mariner and Helen find out that Gregor is one of several other survivors from the atoll. While reading some of the papers the Mariner had found in the chest, Gregor discovers a map similar to the one on Enola's back. Helen tells him that she has seen the land under the sea to which the map points. But the Mariner interrupts her saying, "Some is [still dry]. Enola's been there. I know that now. I saw what she drew. I don't care about Dryland."

What the Mariner cares about is Enola's life, and so he sets out immediately on a jet ski to rescue her from Deacon, who is examining the map on her back. After he finishes with Enola, Deacon salutes a portrait of Joe Hazelwood, former captain of the Valdez, which, when it went a-ground, once spilled gallons of crude oil in Prince William Sound off the coast of Alaska. Meanwhile, the Mariner has found Deacon's ship in fog.

The ship is a heap of rust, full of holes in its sides, and bordered at water level with barnacles wide enough for the Mariner to stand on. Climbing up the side of the ship, the Mariner witnesses Deacon addressing his troops from the bridge. They are getting restless and want to know where Dryland is. With a bottle of Jack Daniels in his right hand, he tells them, "I had a vision. I saw the land." The troops cheer.

Meanwhile, the Mariner pays attention to what's happening, but he also spies a guard examining the watercraft he had left at the base of the ship. He jumps on the guard and kills him. Then, riding the water craft into the hold of the ship, he kills another man and hears Enola's voice.

Deacon continues to rally his troops, saying, "If there's a river [on Dryland], we'll dam it. If there's a tree, we'll ram it." His speech indicates how destructive he is, and it reminds the viewer of Gregor's words early in the movie about the ancients having done something to cause the flooding of the Earth.

The Mariner listens as Enola tells the man guarding her that the Mariner will come to rescue her. The guard asks her what the Mariner's name is. She says, "He doesn't have a name, so death can't find him. He doesn't have a home and people to care for. He's not afraid of anything. He'll come for me. He will." The Mariner, meanwhile, is picking off more of the Smokers, one at a time. Deacon can be heard to say, "Dryland is not only our destination, but it is our destiny." Now, guards, who have found the Smokers the Mariner killed, are searching for him.

The camera switches back to Deacon who is continuing his speech. He says, "How can I find this glorious place? And has said to me: A child shall lead you. A child. And, behold, the instrument of our salvation." Enola is carried out over the shoulder of her guard so that the troops can see the child. Deacon holds her up, and the crowd cheers. He says, "She has shown me the path."

With their confidence restored in Deacon, the Smokers go back to work below deck, sticking their oars through the holes in the side of the ship and rowing it. Meanwhile, Deacon confers with some of his crew, telling them that he doesn't know here they're going but that the Smokers won't figure that out for a while.

The Mariner appears on the deck and walks towards the bridge where Deacon is standing. Enola says, "It's him. You guys are in so much trouble!" The Mariner tells Deacon, "I want the girl." Then, he lights a torch and holds it over the opening to the crude oil tank, saying, "She's my friend." Deacon replies, "Golly gee. A single tear runs down my cheek. You're going to die for your friend." The Mariner drops the torch into the oil tank and the ship begins exploding. Deacon sends his crew after the Mariner, while Enola asks him, "Was this your big vision?"

Grabbing Enola, Deacon gets into his rusty plane on the deck and attempts an escape. But the Mariner shoots a wire to the plane's wing to keep it from taking off. Then, he attaches a second wire to its landing gear, causing it to crash on the deck. He rescues Enola and they hug.

By now the ship is sinking and the Mariner and Enola need to get off of it. Gregor, Helen, and Peacekeeper appear in the balloon above the ship. After Gregor drops down a rope, the Mariner and Enola begin climbing their way to the basket, but Deacon also climbs up the rope and grabs Enola's leg. Helen throws a wrench toward him. It hits his head and he falls into the ocean.

The ship explodes in one giant fire ball and sinks. As it goes down, "Exxon Valdez" can be seen on its hull. But Deacon, who is still not dead, finds an abandoned watercraft with a rifle on it. He fires a shot at the balloon, hitting the basket near Enola and causing her to loose her balance and plunge into the ocean. Several Smokers converge to capture her, but the Mariner, tying a rope to his foot and to the basket, dives into the ocean, picks up Enola, and springs back into the basket, as Deacon and the Smokers collide and explode in a fireball.

Gregor informs the Mariner that he has figured out how to read the map and where Dryland is located. So, they steer the balloon in the direction Gregor indicates, but after several days they are out of water. However, a bird lands on the basket. The Mariner stands up to see Dryland: On the ocean's shore are mountains and valleys with streams of fresh water cascading to the sea. It is the new creation, paradise rediscovered.

While investigating Dryland, Peacekeeper discovers several huts, and in one there are two skeletons. Strewn around are pages, each printed with an identical copy of the map that is on Enola's back. The girl, who has also entered the hut, spies a music box on a table. She winds it up and, as it begins to play, says, "I'm home." The viewer concludes that this is where Enola had been born. The pictures she drew were of her former home and the animals that inhabited it. Somehow, when she was a child, she had been taken to the atoll.

The Mariner, examining a sail, sees a herd of wild horses run by. The viewer can see that he is not comfortable on Dryland. Later, after he has built a new boat, he prepares to leave by saying good-bye to Enola, who is sitting on the beach. "I have to go now," he says. She says, "You came back for me." Mariner: "I like you." Enola: "Why are you leaving?" Mariner: "I don't belong here." Then, looking out to the ocean, he adds, "I belong out there." Enola: "You belong here." Mariner: "It's too strange here. It doesn't move right." Enola responds, "Helen says its only landsickness. We're all feeling it, and it'll go away soon." Mariner: "It's more than that." Enola gives him the music box she found in the hut and runs away from the beach.

Next, the Mariner says good-bye to Helen. No words are spoken, but he touches her cheek with his hand and kisses her. Then, he gets on his boat, which holds several potted green plants, and sails away. From the top of a mountain, Helen and Enola watch him go. Once again, the viewer is reminded of the lines from Coleridge's "The Rime of the Ancient Mariner":

> Alone, alone, all, all alone,
> Alone on a wide, wide sea!

By comparing "Waterworld" to the Book of Revelation, students can get a grasp on the basic characteristics of apocalyptic literature. First, the world is in chaos. Water covers the Earth. In the Book of Revelation, some of the followers of Jesus experienced the crisis of persecution precisely because they chose to follow his way of life rather than that of the Roman government. To the Romans, those early Christians looked like traitors. The crisis they were facing was the stability of the state and its power to rule its citizens. Christians needed the hope that the death of fellow believers was not in vain, much like the survivors of the atoll needed hope that Dryland did exist.

Apocalyptic literature "predicts" the future by using the past. First, the narrator in "Waterworld" explains that the film is set in the future when the ice caps have melted and the Earth is covered with water. From scientific evidence, we know that at one time this already happened and that much of the earth now supporting people was once under the sea. Second, it is no accident that Deacon can quote Scripture, using the text from Isaiah about a little child leading his people. Christians have understood that text to refer to Jesus, who led his people from sin to salvation. Enola is the little child, who leads her people and the Mariner to Dryland. She is an outsider who bears on her back the way to salvation. She is accepted by only a few. When Deacon predicts that she can show the way, he is not aware of the truth of which he speaks. Indeed, Dryland exists, but he will never see it.

Deacon and his Smokers represent the huge force of evil which attempts to wipe out the small force of good. Dressed in black clothes, Deacon and the Smokers many times attack the Mariner, Helen, and Enola, who are usually dressed in white or off-white clothes. Their very name--Smokers--serves as a label for those who kill themselves puffing on cigarettes. In other words, the Smokers are self-destructive, as evil usually is. The Smokers blindly follow Deacon, a Satan, who is de- formed, having only one eye.

The human race, struggling to survive against such odds, finds hope in the child who bears the map on her back, who refuses a cigarette when it is offered to her. She is a type of Christ, who carries a cross that leads to her death through capture, but results in new life on Dryland. If her name is spelled backward, it becomes "Alone," indicating that she alone, literally, carries the weight of the world's salvation on her back. She has come from Dryland and she returns to it, much like the lamb in the Book of Revelation who was slain but now lives.

Dryland, of course, is the new world. In the film, earth is more valuable than gold; it is used as an item for bartering. At first, the Mariner thinks that Dryland is the world that has been covered by the ocean. Later, he comes to believe in Enola and understand that Dryland still exists. In this regard the film's plot resembles the Hebrew Bible's account about Noah and the flood, which destroys every living thing. Only Noah, his family, and the creatures he has saved survive to repopulate the earth.

The Mariner's initial desire to throw Enola overboard turns into a willingness to risk his life in order to save her. His faith is a tested one, carefully examined, and thought through. Dryland, once thought to be a myth, becomes for him the place of salvation for the human race.

The world of "Waterworld" is dualistic. The earth above the ocean, Dryland, is the place of good, the place the remnants of the human race seek. Like the first man and woman cast out of the garden of paradise, a few human beings seek to re-enter it by finding it. The ocean, representing chaos, is the location of evil, where Deacon's ship and the Smokers live. It has covered former cities and it consumes Deacon, the Smoker, and the Exxon Valdez. Dante's inferno is given a nod as the ship, before it sinks, repeatedly explodes in fireballs. Then, hell sinks into chaos.

The battlefield is the ocean. In the Book of Revelation, it is Armageddon, a famous field where the people of Israel won many battles. The survivors of the human race face chaos with their hope. And, though they suffer a lot, they never give up finding the place which represents the incarnation of their hope. Dryland is creation begun again. It is paradise. It is the new city of Jerusalem with its river and fruit-bearing trees. It is pristine beauty with no touch of evil. The old world exists no longer; in fact it was once covered by the sea.

Hope enables people to suffer. Helen suffers through the desire of the Mariner to throw overboard the girl she has adopted as her daughter. Enola suffers through the Mariner's dislike of her and her own fear of the water. The Mariner suffers too; he is shot in the side as he rescues his precious human cargo. Suffering makes humans strong. At least that is what the Book of Revelation seems to imply. Those who stand firm in faith, suffering even death, discover that they have made it to the new Jerusalem.

In such a place the Mariner cannot stay. He is not a human, but a mutation. While he has served as a link between the past and the future (the sea and Dryland--he is made with both gills and feet), he belongs to the ocean and cannot live on Dryland. So, he must sail away. However, he sails away changed by the faith of a few human survivors, much as the reader leaves the Book of Revelation. Life continues for the Mariner on the sea, and life continues for the human race on Dryland.

Exercises and Questions for Discussion

1. Make a list of five comparisons of themes between "Waterworld" and the Book of Revelation.

2. Make a list of three comparisons of characters between "Waterworld" and the Book of Revelation.

3. Outline the plot of the film by scene. For each scene indicate its importance to the whole story and what purpose it serves.

4. Outline the plot of the Book of Revelation by scene. For each scene indicate its importance to the whole story and what purpose it serves.

5. What do you think is the major truth which the movie attempts to communicate? Is this truth one that endures? Explain.

6. What do you think is the major truth which the Book of Revelation attempts to communicate? Is this truth one that endures? Explain.

7. In both "Waterworld" and the Book of Revelation, evil is destroyed by using violent means, such as killing, destruction of property, maiming. In what other ways can evil be conquered?

8. Compare and contrast life on the atoll, life on the sea, and life on Dryland in "Waterworld" with life in the seven churches, life on the earth, and life in the new Jerusalem in the Book of Revelation. What do you discover?

9. Why do you think "Waterworld" presumes that Enola came from Dryland and must return there? Why do you think the Mariner cannot remain with Helen and Enola on Dryland but must sail away?

Teaching the "Vineyard" Metaphor

A Walk in the Clouds

In the very first book of the Hebrew Bible, we are told that Noah was the first man to ever plant a vineyard. Once the Hebrew slaves escape from Egyptian bondage and enter the land promised to them by God, "vineyard" becomes a metaphor for the land and the nation. When King Ahab wants to buy Naboth's vineyard and turn it into his vegetable garden, Naboth refuses because it is his ancestral inheritance. In the First Book of Kings, Naboth's vineyard represents his past, his ties to the land, and his dependence upon God for fruitfulness.

The "vineyard" metaphor is further developed by the prophet Isaiah, who portrays God as accusing the elders and princes of the Israelites of having devoured the vineyard, the people, as the nation was attacked and captured by its enemies. In the first seven verses of the fifth chapter of Isaiah, we find a love song about a vineyard. An anonymous singer tells about his beloved who had a field which had been cleared and planted with choice vines. A watchtower and wine press were built to process the grapes, but the vineyard yielded only wild grapes. The owner decides to tear it down.

Then, the prophet declares that the vineyard is the house of Israel. The love song about the vineyard represents God's love for the people who have produced only wild grapes. Because no good fruit was found, God permitted the vineyard to be attacked and torn down by Israel's enemies. Later, Isaiah uses the "vineyard" metaphor again to envision the people's redemption by God, who will replant the vineyard and make it fruitful.

In a similar vein, the prophet Jeremiah employs the "vineyard" metaphor. God is portrayed as accusing the shepherds, the leaders, of Israel as being responsible for having destroyed the vineyard, the nation.

Likewise, does the prophet Ezekiel use the "vineyard" metaphor, declaring to the Babylonian captives that their mother, their nation, was once like a fruitful vine in a vineyard, the land of Israel, but it was transplanted by its enemies to the wilderness.

Psalm 80, a prayer for Israel's restoration, uses the "vineyard" metaphor for the nation of Israel in a plea to God to lead the people out of their captivity and back to their homeland. The psalmist first reminds God that Yahweh once brought a vine, the Hebrew people, out of Egypt and planted it in the land of Canaan, where it, the nation, took root and, conquering its neighbors, spread over the mountains to the sea and across the Jordan River. But first the Assyrians and then the Babylonians destroyed the nation of Israel, breaking down its walls, plucking its fruit, taking the people into captivity, and leaving the land desolate. The psalmist begs God to have regard for the vine, the stock that God planted, and bring the people home, creating another exodus for them out of captivity to freedom.

The "vineyard" metaphor reaches a crescendo in the Christian Bible. It becomes the basis for the analogy of the wicked tenant farmers at the beginning of chapter 12 in Mark's Gospel. It is copied by the authors of Matthew's Gospel and Luke's Gospel into their works. The Markan Jesus tells a story about a man, God, who planted a vineyard, the land of Israel, and leased it to tenant farmers, the people of Israel. When harvest time arrived, the owner, God, sent a slave, a prophet, to collect his share of the grapes, but the tenants beat him and sent him away with nothing. Two more times the owner sent slaves, prophets, and repeatedly they were beaten, insulted, and killed.

Finally, the owner sent his son, Jesus, thinking that they would respect him. But thinking that if they got rid of the son, they would inherit the owner's property, they killed him, crucified Jesus, and threw him out of the vineyard, outside of Jerusalem. Then, the story-teller poses a rhetorical question to the hearers: What will the vineyard owner do? The answer: He, God, will destroy the tenants, the nation of Israel, and give the vineyard to others, to the Gentiles. By 70 C.E., when Jerusalem and the Temple were destroyed by the Romans, the "Christian" author of Mark's Gospel thought that God had taken the "vineyard" away from the Jews and handed it over to the Gentiles.

With little editing, the author of Matthew's Gospel retains the wicked tenant analogy, but he prepares for it with two other stories: the parable of the laborers in the vineyard and the parable of the two sons sent to work in the vineyard.

In the unique story of the laborers in the vineyard at the beginning of chapter 20 in Matthew's Gospel, the "vineyard" metaphor is stretched from its Hebrew Bible reference to the land of Israel to include the kingdom of heaven. The landowner, God, hires laborers, both Jews and Gentiles, to work in the kingdom at different times of the day. No matter what time of the day they are called, they respond and work. Those who worked longer presume that they will be paid more, but all receive the agreed-upon wage for a day of labor. The parable is addressed to Jews, who thought they should be rewarded more because they worked longer in the vineyard and were its original laborers, and to the Gentiles, who wondered what share they might have as latecomers into the kingdom. What the Matthean Jesus makes clear is that God gives to each as the Holy One wills, and no one has any right to argue about any injustice done to anyone.

In the unique Matthean analogy of the two sons, immediately preceding the analogy of the tenant farmers in chapter 21 of Matthew's Gospel, the author portrays Jesus as using the response of the sons to parallel the response of Jews and Gentiles to the proclamation of the kingdom of heaven. The first son, who says no to his father's, God's, request to work in the vineyard but later changes his mind and goes, represents those who heard Jesus, such as tax collectors and prostitutes-- the outcasts of society--and responded to his message by following him and changing their lives. The second son, who says yes to his father's, God's, request to work in the vineyard but never goes, represents those who heard Jesus--anyone who hears or reads the story--and failed to respond to his message and did not change their lives. It's the first group of whom the vineyard owner, God, approves.

As did the author of Matthew's Gospel before him, the author of Luke's Gospel did little editing of Mark's analogy of the wicked tenants. However, he prepares for it with the unique parable about a barren fig tree planted in a vineyard. The fig tree represents anyone who is not at first fruitful. The owner of the vineyard, God, wants the tree removed due to its lack of fruitfulness, but the gardener, Jesus, pleads for one more year before taking such drastic action. The owner grants the gardener's request. The author of Luke's Gospel gives Gentiles time to change, since he believes that they are rooted and grow out of the vineyard of Israel.

While John's Gospel contains no vineyard parables or analogies, the author does manage to employ the "vineyard" metaphor in chapter 15. The Johannine Jesus declares himself to be the true vine and God, the Father, the vinegrower. God prunes the branches, followers or believers, so that they produce more fruit, more faith. Unless the branches, people, remain firmly attached to the vine, Jesus, they wither, and die, and are burned.   However, through nourishment from the vine, Jesus, the branches keep growing and producing abundantly.

In order to help students understand the use of the "vineyard" metaphor, "A Walk in the Clouds" (20th Century Fox, 1995) can be shown. The film, an old fashioned romance, begins with the return of a ship full of veterans following World War II. The boat docks in San Francisco, California, as Paul Sutton (Keanu Reeves) reveals to another man that he last saw his wife four years ago on their wedding day. He had met her on a Friday, married her on a Saturday, and shipped out on a Sunday. But as the reunion of other men and their wives on the dock is completed and couples disperse throughout the Golden Gate city, Sutton can't find his wife, Betty.

Walking to her apartment, he opens the door with a key he has. Inside, she is startled to see him, but immediately confesses that she hasn't read the daily letter he has sent her for the past four years. She has all of them stacked neatly in a box. She reveals that she has asked his former boss to hold his job as a chocolate salesman for him. All Sutton can say is that he has had time to think about what's important to him.

After a reunion sex scene, Sutton leaves early the next morning, dressed in his uniform and taking the train to Sacramento to sell chocolates. After helping a woman on the train who is struggling with getting a suitcase on the overhead rack, she, Victoria Aragon (Aitana Sanchez-Gijon), vomits on his uniform and he must change into a brown suit he carries with him. After finally getting settled into a seat on the train, he daydreams about an orphanage which was destroyed by the war.

Because he and Victoria inadvertently ended up changing train tickets, without knowing it both get off at the same stop and catch the same bus headed toward Sacramento. On the bus, Sutton spots Victoria, sits across the aisle from her, finds out that she is on her way to the Napa Valley, and that she has his ticket. At the next stop two men, Bill and Herman, sit next to and behind Victoria, respectively, and begin to harass her. Sutton defends her by throwing a punch at Bill and Herman. The bus driver, a woman, stops the vehicle and puts all three of them off. Bill and Herman walk one direction on the road and Sutton takes the other. After a while, who should he come upon sitting on her suitcase in the middle of the road and crying but Victoria Aragon.

Interspersed with sobs, Victoria tells Sutton that she's waiting for a miracle. He offers to listen to her tale of woe. She tells him about an affair she had with a professor in school who, before he dumped her, got her pregnant. She tells Sutton that her father said that he would kill anyone who dishonors his family. Then, Victoria tells Sutton that her father will kill her if she comes home pregnant without a husband. In order to save her life, Sutton offers to play the role of her husband for one day. Then, he will disappear as if he had abandoned her.

Taking her bag, they walk together down the gravel road toward Victoria's home, while Sutton tells her about his plans for the future with his wife in San Francisco. She can't believe that anyone would do this for her, but Sutton tells her that he is doing it for both her and her baby.

Approaching a view through the trees of the valley below, Victoria tells Sutton that the vineyard, whose vines crisscross all the hills like stitches on a sampler, is called "The Clouds." Opening his sample box of chocolates, he takes a gold-like ring off of a piece of candy, puts it on Victoria's finger, and, taking another one, puts it on his. Little does the viewer realize that this is a flashforward of things to come. But just as the "wedding" ceremony is completed, gunfire is heard, and they fall to the ground to get out of the way. Her father, Alberto Aragon (Giancarlo Giannini), approaches with several other hunters, and Victoria introduces Sutton to her father as her husband.

The next scene takes place in the Aragon home, where Victoria introduces Sutton as her husband to her mother and the household servants. Meanwhile, Alberto swears that her marriage to Sutton cannot be true. However, contrasted to Alberto's inhospitality is Don Pedro Aragon's warm welcome. Don Pedro (Anthony Quinn) introduces himself to Sutton and tells him that he wants to try his chocolates. After eating one, he says that it is delicious.

Before dinner, Victoria and her mother discuss her father and the difficulty he has with change. When all are seated for supper, Victoria's grandmother says grace. Then, Sutton and Victoria are invited to tell everyone how they met, but their stories do not always coincide. So, one after the next, they must quickly clarify details. Sutton reveals that he is originally from Moline, Illinois, where he grew up in an orphanage. Alberto, dismayed by this, since he declares his daughter can trace her ancestors back 400 years, says, "My daughter has married a man who has no past, and he has no future." Victoria retorts that Alberto doesn't know that Paul has not future. Both Sutton and Victoria get up abruptly and leave the table.

Outside the house, Sutton and Victoria engage in their first real conversation. Paul begins by stating that Alberto doesn't pull any punches. Then he reveals that as a young boy every night he would climb on the roof and make a wish on every star he saw. Victoria tells Paul that is a lot of wishing. Sutton clarifies that he has only one wish, and Victoria asks what it is. Sutton answers that he wishes he had a family like she does.

Victoria tells Paul that her father, Alberto, has no right to treat him the way he does, but Sutton says that if a strange man came into his house and told him that he had married his only daughter, he would probably act the same way. Once Sutton has revealed his depth of understanding of his foe, Alberto, Victoria tells him that he would not act the same way. Sutton says he is not sure how he would act. Then, he concludes that in another eight hours he will be back on the road and that he thinks the worse part is over.

But the worse part is not over. The next scene is set in Victoria's parents' bedroom. While her mother makes the bed, she tells them that her grandmother, her mother, and she spent their wedding night in it and wants Victoria and Sutton to spend their first night home in it also. Receiving a single rose from a maid, she lays it on the pillow on the bed, saying, "Love each other always." Then she and the maids exit the room, close the door, and leave Victoria and Sutton alone.

In a smaller room, Alberto and his wife prepare for bed. She defends her daughter's action and tells him that he needs to accept Sutton as her husband. She tells him that he needs to go to the room where Victoria and Sutton are and wish them a good night.

Meanwhile, Victoria and Sutton have prepared for bed. He is dressed in pajamas and she in a gown with a house coat over it. As they talk, he takes bed linens and a pillow and makes a pallet on the floor near the fireplace which is glowing with burning logs. Sutton tells her that he believes that there is a perfect someone for everyone--someone who will love her no matter what. She asks him if he would marry someone if it wasn't his baby she was carrying, and he responds that he would marry her if he loved her.

Their conversation is interrupted with a knock on the door. Quickly grabbing some of the bed linens, he rushes into bed with Victoria. She invites in the person on the other side of the door. Her father sticks his head through the door and wishes them goodnight. Then, Alberto leaves, but not before spying some of the bed linens on the floor near the fireplace.

Victoria and Sutton agree that they should stay in bed together in case someone else comes along. After scooting as far away from each other as possible, they sleep. But Sutton dreams of the orphanage and the children killed in war again and wakes up screaming, "Victoria." Just as she is comforting him, they hear the sound of a bell ringing. Sutton asks about it, and Victoria tells him that it means frost.

Sutton and Victoria rush to the vineyard, where all the other members of the family and the household are already fighting the frost off of the grapes. Sutton helps by taking a set of wings in his hands and following Victoria, who shows him how to wave them in order to keep the frost off of the grapes. Called "flying," the waving of the wings brings the heat down from the warmers to the grapes. In a wide-angle shot, the viewer sees the whole vineyard interspersed with fire pots and people "flying," while Alberto keeps an eye on Victoria and Sutton.

The next morning, Sutton prepares to leave according to the original plan. Victoria and Paul wish each other the best of luck. But on the way out, as a rooster is heard crowing, Sutton meets Don Pedro, Victoria's grandfather, who tells him, "It's the cold of the grape that robs our sleep. When she's ripe, she calls to man." Then, he invites Sutton to walk with him through the vineyard and tells him to bring his chocolates with him.

Don Pedro tells Sutton that his doctors have told him no chocolates, no salt, no cigars, and just a little brandy. Don Pedro says that the doctors don't know about the needs of a man's soul. Then, after picking a chocolate from the box Sutton holds, he examines a ring on one piece and says that it looks like his granddaughter's ring. Sutton says that he hasn't noticed that.

Then, Don Pedro proceeds to give Sutton a history lesson about the Aragon family. He tells him about the first priest who came from Spain to Mexico with only a dream, the clothes on his back, and the root from the family's vineyard inside his pulpit.

Next, Don Pedro takes Sutton to a small hill in the vineyard upon which is a shrine and one vine growing in front of it. Don Pedro says,

> This is the root I brought with me, a descendant from the root the first Pedro brought with him. Our vines come from this one. It's not just the root of "The Clouds," it's the root of our lives, Victoria's life. Now that you are a part of all this, a part of us, now it is the root of your life. You are an orphan no longer. So, you will stay with your family while we harvest the fruit. It's a special time, a time of magic.

Don Pedro uses the "vineyard" metaphor to reference his family, which has been in the vine-growing business for 400 years. He has also adopted Sutton into his family in contrast to Alberto, who cannot accept him. To Don Pedro's invitation to stay for the harvest, Sutton says that he cannot because he has commitments. Don Pedro asks him about his commitment to his family, but Sutton insists that he must leave.

Don Pedro, seeing that he getting nowhere, uses some reverse psychology, telling Sutton that Alberto said he would not stay. Don Pedro tells him that Alberto said that the first chance the gringo got he would leave Victoria. Sutton declares that is not leaving her. Don Pedro says that he understands but that Alberto will remind Victoria that he wasn't there for harvest and she will pay for his commitments. Sutton says that it would just be the difference of a day. Don Pedro replies that the harvest is the most important day of the year in the vineyard and if Sutton leaves, Alberto will remind Victoria about it for the rest of her life. Seeing that he has lost this battle, Sutton declares Don Pedro to be correct and states that he will stay one more day. After eating another chocolate, Don Pedro reminds Paul that he has no more chocolates to sell anyway.

Finding Victoria, Sutton tells her that he is staying until after the harvest. Looking at her father, Alberto, Sutton tells him, "Family comes first."

In the next scene, Victoria's brother, Pedro, drives his car into the vineyard in order to participate in the harvest. After Victoria introduces him to Sutton, he welcomes Sutton to the family and calls himself "Pete," which causes his father to scowl. But the harvest begins, and the Aragons, Sutton, and field hands begin to cut the ripe grapes from the vines. Once Sutton is shown how to cut the clusters quickly, he and Alberto engage in a contest to see who can harvest more grapes.

In the next scene, Don Pedro, who has loaned Sutton a pair of pants, asks him about how they feel. Demonstrating that there is enough room for two men in them, Sutton responds that they are a little big. Then Don Pedro proceeds to teach Sutton another lesson about family, saying, "Clothes are like family. You have to live in them for a while before you get the perfect fit." Sutton says that he doubts if everyone shares Don Pedro's opinion. Don Pedro says that it was not easy for him, and that it is not easy for Alberto to be in charge. He adds, "Every man has to find his own way. But I have faith in my son, and I have faith in you."

Now, the stomping of grapes begins. Musicians play while the women dance on the grapes in a huge wooden vat. Some of the men remove Sutton's shoes and put him in the vat near Victoria. After a while, both of them run to their room in her father's house and engage in passionate kissing, but Sutton stops abruptly. He tells Victoria, "I want you more than anything, Victoria. You can't imagine how I want you. But I'm not free. And I won't hurt you that way." As he leaves the room, Victoria curls up in the fetal position on the bed.

The next morning, Paul is found in a chair in the living room where he has spent the night. Alberto and his son, Pedro, enter the room discussing partnerships for the vineyard business. Alberto sees Sutton and tells him to stick to his own business of selling candy. Then, Alberto asks Sutton about what is going on. He tells Sutton that he has observed that he sleeps one night on the floor and the next on the couch. But just as he finishes, Victoria walks into the room accusing her father of making Sutton feel unwelcomed. Alberto says that there is something wrong with Paul's and Victoria's scenario. He also tells Victoria that he noticed that she brought home all her clothes, "like she has no place else to go."

Victoria says that if he doesn't want her there, that she will leave. Her father states that he wants the truth. Victoria tells him that the only truth he wants is his own truth because that is the only truth he can accept." As Victoria leaves the room, Sutton says, "The truth is she came home because she loves her family." Alberto, staring into Sutton's face, says, "I told you: Stay out of our business." Sutton retorts, "She is my business."

Again dressed in his brown business suit, Sutton prepares to leave "The Clouds." He finds the laundry woman preparing to wash his uniform. As she shakes his pants before putting them into the tub of water, a locket with his wife's picture falls out, and he moves quickly toward the woman to pick it up before she can see it. He tells her that he doesn't have time to wait while she washes his clothes because he has business to attend. She says that Don Pedro has finished his business and that he must follow his fate, what brought him there.

Just as he is finishing his conversation with the laundry woman, who puts his clothes into the tub, he catches a glimpse of Victoria doubling up in pain. He runs to her, but she tells him to stick to their plan and to go home to his wife. She tells him that he can't help her. Then, she runs into the wine cellar. He follows her, shouting, "Victoria? Victoria?"

Who should appear on a wooden walkway above the vats in the cellar but Alberto, who tells Sutton that his marriage to Victoria does not entitle him to her half of the vineyeard and its wines. Sutton asks him what he means. Alberto states that he didn't see a wedding, not even a wedding certificate. Then, he reminds Sutton that just because he speaks with an accent that Sutton should not conclude that he thinks with one.

Sutton turns the conversation to the topic of Alberto's aloofness. He says that for the four years that he had been at war he had to keep himself closed off. Then, he asks Alberto why he is closed off. Alberto, getting angry, asks Sutton what he is talking about. Paul tells him that he has shut his daughter out of his life. Then, Sutton asks Alberto, "Can't you see how amazing she is, how alive?" He adds, "My whole life I've been dreaming of getting the kind of love your daughter gives to you. I would die for what you have. Why can't you just love her? She's so easy to love."

While Victoria, hiding behind a vat, listens to their conversation, Alberto states that Paul knows nothing about his daughter. Sutton responds, "I know that she is good and strong and deserves all the love this world has to give. Can't you see that--how wonderful, how special she is?"

Looking out the window at the vineyard, Alberto says that he cultivates the vineyard for his family." Sutton tells him that he should let his family know how much he cares.

After going to the wash tub to rescue his wet uniform, Sutton puts it into his satchel and begins to leave "The Clouds." But, as has happened to him previously, Don Pedro appears on the scene with a bottle of twenty-one-year-old brandy and a glass. Then, using the brandy as his taking-off point for another lesson for Sutton, he says, "The secret about brandy is age. The secret of everything is age."

While Don Pedro shuffles Sutton off to the brandy cellar, Victoria's mother comforts her. Victoria says, "He will come back." Meanwhile, Don Pedro continues the lesson he had started, telling Sutton that newlyweds always make love and war. He asks Sutton if he talked to Victoria. Sutton says he tried. Don Pedro states, "Wouldn't make a difference. Talking between men and women never solves anything. When we think, they feel."

Motioning to Sutton to take one of the seats at the table in the brandy cellar, Don Pedro tells Paul to sit down, but he protests that he will miss his bus. Then, Don Pedro says, "Make yourself comfortable, please. Tomorrow we'll go to the festival for the wine blessing. The bus will be there. I have the perfect solution for you." They begin drinking brandy. Sutton guzzles his first glass while Don Pedro watches in astonishment.

In the next scene, musicians have joined Don Pedro and Sutton in the brandy cellar, and the table has been spread with food. Don Pedro teaches Sutton a love song in Spanish, and Sutton sings with him and the four musicians. Afterward, as they walk through the courtyard, Don Pedro reminds him that he's a gringo, the wife he is talking to is Mexican, and that he needs to speak to her in a language she understands.

Sutton, with the musicians accompanying him, serenades Victoria with the love song Don Pedro taught him. After a few verses, Don Pedro tells him to keep watching in the window; when the light comes on, he will be saved. But no light comes on. Victoria is awakened by the singing, but she watches in the dark through the window. Likewise, Alberto and his wife are awakened by the serenade. Alberto tells his wife that Paul seems to love Victoria and that maybe he has been too tough on him. But Sutton walks out of "The Clouds," the vineyard, and Victoria turns on no light to call him back as he looks over his shoulder toward her window several times.

The next day the blessing of the wine festival takes place in the local town. The Aragon family, after arriving on horseback, takes part in the dancing in the street. Victoria spies Sutton, dressed in his uniform and standing on a walkway leading to the bus station, as the priest says the prayer blessing the harvest after which he tastes some of the first vintage and pronounces it good.

Carrying two glasses of wine, Victoria approaches Sutton, asking him to toast with her. He asks about what they are toasting. She answers, "To 'what if.'" Holding up their glasses, Sutton says, "To 'what if,'" and they drink. Just as they are swallowing, Alberto approaches them with the priest and introduces Sutton as his son-in-law and "a bonafide war hero." He tells the priest that Sutton had helped bring in the harvest. Then, Alberto declares that his daughter's marriage in city hall was not an appropriate place for the exchange of marriage vows. Making a public announcement and putting Sutton and Victoria on the spot, Alberto tells the crowd that he has arranged for Paul's and Victoria's marriage that evening and he wants everyone to attend.

Sutton tells Victoria, "We have to tell them." She responds, "No, I have to tell them. I'm not scared now." Taking a war medal out of his satchel, he hands it to Victoria as a present for the baby. She asks him about it, and he tells her it was awarded to him for courage under fire. Victoria states that he is the most honorable man she has ever known. They kiss, and she walks away to tell her parents the truth--that she is not married to Sutton and that her pregnancy is the result of an affair she had with her professor.

Sutton, walking and hitchhiking, heads toward San Francisco. One man, driving a truck, picks him up. Before he falls asleep in the passenger seat and has another dream of the orphanage in the war, tempered this time with Victoria and a child in it, Sutton tells the driver that he has been "walking in the clouds." Meanwhile, Victoria's father, who is terribly upset by what she told him, sits at a table under a huge tree in the vineyard and drinks until he is drunk, while his daughter watches from afar.

Back in San Francisco, Sutton goes to his apartment and, upon opening the door, notices that his wife, Betty, has opened all the letters he had sent her. She tells him that she has now read them and that what he wants she doesn't. Then, Sutton hears a man call her name from behind a curtain petitioning a sleeping area from the rest of the one-room apartment. Betty has been cheating on Sutton. She tells him that they could still be friends, that an annulment would be easiest, and all he has to do is sign it. He does.

Sutton is not visibly shaken by any of this. In fact, it is exactly for what he had dared not hope. He does not demonstrate any anger, even when the man with whom Betty has been having an affair stands in front of him and begs Sutton not to hit him. Sutton tells him that he has no intention of hitting him. From the apartment window, the man and Betty watch as Sutton heads out of town and hitches a ride back to "The Clouds."

Upon his return to the vineyard, he finds Alberto passed out with his head on the table in the vineyard. Keeping his distance, Paul tells Alberto that he owes him an apology. Alberto, raising his head, tells Sutton to get off his land. Sutton tells him that his intentions were good, that he wanted to protect Victoria. Alberto tells him to stay away from her. Sutton says: "I can't. She's like the air to me. I've come to ask you for her hand in marriage."

Getting very angry, Alberto declares that Paul is already married. Then, calling Jose, one of the men standing around the area, Alberto asks for his gun. Interrupting him, Sutton says that his marriage to Betty was never meant to be, that it was a mistake, and that it's over. Then, Sutton shows him the annulment paper. That, however, does not appease Alberto, who tells Sutton that he has deceived him in his own house and in his own bed. Again, he warns Sutton to stay away from her. But Sutton declares: "I love her. I want to be with her for the rest of my life. I want to take care of her." Again, Alberto asks for his gun. But Sutton just shouts, "Victoria, Victoria, Victoria." And from her room, she hears him and proceeds to go to meet him.

Alberto continues the dialogue, saying that it is not his child she carries. Sutton says he will claim it as his if Victoria will marry him. Alberto lunges at Sutton as Victoria runs toward him, stating, "I love him." But Alberto grabs the kerosene lantern and hurls it at Sutton, who dunks. However, when the lantern hits the ground it bursts open and sets fire to the area. The fire begins to spread rapidly, jumping from one dry vine to the next. Both Sutton and Victoria try to put it out, but they cannot. By the time others arrive to help extinguish the fire, it is out of control. One by one, the dry grape vines go up in a single fireball, until the whole vineyard lights up the night.

So determined is Sutton to continue to attempt to put out the flames that Don Pedro has to restrain him from going into the burning hell. Sutton does manage to reach Pete, whose clothes on his back have caught on fire. Sutton stops him from running and, rolling him on the ground, extinguishes the flames and saves his life. All the members of the Aragon family watch in amazement with sooted faces as the entire vineyard burns over the hills.

The next morning the family is found at a shed along with Sutton. Their faces are streaked with soot as we see them either sitting or standing in a state of disbelief. Victoria breaks the silence, saying, "Papa." Alberto, who has been converted, says that he was afraid of losing all of them and that he didn't know any other way to love. Then, he asks them to teach him how to love.

Don Pedro states, "The fire burned through everything. There's no root stock left to replant. It's finished." But Sutton, recalling the shrine that Don Pedro had showed him earlier and the talk about family roots that Don Pedro had given to him there, walks to the hill where he finds a root, pushes it over, and discovers that it is not burned through. Bringing the root to Alberto, Sutton asks him if the fire reached the inside. Cutting off a small piece with his pocket knife, Alberto declares, "It's alive. 'The Clouds' lives."

Cutting off another piece of the living vine, Alberto hands it to Sutton, saying, "This is the root of your life, the root of your family. You are bound to this land and to this family by commitment, by honor, and by love. Plant it. It will grow." Sutton, who up to this point has always known what ought to be done, says, "I don't know how." Alberto, looking at Victoria, says, "Victoria, help your husband." After handing her the root, Sutton removes a ring from his pocket and places it on her finger. They kiss. Don Pedro gets the last word: "Beautiful."

In "A Walk in the Clouds," the student can learn the polyvalent quality of the "vineyard" metaphor as it is found in the Hebrew Bible and used in the Christian Bible. First, like the "The Clouds" vineyard represents the Aragon family, the vineyard represents the people of Israel. And just as "The Clouds" stands for the wealth of the Aragon family, so does the fruitfulness of the vineyard stand for the Israelites. Both the Aragons and the Israelites acknowledge that prosperity, plenty, and fruitfulness come from God.

Second, the fruitfulness of the Aragon vineyard is an appropriate setting for the blossoming of the love between Paul Sutton and Victoria Aragon. Sutton is like the transplanted vine, who takes root and grows in the Aragon vineyard, enjoying its beauty, saving it from frost, and helping to harvest its produce. While working in the physical vineyard, he is also taking root, growing, and saving the vineyard (who is Victoria in terms of love). Likewise, he takes root, grows, and, ultimately, saves the vineyard that is the Aragon family as one by one the members accept him as one of their own. After God settles the Israelites in the promised land and makes them like a vineyard, they enter into a covenant of love with

God, always succeeding, growing stronger, and being saved by their God.

However, at times, the vineyard is destroyed, sometimes torn down from within by leaders and sometimes from without by Israel's enemies. In "A Walk in the Clouds," Alberto Aragon destroys his own vineyard by refusing to admit Paul Sutton to marry his daughter, Victoria, and by tossing the lantern that sets the vineyard ablaze. The death of the vineyard removes the one way that Alberto had used to express his love for his family, namely, by providing for them. Now, he needs a new way, the way of love. Once he realizes the error of his ways, repents, and learns to love, Alberto is converted and welcomes Sutton to his family, the vineyard. Likewise, once the people of Israel repented, God accepted them back. Their old roots were found still to have life in them, like Sutton found the old root of the vineyard to be still alive after the fire. There will be a new beginning of the vineyard, like there is a new Alberto, a new Paul, a new Victoria, a new family.

From a gospel point of view, "The Clouds" is taken away from the Aragons and given to Sutton, who will make the vineyard fruitful once again. At first, he is like the son who said yes but never went to work in the vineyard, as he was to be Victoria's husband for only a day. In the end, he is like the son who said no, but later changed his mind, married Victoria, claimed her child as his own, and worked to make the vineyard fruitful.

The Aragon family is like a vine and Paul is like a branch who wants to be connected to it. Sutton can be seen as a Gentile, who desires to be attached to the Jewish vine of the Aragon family. At first there are difficulties, but Sutton is grafted on as the problems melt into love and one family emerges filled with the promise of new life. Family life is for what Sutton has searched all his life. He was an orphan who continued to have dreams about the orphanage he had been a part of destroying during the war. Without a family connection, Sutton realizes that he has no life; he is an unattached branch. Once Alberto is willing to accept him as a member of his family, Sutton's dreams cease because he is grafted onto the Aragon family vine and serves as its instrument of restoration.

The fruitfulness and new life of the Aragon's vineyard and family which Sutton desires is contrasted to his marriage to Betty. He had met her one day, married her the next, and shipped out to war on the third day. Theirs was not a marriage at all. For Sutton is was a dream; for Betty it was nothing, as at first she never even read the letters he had sent her for four years, and, after she does read them, she concludes that what he wants is not what she wants. Because she hasn't read his letters, she doesn't even know that he was coming home. Betty's fruitfulness is with another lover. Once he experiences real love, Sutton realizes what he doesn't have with Betty and willingly and joyfully accepts the annulment papers she presents to him. There is no divorce, because there never was a marriage to begin with. The annulment decrees and declares Sutton to be free to marry Victoria. Sutton is transplanted to a vineyard where he will produce abundantly, like the Hebrews led out of Egypt to the promised land. His wife, who is pregnant, echoes Psalm 128, a song about home and family life: "Your wife will be like a fruitful vine within your house; your children like olive shoots around your table."

The lack of acceptance of Sutton on the part of Alberto is contrasted to the full acceptance of Sutton by Don Pedro, who, because of his age and experience, is more closely connected to the life of the family and the vineyard, the root of their lives. Every time Sutton attempts to leave, Don Pedro manages to detain him and teach him more about the vineyard, about being a member of a family, about serenading a woman, about the rhythm of death and life. Sutton exceeds his teacher. After the fire, Don Pedro declares there to be no life left, but Sutton finds it. Like the destroyed land of Israel and like the Israelites taken into captivity where they experienced death, "The Clouds" was burned. But the Israelites returned and the land became fruitful once again. The marriage of Paul Sutton and Victoria Aragon, who already carries a child, guarantees the future of the family, and Sutton's finding of the root of a vine guarantees the future of the vineyard.

Exercises and Questions for Discussion

1. What is the significance of Betty Sutton not being at the dock to meet the ship upon which Paul Sutton arrived? What parallel can you find in the biblical vineyard metaphor?

2. What is the significance of the setting for Paul and Betty Sutton's relationship in a city and Paul Sutton's and Victoria Aragon's relationship in a vineyard?

3. While the "vineyard" metaphor for family dominates "A Walk in the Clouds," what other metaphors are operative for family in the film?

4. What five aspects of the biblical vineyard metaphor are best portrayed in "A Walk in the Clouds"? Be specific and explain each.

5. Does "A Walk in the Clouds" help to better understand the Hebrew Bible's use of the vineyard metaphor or the Christian Bible's use of the vineyard metaphor? Explain.

6. Compare and contrast God's role in the biblical vineyard metaphor and Don Pedro's role in "A Walk in the Clouds." What do you discover?

7. Compare and contrast the parable of the laborers in Matthew's Gospel to "A Walk in the Clouds." What do you discover?

8. Compare and contrast the parable of the tenant farmers in either Mark's Gospel, Matthew's Gospel, or Luke's Gospel to "A Walk in the Clouds." What do you discover?

9. Compare and contrast the Johannine Jesus' saying about he being the vine and everyone else being branches to "A Walk in the Clouds." What do you discover?

10. What is the biblical definition of love? In which character(s) in "A Walk in the Clouds" is that definition best reflected? Explain.

Teaching Hermeneutics

Romeo and Juliet

Hermeneutics, literally meaning "interpretation," is derived from the name of the Greek god Hermes, who served as a messenger of the other Greek gods. The task of biblical hermeneutics is to build a bridge from an ancient text to the present. After answering the question, "What did the text mean to the people to whom it was written," hermeneutics enables us to answer this question: "What does the text mean to us today?"

The methodology of hermeneutics can be summarized in the following manner:

(1) Identify presuppositions or pre-understandings that the reader brings to the text. Assumptions, such as personal experiences, biases, culture, language, etc., can get in the way of answering the first question, "What did the text mean to the people to whom it was written?" Students often assume that a biblical text is addressed to them because it appears in English translation. By presenting a copy of the New Testament in Greek and asking a student to read a few verses, students immediately begin to grasp the fact that the New Testament was written to people who spoke and read Greek--not them.

For another example, today most people do not consider leaven or yeast to be an agent of evil or corruption, as it is in the parable of the leaven (Matthew 13:33, Luke 13:20-21). Ancient people did not understand how leaven worked, so they concluded that it must be the result of evil or corruption. That is why only unleavened bread could be used during high holy day celebrations in honor of God. Without that understanding, the tension cannot be experienced when Jesus compares the reign of God to a woman who hides leaven in flour. Jesus says that God corrupts everything God touches.

(2) Once we become aware of our pre-understandings or assump-

tions, step two in the hermeneutical process is for students to record their initial understanding of a text. A person answers this question: "What does the text mean to me the first time I read it?"

In the case of the parable of the leaven, students usually say that it refers to the way the church spreads throughout the world. Without any hint of the corruptive influence of leaven, since yeast is assumed to be a good ingredient in our culture, students conclude that the church or Christianity will spread throughout the universe.

(3) Step three in biblical hermeneutics is for students to begin to ask questions about their initial understanding of a text. This is a difficult stage, because it implies that a person has a biased point of view --which, of course, is true. Every person has biases, a perspective from which he or she begins the process of interpretation. Being biased is not negative; it's just natural. In this step, the student identifies what he or she is contributing to the interpretation process.

In the example of the parable of the leaven, the student might become aware that he or she has interpreted the reign of God to refer to the church, or that leaven or yeast has a positive connotation.

(4) As one's biases are questioned and set aside, the student begins to realize that more information about the culture out of which the parable emerges is needed. In order to answer the question, "What did the text say to the people to whom it was written?," we must know something about the intended audience and its culture and its presuppositions and its biases.

For example, in the parable of the leaven, the student discovers that leaven was understood by ancient people to be corruptive or evil. A woman, the agent who hides the leaven in the parable, while acceptable today, should have been a man in terms of a metaphor for God's reign. Three measures of flour, a huge amount, signifies a biblical epiphany, a manifestation of God, such as Abraham's three visitors and Sarah's preparation of three measures of flour, or Gideon's offering of three measures of flour and its disappearance in fire, or Hannah's offering of three measures of flour and the promise of a son in her old age.

(5) Once the student discovers what the text meant to the people to whom it was written, interpretation begins. The student begins to build a bridge from the text and its meaning to today and what the text might mean now. Usually, this takes the form of a question and answer dialogue. By asking questions, such as, "What else do I need to know about the culture and its presuppositions that produced this text?," the student discovers answers that lead to interpretation.

This part of the process of hermeneutics might take the form of arguing with the text, such as debating why Jesus would compare God's reign to something as corrupt as leaven. Or it might consist of a moment of aha, when understanding seems to come from nowhere. No matter how interpretation comes, the student is led to the next step: testing.

(6) Testing presumes an understanding of context. For example, the parable of the leaven appears only in Matthew's Gospel and Luke's Gospel. And in each gospel it is found in a different place. Matthew places it in his Jesus' second sermon which he delivers while sitting in a boat on the sea, while Luke locates it within a teaching narrative in a synagogue. Luke also turns the first part of the parable into a question. So, the student must ask if his or her interpretation fits within the immediate context of the parable's location. Does the material surrounding the parable convey the same or a similar meaning?

Context also includes an understanding of the whole gospel. Are similar themes found in Matthew and Luke that shed light on the parable's meaning? If these can be named, then the student has tested his or her interpretation. If they cannot, then the process of interpretation must begin all over again.

(7) Once the testing phase is complete, the student must decide on a meaning for a text. In the case of the parable of the leaven, the text means that God's reign spreads undetectably throughout the world, corrupting everything and everyone it touches. And the agent for God's reign is most likely who we wouldn't expect.

One way to be sure that students have understood adequately the answer to the question, "What did the text say to the people to whom it was written?," and that they have interpreted a text authentically, answering "What does the text mean to us today?," is to ask them to rewrite the text as if it were written to us today.

The parable of the leaven might be rewritten this way: God's presence in the world is like radioactive waste which a scientist took and hid in a bag of garbage. The garbage collector took the bag to the dump, where the radioactive waste contaminated the whole fifty acres of the waste-management site.

An effective way to teach the methodology of hermeneutics is by using the film "Romeo and Juliet" (20th Century Fox, 1996). In this modern adaptation of William Shakespeare's classic love story, Baz Luhrmann builds a bridge from Elizabethan England to contemporary United States culture. Keeping only the dialogue he deemed necessary to help the viewer in the progression of the story, Luhrmann directs Leonardo DiCaprio (Romeo) and Claire Danes (Juliet), the youthful star-crossed lovers of the past, and transforms them into a tragic love affair of the present.

The film begins with a view of a TV screen filled with "snow." Suddenly, a female newscaster appears and begins to report on the recent death of Romeo Montague and Juliet Capulet. Her text is the prologue of the play. The time is not the sixteenth century, but the twentieth and twenty-first centuries. The setting is not Verona, but Verona Beach.

As the TV news reporter fades away, the Dramatis Personae are presented. Each character's face, name, and role appears on the screen. Shakespeare's "Montague and Capulet, heads of two houses at variance with each other" are given first names and identified for the viewer. Thus, we have Fulgencio Capulet, Juliet's father, and Gloria Capulet, Juliet's mother; Ted Montague, Romeo's father, and Caroline Montague, Romeo's mother. "Escalus, prince of Verona" becomes Captain Prince, chief of police. "Paris, a young nobleman, kinsman to the prince," becomes Dave Paris, the governor's son. And "Mercutio, kinsman to the prince, and friend to Romeo" becomes Mercutio, Romeo's best friend.

The public place of Act 1, Scene 1, in which a fight ensures between members of the houses of Capulet and Montague, is set at a gas station to which three members of the Montague gang arrives in a convertible while listening to loud rap music. They wear open, bold-colored beach shirts and gold necklaces, sporting shoulder holsters with handguns and sunglasses propped on top of their heads. The license plate on their car reads "Montague."

The rival gang, the Capulet boys, arrives at the same gas station in a hard top car with this license plate: CAP-005. While each is parked for refueling, members of the gang taunt each other.

Meanwhile, the viewer is introduced to some of the members of the gang. Shakespeare's "Benvolio, nephew to Montague, and friend to Romeo" becomes Benvolio Montague, Romeo's cousin. He waves his handgun, which has "Sword 9 mm" inscribed on the side. "Tybalt, nephew to Lady Capulet" becomes Tybalt Capulet, Prince of Cats and Juliet's cousin, who lights a cigar and drops the lit match onto the cement. For a second and as a prediction of things to come, the camera focuses on the banner hanging on the gas station: "Phoenix: Add more fuel to your fire."

As a gun fight erupts, the Montague gang pulls away from the gas pump, permitting the gas nozzle to fall to the pavement and spread the liquid everywhere. As Tybalt drops his cigar, an inferno envelops the place as a police helicopter circles overhead and the reporter on the TV announces that this has been the third civil brawl between the two rival gangs.

The aerial view from the helicopter shows signs on the tops of two skyscrapers of equal heights and directly across the street from each other. One sign reads "Montague" and the other "Capulet." The street between the buildings leads to a huge church with a statue of the Sacred Heart of Jesus perched on the top of its dome. The viewer concludes that Shakespeare's rival houses have become rival businesses and the very "lay of the land" or design of the city of Verona Beach speaks to the tension between them.

Meanwhile, Romeo walks along the beach, smoking a cigarette and stopping to write in his journal. Dave Paris, bachelor of the year, talks with Fulgencio Capulet, asking him for his daughter's hand in marriage. Benvolio finds Romeo walking along the beach and they enter a pool hall and play a game of pool while Romeo talks about his feelings of love for Juliet. A news report on the TV in the pool hall reveals that the Capulets are preparing for their annual feast. This bit of news gives Romeo an idea of how to see Juliet.

At the Capulet mansion, servants are preparing the place for the annual party. Juliet's nurse, dressed in traditional black-trimmed-in-white maid clothes, and her mother, dressed in a gown over her underwear, search for the young lady, find her, and tell her about Dave Paris' desire to marry her. While they talk, Gloria Capulet puts on her costume--that of an Egyptian princess--for the party. Juliet dresses as an angel.

Meanwhile, the Montague gang and Romeo meet at the Sycamore Grove, a theme park. They, too, are dressed in costume. Romeo is clothed with mail and partial armor and carries a sword. He looks like Robin Hood. Mercutio, dressed in drag, produces a fake invitation to the Capulet party and also gives Romeo a love potion, a drug.

Dancing and entertainment begin the costume party inside the mansion. Groups of musicians play contemporary music and solo performers sing songs as guests mingle and dance. Feeling the effect of the drug, Romeo steps into a bathroom and washes his face. After emerging, he spies Juliet through a large aquarium, which is filled with all types of tropical fish. They peer at each other for a long time through the sides of the tank. Just as they are smiling, Juliet's nurse finds her and takes her to her mother and Dave Paris, who is dressed as an astronaut and who invites Juliet to dance with him. The camera focuses on Fulgencio Capulet, who is appropriately dressed as a Roman emperor, while Gloria Capulet and the nurse watch Juliet and Paris dance.

Romeo cuts in on Paris and steals Juliet away behind some columns so that they can talk. At first they talk about kissing, then, getting into the elevator, they kiss passionately. As the elevator stops, the nurse pulls Juliet out of it and takes her back to her mother and Paris. As she does so, the nurse tells Juliet that Romeo is the only son of her enemy, the Montagues.

As the Montague gang is leaving the party with Romeo, he jumps out and goes back toward the Capulet mansion. Meanwhile, Tybalt Capulet, dressed as the devil, pledges revenge on the Montagues for their party intrusion. Romeo first climbs over the wall and then the trellis to Juliet's window which overlooks the swimming pool. Making noise, he alerts the security guard, but he quickly darts out of sight of the security camera. Juliet, who sees him, meets him in the garden by the pool into which both fall. When the security guard arrives to investigate, he sees only Juliet in the pool, as Romeo stays under the water. Once the guard disappears, Romeo surfaces and he and Juliet kiss passionately. They agree to elope and marry secretly. Meanwhile, from upstairs the nurse keeps calling, "Juliet, Juliet."

The scene changes to the roof of the priest's residence where he speaks to school boys about the plants he grows and the effects they can have on people who use them. He tends the plants shirtless, so that the large tattoo in the form of an Irish cross can be seen on his back. Romeo arrives and asks the priest, Father Laurence, to secretly marry him and Juliet. Father Laurence agrees. They set the date and time.

Romeo finds his friends on the beach as Juliet's nurse arrives to talk to him. He tells her about their plan to marry, and when the nurse returns home, she tells Juliet that all is arranged for the ceremony.

In the church, Juliet walks down the aisle as her nurse and chauffeur watch. Romeo, standing in the front of the altar with his best man and Father Laurence, watch Juliet walk toward them. In the choir loft, a boys' choir sings a contemporary love song. In a simple ceremony, Romeo and Juliet are married.

Back on the beach the Montague gang sees the Capulet gang arrive. The Capulets have come seeking revenge on the Montagues for their attendance at the masquerade ball. All members of both gangs are armed with shoulder holsters and hand guns. The gun fight begins just as Romeo arrives. Tybalt challenges Romeo to fight, but Romeo refuses, turns around, and walks away. Tybalt follows him, tackles him, kicks him, and beats him with his fists. When Romeo fails to respond to the beating he is receiving, Mercutio takes up his cause and fights Tybalt. However, Mercutio falls on broken glass and mortally slashes his side. Before he dies in Romeo's arms, Mercutio curses both houses of Capulet and Montague. Meanwhile, a windstorm comes in from the ocean and all flee the beach.

The handguns carried by the rival gangs are in contrast to the religious images seen throughout the film, especially the heart. The statue on the top of the church is the Sacred Heart of Jesus, an image of Christ with a huge pierced heart exposed on his chest. On the beach, Romeo wears a brightly-colored shirt with the image of heart on it. The priest's alb has the same heart embroidered in gold on the front. Tybalt bears the image of the heart in a tattoo on his chest, and his gun handle has a picture of the Immaculate Heart of Mary, the Virgin with a huge pierced heart on her chest. The heart signifies love and is contrasted to all the hate shown by the rival gangs.

After Mercutio dies, Romeo gets into his car and drives toward the Capulet mansion, where Juliet awaits him, sitting on her bed surrounded with candles. She yearns for Romeo on her wedding night. Meanwhile, in a drag race, Romeo's car causes Tybalt's car to overturn. Both get out and fight. Tybalt drops his gun. In front of the church, Romeo, picking up Tybalt's gun, shoots him as he flees. Rain begins to fall. Before he dies, Tybalt sees in the pool of his own blood the reflection of the huge figure of the Sacred Heart of Jesus above him. The viewer concludes two things: It was no accident that Tybalt was dressed as the devil at the costume party, and he has not loved but, rather, hated.

Police arrive with Fulgencio and Gloria Capulet, who demand justice--Romeo's death--for Tybalt's death. Romeo's parents, Ted and Caroline Montague, also arrive. Romeo, who has fled into the church for sanctuary, can't hear the chief of police using a megaphone declare that Romeo will be banished from Verona Beach.

Inside the priest's residence, Father Laurence bandages the wound in Romeo's side and tells him of his banishment. Juliet's nurse arrives with a message. The nurse tells Romeo that Juliet weeps and gives Romeo a ring from Juliet. The ring has a heart on it and the words "I love thee" engraved on it. The priest instructs Romeo first to go to Juliet and then to flee to Mantua, where he should stay until the priest has time to fix the problem that has developed in Verona Beach.

Juliet prays before statues of Mary and the angels, surrounded by candles. Dave Paris appears to court Juliet, whose mother tells him that she is burdened by the heaviness of Tybalt's death. But Romeo appears in Juliet's room. They kiss passionately, undress each other, and make love on their wedding night. Fulgencio Capulet declares to Gloria that Dave Paris will marry Juliet on the next Thursday, and he instructs Gloria to tell Juliet of his decision the next morning.

The next morning, however, Juliet and Romeo awaken in bed together. Romeo dresses and prepares to leave, but Juliet begs him to stay a while longer. Playfully, they kiss under the sheets. Abruptly, the nurse enters and finds them together. Romeo flees through the window and falls into the swimming pool. Juliet has a vision that Romeo in the swimming pool is in a tomb--a foreshadowing of the end of the movie.

Gloria Capulet arrives to tell Juliet of her father's decision that she will marry Dave Paris in St. Peter Church on Thursday. Juliet objects. Fulgencio arrives and is angry that Juliet rejects Paris. In a tussle, he tosses her onto her bed. The nurse intercedes, but Fulgencio pushes her aside. Fulgencio tells his daughter that if she doesn't marry Paris, that he'll disown her. Angrily, he leaves the room. Shakespeare's scene of a father disowning his daughter has been transformed into a contemporary domestic dispute complete with abuse.

Juliet asks her mother to delay the marriage. But Gloria leaves Juliet, refusing to help. Juliet's nurse comforts her, but says it is best if she marries Paris. Juliet decides to go see Father Laurence under the pretext of going to confession and preparing for her marriage to Dave Paris.

Meanwhile, Paris has gone to see Father Laurence about arrangements for the wedding. Juliet arrives at the church and Paris kisses her on his way out. In the priest's room, Juliet draws a handgun and threatens to kill herself. Father Laurence tells her about a plan he has. He will give her a drug to take that will make her look like she is dead for twenty-four hours. Her body will be put in the crypt, while he sends a letter to Romeo to come and get her. When she awakens, Romeo will be at her side to take her away.

The priest writes his letter to Romeo and sends it special delivery. The delivery man, finding no one home in Romeo's trailer in a desert in Mantua, leaves a notice on the door that he will call again. Meanwhile, Juliet's mother wishes her a good night, after which Juliet drinks the potion the priest had given her and falls into a deep sleep in her bed, where she is discovered the next morning and thought to be dead. The priest arrives and administers the last rites. Only he knows the truth of the situation.

Entering the church and seeing Juliet lying on a bier, Balthasar, Romeo's servant, presumes that she has died and drives to Mantua in search of Romeo, whom he finds writing a letter to Father Laurence. The desert, a wasteland, is what life is like for Romeo without his true love, Juliet. Balthasar proceeds to tell Romeo about Juliet's death. The notice left by the special delivery mail carrier has blown off the door of Romeo's trailer. The camera focuses on it as the wind drives it across the desert. When Romeo hears Balthasar's news, he weeps uncontrollably and cries, "Juliet."

Next, Romeo puts on his shoulder holster and gun, gets into Balthasar's car, and with him heads for the church, where Juliet's body lies in state. Romeo asks Balthasar if he carries a letter from the priest, but Balthasar can only shake his head no. As their car is heading toward Verona Beach, unknowingly they pass the truck with the courier who is returning to attempt to deliver the letter from Father Laurence to Romeo.

Meanwhile, the priest finds out that his letter was not able to be delivered and concludes that something dreadful is going to happen. A police helicopter with a search light hovers over the city looking for the banished Romeo who has returned to see his supposedly-dead Juliet. Slipping in through a dark alley, Romeo pays a drug dealer for a vial of poison which he can take that will kill him almost immediately. The helicopter with Captain Prince in it continues to search the city for the banished lover who slips out of the drug dealer's apartment and is driven to the church by Balthasar.

The priest, realizing that Juliet will awaken within one hour, heads toward the church. Captain Prince spots Balthasar's car as it stops in front of the church and the passenger door opens and Romeo gets out and rushes up the steps toward the front door of the church. Several police cars arrive with their flashing lights as Romeo reaches the middle of the steps, where he grabs a passerby and takes him hostage until he can get into the door of the church. Once the hostage is released, gunfire is exchanged, but Romeo has made it into the church. While all this violence ensues, the camera continues to flash images of the statue of the Sacred Heart of Jesus on top of the church.

Romeo proceeds to walk down the center aisle of the church which is lined with neon crosses and electric candles and flowers. As he gets closer to the bier where Juliet supposedly rests in death, real candles blaze all around her, imitating her room on their wedding night. Romeo cries when he gazes upon her and sees that she holds a lily in her hand. He touches her cheek, saying, "My love, my wife." Noticing that she still has color in her checks, he touches his cheek to hers and wonders why she is still so fair and not pale, as is usual in death. After kissing her, he takes the ring she had given him from a chain around his neck and puts it on her finger and caresses her again.

Taking his last look at Juliet, Romeo embraces her one last time, kisses her, and drinks the vial of poison he had purchased from the drug dealer. He desires to join her in death. But just as he finishes the last drop of the poison, Juliet awakens from her deep sleep and touches him on the cheek with her hand. Quickly, she concludes that he has consumed poison and kisses his lips in the hopes of getting some for herself. Romeo dies. Juliet begins to weep uncontrollably. Taking Romeo's gun, she cocks it, places it to her head, and kills herself. As the camera moves away from the bier, the viewer sees that both Romeo and Juliet now lie in death together, just like they had lain in love together in Juliet's bedroom.

In order to counteract the effects of the tragedy, flashbacks to the scene of their first meeting at the aquarium, the scene where she gave him the ring with "I love thee" engraved on it, the scene of their first night together under the sheets in her bedroom, and the scene of them together in the swimming pool are flashed before the viewer.

At the front door of the church, the viewer watches as the bodies, covered in white sheets, are removed on gurneys and placed in an ambulance, while the red, blue, and white lights on top of the police cars illumine the night. Both Romeo's and Juliet's parents are present. Captain Prince tells them that this tragedy is the result of their hate and that now all of them are punished.

The camera returns the viewer to the TV and the newscaster, who concludes her report by saying, "For never was a story of more woe / Than this of Juliet and her Romeo." "Snow" appears on the TV screen as the camera pulls away and fades out.

What makes the film, as compared to Shakespeare's original play, such a good study in hermeneutics is the characters. They have been adapted to fit the current culture. Instead of sixteenth-century dress, they wear business suits, beach attire, leather clothes. The younger characters are members of gangs with appropriate gang signs, such as their clothes, handguns, and tattoos. Instead of the single name each character bears in the original play, the film gives them first names. Instead of Capulet and Lady Capulet, the film presents Fulgencio and Gloria Capulet. Instead of Montague and Lady Montague, the film presents Ted and Caroline Montague. The apothecary in the play becomes a drug dealer in the movie. And the swords and daggers the characters carry in the play become handguns in shoulder holsters in the film.

The film-maker has turned Capulet's feast, during which Romeo and Juliet meet, into a costume ball complete with a floor show, orchestra, and solo performers. Shakespeare's torch bearers are omitted, as automobiles provide transportation and their headlamps provide light. Likewise, there is no need for a chorus, as the TV news reporter fills that role.

Shakespeare's orchard scenes, limited by space on the stage, become a garden with a swimming pool, a modern kitchen, or Juliet's bedroom in a mansion. Shakespeare's public places are transferred to modern public places, such as the beach, city streets, and a gas station.

Likewise, Shakespeare's scenes set in Friar Laurence's cell are moved to the roof of the priest's living quarters, a room in his house, and a large church. Friar Laurence has become Father Laurence, a parish priest instead of a Franciscan friar.

The appearance in the play of a Friar John, who is responsible for bearing Friar Laurence's letters to Romeo, is omitted in the movie. The director has chosen a special delivery mail courier instead. Likewise, Shakespeare's repeated mention of a Rosaline, a former love of Romeo, is omitted in the film except for the initial dialogue between Romeo and Benvolio in the pool hall. The scene at Juliet's tomb is transferred to the church where she is waked and where they were married.

The ending of the play is changed in the movie version. Paris and Romeo do not engage in a fight at Juliet's tomb during which Paris is killed by Romeo. We do not find out what happens to Paris in the film. Likewise, in the film, Friar Laurence doesn't go the tomb to discover what's happened and interpret these events for the audience. Neither does he dialogue with Juliet about going to a convent for the rest of her life before she takes her own life. Instead of drawing a gun and killing herself, in the play Juliet takes Romeo's dagger and plunges it into her heart. Finally, the friar does not explain to the parents of the slain lovers what has happened. The viewer, who has observed what many of the characters have not seen, is left to put all the pieces together on his or her own and must presume that the parents of the dead lovers have done the same.

The screen writers had to change the ending of Shakespeare's play because tragedy does not appeal to United States culture. So, Paris' death is omitted. Romeo's death and Juliet's death cannot be changed in the film, but they are adapted. Once they are both dead, flashbacks from their previous encounters are seen, and the camera focus on the bier holding both of their bodies reminds the viewer of the same setting in Juliet's bed when both awaken after their wedding night. Thus, the viewer is led to believe that they live happily ever after, even though both are dead. Shakespeare's tragedy has been redeemed by the movie-maker.

Much of the dialogue of Shakespeare's play has been omitted in the screen play because the camera can do the work of telling the story. When the medium of story-telling changes, the method must also change. Of the dialogue that the screen play keeps from the play, the words are not altered, giving the viewer a feeling that the movie is still a Shakespearean play. Likewise, the multiple images which a camera can flash before a viewer and its ability to take the viewer from one scene to another quickly can't be done on a stage where scenes are limited by space and props.

Thus, Shakespeare's tragic love story has been adapted to a contemporary story of love and tragedy that ends with the couple living happily ever after in the life after this one. And all of it has been effectively accomplished through hermeneutics.

Exercises and Questions for Discussion

1. Comprehensively define "hermeneutics." Outline the process in which one engages when preparing an interpretation using hermeneutics.

2. Identify the hermeneutics used in the 1996 film version of "Romeo and Juliet" for each of the following: swords, houses, public place, prince, torches, orchard, apothecary, and chorus.

3. Identify five ways the 1996 film version of "Romeo and Juliet" helps the viewer remember to what family the characters belong.

4. In what three ways do the hermeneutics used in the 1996 film version of "Rome and Juliet" help you understand the story?

5. Do you think the film director, Baz Luhrmann, was justified in changing the ending of Shakespeare's play in the 1996 film version of "Romeo and Juliet"? Explain.

6. What hermeneutic would you use for each of the following: the cure of a demoniac (Mark 1:21-28), the parable of the lamp (Mark 4:21-23), the parable of the weeds among the wheat (Matthew 13:24-30), the workers in the vineyard (Matthew 20:1-16), raising the widow's son (Luke 7:11-17), the parable of the rich fool (Luke 12:16-21), the wedding at Cana (John 2:1-11), and the vine and the branches (John 15:1-10).

About the Author

Since 1989, Mark G. Boyer has served as a per course instructor in New Testament in the Religious Studies Department of Southwest Missouri State University, where he continues to teach two courses each semester: Introduction to the Literature and World of the New Testament and The Bible on Film.

Besides teaching, Boyer has served for over 14 years as editor of the Catholic newspaper serving the 39 counties in southern Missouri. Since he became editor of *The Mirror*, it has won a total of 28 journalism awards from the Associated Church Press and the Catholic Press Association.

Over 60 of Boyer's articles have appeared in such national magazines as *U.S. Catholic*, *Liturgy 90*, *Rite*, *The Priest*, *The Critic*, *Markings*, *Environment & Art Letter*, *Modern Liturgy*, *Design*, and others.

He is the author of 21 books in the areas of biblical and liturgical spirituality. They, their publishers, and years of release include:

–*Day by Day Through the Easter Season*, Liguori, 1987.

–*Following the Star: Daily Reflections for Advent and Christmas*, Liguori, 1989.

–*Mystagogy: Liturgical Paschal Spirituality for Lent and Easter*, Alba House 1990.

–*The Liturgical Environment: What the Documents Say*, The Liturgical Press, 1990.

–*Return to the Lord: A Lenten Journey of Daily Reflections*, Alba House, 1991.

–*Breathing Deeply of God's New Life: Preparing Spiritually for the Sacraments of Initiation*, St. Anthony Messenger Press, 1993.

–*Mary's Day–Saturday: Meditations for Marian Celebrations*, The Liturgical Press, 1993.

–*Why Suffer?: The Answer of Jesus*, The Pastoral Press, 1994

–*A Month-by-Month Guide to Entertaining Angels*, ACTA, 1995.

–*Biblical Reflections on Male Spirituality*, The Liturgical Press, 1996.

–*"Seeking Grace with Every Step": The Spirituality of John Denver*, Leavenhouse Publications, 1996.

–*Home is a Holy Place: Reflections, Prayers and Meditations Inspired by the Ordinary*, ACTA, 1997.

–*Day by Ordinary Day with Mark: Daily Reflections for Ordinary Time: Weeks 1-9*, Alba House, 1997.

–*Day by Ordinary Day with Matthew: Daily Reflections for Ordinary Time: Weeks 10-21*, Alba House, 1997.

–*Day by Ordinary Day with Luke: Daily Reflections for Ordinary Time: Weeks 22-34*, Alba House, 1997.

–*Baptized into Christ's Death and Resurrection: Preparing to Celebrate a Christian Funeral: Volume 1: Adults*, The Liturgical Press, 1999.

–*Baptized into Christ's Death and Resurrection: Preparing to Celebrate a Christian Funeral: Volume 2: Children*, The Liturgical Press, 1999.

–*The Greatest Gift of All: Reflections and Prayers for the Christmas Season*, ACTA, 1999.

–*Meditations for Ministers*, ACTA, 2000.

–*Waiting in Joyful Hope: Reflections for Advent 2001*, The Liturgical Press, 2001.

–*Filled with New Light: Reflections for Christmas 2001-2002*, The Liturgical Press, 2001.

–*Lent and Easter Prayer at Home,* Ave Maria Press, 2002.

In addition to those books, Boyer has a series of two books each for the next two years coming from The Liturgical Press: *Waiting in Joyful Hope: Reflections for Advent* 2002 and *Filled with New Light: Reflections for Christmas 2002-2003* and *Waiting in Joyful Hope: Reflections for Advent 2003* and *Filled with New Light: Reflections for Christmas 2003-2004*.

Boyer, who holds undergraduate degrees in philosophy and education and graduate degrees in theology, religious studies, and religious education, was ordained a Roman Catholic priest for the Diocese of Springfield-Cape Girardeau, Missouri, in 1976. He has served as an associate pastor, a full-time high school faculty member, and an adult educator.